Machine Trading

Founded in 1807, John Wiley & Sons is the oldest independent publishing company in the United States. With offices in North America, Europe, Australia, and Asia, Wiley is globally committed to developing and marketing print and electronic products and services for our customers' professional and personal knowledge and understanding.

The Wiley Trading series features books by traders who have survived the market's ever-changing temperament and have prospered—some by reinventing systems, others by getting back to basics. Whether a novice trader, professional, or somewhere in between, these books will provide the advice and strategies needed to prosper today and well into the future.

For more on this series, visit our website at www.WileyTrading.com.

MACHINE TRADING

Deploying Computer Algorithms to Conquer the Markets

Ernest P. Chan

WILEY

Published by John Wiley & Sons, Inc., Hoboken, New Jersey.
Published simultaneously in Canada.

For general information on our other products and services or for technical support, please contact our Customer Care Department within the United States at (800) 762-2974, outside the United States at (317) 572-3993, or fax (317) 572-4002.

Wiley publishes in a variety of print and electronic formats and by print-on-demand. Some material included with standard print versions of this book may not be included in e-books or in print-on-demand. If this book refers to media such as a CD or DVD that is not included in the version you purchased, you may download this material at http://booksupport.wiley.com. For more information about Wiley products, visit www.wiley.com.

Library of Congress Cataloging-in-Publication Data is available:

ISBN 978-1-119-21960-6 (Hardcover)
ISBN 978-1-119-21967-5 (ePDF)
ISBN 978-1-119-21965-1 (ePub)

Cover Design: Wiley
Cover Images: Wave © kdrkara90/Shutterstock; Abstract background © Marina Koven/Shutterstock; Fractal Realms © agsandrew/Shutterstock

Printed in the United States of America

V10010964_060719

To my mom, Ching, my spouse, Ben, and to the memory of my beloved father, Hung Yip.

CONTENTS

PREFACE

The best way to learn something really well is to teach it to someone else (Bargh and Schul, 1980). So I confess that one major motivation for my writing this book, the third and the most advanced to date in a series, is to force myself to study in more depth the following topics:

- The latest backtesting and trading platforms and the best and most cost-effective vendors for all manners of data (Chapter 1);
- How to pick the best broker for algorithmic executions and what precautions we should take (Chapter 1);
- The simplest way to optimize allocations to different assets and strategies (Chapter 1);
- Factor models in all their glory, including those derived from the options market, and why they can be useful to short-term traders (Chapter 2);
- Time series techniques: ARIMA, VAR, and state space models (with hidden variables) as applied to practical trading (Chapter 3);
- Artificial intelligence/machine learning techniques: particularly methods that will reduce overfitting (Chapter 4);
- Options and volatility trading strategies, including those that involve portfolios of options (Chapter 5);

- Intraday and higher frequency trading: market microstructure, order types and routing optimization, dark pools, adverse selection, order flow, and how to backtest intraday strategies with tick data (Chapter 6);
- Bitcoins: bringing some of the techniques we covered to this new asset class (Chapter 7);
- How to keep up with the latest knowledge (Chapter 8);
- Transitioning from a proprietary trader to an investment advisor (Chapter 8).

I don't know if these topics will excite you or bring you profits, but my study of them has certainly improved my own money management skills. Besides, sharing knowledge and ideas is fun and ultimately conducive to creativity and profits.

You will find most of the materials quite accessible to anyone who has some experience in a quantitative field, be it computer science, engineering, or physics. Not much prior knowledge of trading and finance is assumed (except for the chapter on options, where we do assume basic familiarity). However, if you are completely new to trading, you may find my more basic treatments in *Quantitative Trading* (Chan, 2009) and *Algorithmic Trading* (Chan, 2013) easier to understand. This book can be treated as a continuation of my first two books, with coverage on topics that I have not discussed before, but it can also be read independently.

Although many prototype trading strategies have been included as examples, one should definitely not treat them as shrink-wrapped products ready to deploy in live trading. As I have emphasized in my previous books, nobody should trade someone else's strategies without a thorough, independent backtest, removing all likely sources of biases and data errors, and adding various variations for improvement. Most, if not all, the strategies I describe contain hidden biases in one way or another, waiting for you to unearth and eliminate.

I use MATLAB for all of my research in trading. I find it extremely user-friendly, with constantly improving and new features, and with an increasing number of specialized toolboxes that I can draw on. For example, without the Statistics and Machine Learning Toolbox, it would take much longer to explore using AI/ML techniques for trading. (See why Google scientist and machine learning expert Kevin Murphy prefers MATLAB to R for AI/ML research in Murphy, 2015.) In the past, readers have complained about the high price of a MATLAB license. But now, it costs only $150 for a

"Home" license, with each additional toolbox costing only $45. No serious traders should compromise their productivity because of this small cost. I am also familiar with R, which is a close relative to MATLAB. But frankly, it is no match for MATLAB in terms of performance and user-friendliness. A detailed comparison of these languages can be found in Chapters 1 and 6. If you don't already know MATLAB, it is very easy to request a one-month trial license from mathworks.com and use its many free online tutorials to learn the language. One great advantage of MATLAB over R or other open-source languages is that there is excellent customer support: If you have a question, just email or call the staff at Mathworks. (Often, someone with a PhD will answer your questions.)

I have taught many of these topics to both retail and institutional traders at my biannual workshops in London, as well as online (www.epchan.com). In order to facilitate lecturers who would like to use this as a textbook for a special topics course on Algorithmic Trading, I have included many exercises at the end of most chapters. Some of these exercises should be treated as suggestions for open-ended projects; there are no ready-made answers.

Readers will also find all of the software and some data used in the examples on epchan.com/book3. The userid and password are embedded in Box 1.1. But unlike my previous books, some of the data involved in the example strategies are under strict licensing restrictions and therefore are unavailable for free download from my website. Readers are invited to purchase or rent them from their original sources, all of which are described in Chapter 1.

I have benefited from tips, ideas, and help from many people in putting the content together. An incomplete list would include:

- Stephen Aikin, a renowned author (Aikin, 2012) and lecturer, who helped me understand implied quotes due to calendar spreads in the futures markets (Chapter 6).
- David Don and Joseph Signorelli of Lime Brokerage, who corrected some of my misunderstanding of the market microstructure (Chapter 6).
- Jonathan Shore, infinitely knowledgeable about bitcoins, who helped compile some order book data in that market and shared that with me (Chapter 7).
- Dr. Roger Hunter, CTO at our firm, QTS Capital Management, who reviewed my manuscript and who never failed to find software bugs in my codes.

- The team at Interactive Brokers (especially Joanne, Ragini, Mike, Greg, Ian, and Ralph) whose infinite patience with my questions about all issues related to trading are much appreciated.

I would like to thank Professor Thomas Miller of Northwestern University for hiring me to teach the Risk Analytics course at the Master of Science in Predictive Analytics program. In the same vein, I would also like to thank Matthew Clements and Jim Biss at Global Markets Training for organizing the London workshops for me over the years. Quite a few nuggets of knowledge in this book come out of materials or discussions from these courses and workshops.

Trading and research have been made a lot more interesting and enjoyable because I was able to work closely with our team at QTS, who contributed to research, ideas, and general knowledge, some of which find their way into this book. Among them, Roger, of course, without whom there wouldn't be QTS, but also Yang, Marcin, Sam, and last but not least, Ray.

Of course, none of my books would come into existence without the support of Wiley, especially my long-time editor Bill Falloon, development editor Julie Kerr, production editor Caroline Maria, and copy editor Cheryl Ferguson (from whom no missing "end" to a "for"-loop can escape). It was truly a great pleasure to work with them, and their enthusiasm and professionalism are greatly appreciated.

Machine Trading

CHAPTER 1

The Basics of Algorithmic Trading

An algorithmic trading strategy feeds market data (historical or live) into a computer (backtest or automated execution) program. The program then submits orders to the broker through an API, and receives order status notifications back from the broker. The flowchart in Figure 1.1 illustrates this process.

Notice that I deliberately use the same box to indicate the computer program that generates backtest results and live orders: This is the best way to ensure we are trading the exact same model that we have backtested.

In this chapter, I will discuss the latest services, products, and their vendors applicable to each of the blocks in Figure 1.1. In addition, I will describe my favorite performance metrics, the way to determine the optimal leverage, and the simplest asset allocation method. Though I have touched on many (but not all) of these issues in my previous books, I have updated them here based on the state of the art. The FinTech industry has not been standing still, nor has my understanding of issues ranging from brokers' safety to subtleties of portfolio optimization.

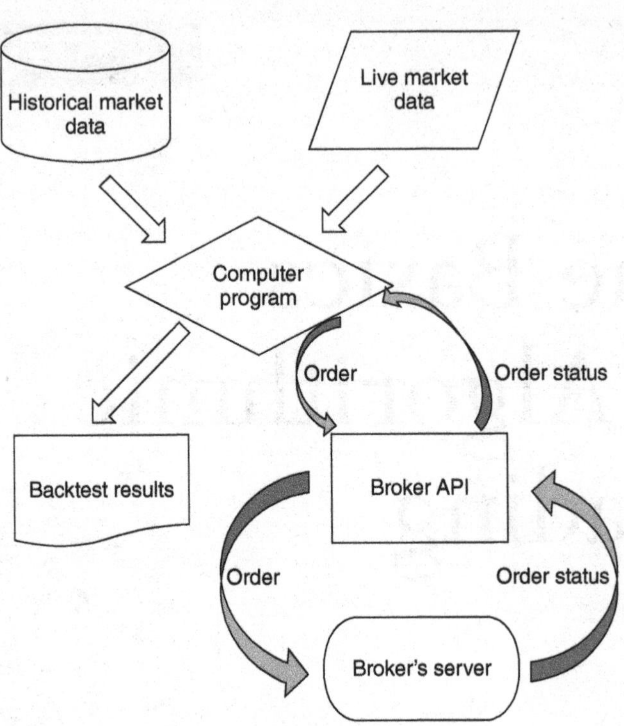

FIGURE 1.1 Algorithmic trading at a glance

Historical Market Data

For **daily historical data in stocks and futures**, I have been using CSI (csidata.com) for a long time. CSI has a very flexible, and robust, desktop application. The beauty of this application is that we can set a time in the evening when the data are automatically updated through an Internet connection with CSI's server. Also, the data can be stored in various convenient formats such as .txt, .csv, or .xlsx. We can ask it to automatically adjust historical stock (and ETF) prices for splits and dividends. For a little extra, CSI can also provide delisted stocks' historical data, so that you can have a survivorship-bias-free data set.[1] (By the way, CSI data powers Yahoo! Finance's historical stock data.) For futures, we can choose different rollover methods to create continuous contracts. Or not, since the original contract prices are also available, and many professional traders prefer to backtest futures using original contract prices instead of back-adjusted continuous contract prices. This is because the latter depends on a particular roll method, and may have look-ahead bias embedded (see Chan, 2013, for a detailed exploration of this issue). Finally, CSI has excellent customer support through email and phone.

An alternative to CSI is Quandl.com, which is a consolidator of many kinds of data from many different vendors. It also provides an API in different languages (including MATLAB, which I use in this book, or Python, which many other traders use) that we can use for data selection and download. Some of Quandl's data are free (daily data for stocks is one example), and others require payment. I have purchased, for example, fundamental stock data from them (see Chapter 2, Factor Models), and they are much more economical than established vendors such as Compustat.

Serious traders or academic finance researchers may prefer stock, ETF, and mutual fund data from CRSP (www.crsp.com). Their historical data are carefully compiled to be survivorship-bias-free, and dividends and splits are provided separately so you can decide how to utilize them in a backtest. But most importantly, they provide the best bid and offer (BBO) prices at the close. These are important because, as is explained in Box 6.2 in Chapter 6, using the usual consolidated closing prices from CSI or Quandl can inflate backtest performances for certain strategies. A similar issue arises from using the consolidated opening prices. The best open and close prices to use are the auction prices from the primary exchange. (See also Box 6.2 for an explanation of how we can extract such auction prices from tick data.) The second best open and close prices to use are the BBO prices that can be used to compute the midprices at the open and close. Unfortunately CRSP does not provide the BBO prices at the open, so one must use intraday data for that purpose. For academic researchers, CRSP data can be obtained at a lower cost through WRDS (wrds-web.wharton.upenn.edu), which is a consolidator of many high quality historical databases for scholarly research.

Of course, those serious traders who can afford to buy data from CRSP may also be able to afford a Bloomberg terminal subscription. One advantage of a Bloomberg terminal is that we can download the "primary exchange" close price for US stocks. Of course, a Bloomberg subscription also includes access to many historical and live data spanning a wide variety of instruments and, importantly, breaking news on every stock. I have found Bloomberg's news service to be superior to many other vendors'. Often, we will see a stock moves suddenly, and are not able to find the reason anywhere else but on Bloomberg's news feed. They do capture the most obscure news on the most obscure stocks in the shortest time frame, which is important when you have an event-driven strategy. Bloomberg's historical US stock data are also survivorship-bias-free. (To be fair to Thomson Reuter's Eikon platform, which is a keen competitor to Bloomberg's, I have not tested its news feed. So it is possible that it provides just as wide and timely coverage as well. There is one feature on Eikon that impressed me in a demo: I was able to see the geographical locations of individual oil tankers and where they were headed. Apparently, this is useful to oil traders to predict short-term oil inventory, supply, and demand.)

For **futures traders**, daily data does not present much of a problem. CSIs and the free data on Quandl are as good as any.

Daily options data can be obtained from ORATS.com as well as ivolatility.com. Both offerings are survivorship-bias-free. The institutional trader or academic researcher may also purchase from Option Metrics, which is often part of the WRDS package (see above). One nice feature of all these databases: They do not include just option closing prices, but also the bid-ask quote at the close as well. This is important because some options, especially ones that are out-of-the-money or have long tenor, may be traded infrequently. So the last trade price of the day may be very different from the bid-ask quotes at the close, and is not indicative of the price we can actually trade at or near the close. These databases also include auxiliary but important information such as the Greeks and implied volatilities. Furthermore, they may include an implied volatility surface. This uses implied volatilities computed on actual options and interpolates them to yield implied volatilities for strikes and tenors that did not actually exist.

Options historical data tend to be more expensive than stock or futures data, due to their voluminous nature. However, it can be cheaper to rent *intraday* option prices from QuantGo.com than to buy *daily* option prices from other vendors. We will talk more about QuantGo when we discuss intraday data in general. It would be a trivial programming exercise to extract the end-of-day quotes from the intraday data, by looking for the quotes with timestamps at or just before the daily closing time.

Beyond daily price data, there are, of course, **fundamental financial data** for companies. I already mentioned that Quandl carries such data. Institutional traders would most likely look to Compustat for such data. For corporate earnings estimates by analysts, Thomson Reuters' IBES database is the standard. Both Compustat and IBES are available from WRDS. Meanwhile, crowd-sourced earnings estimates are available from Estimize. There is some research that suggests Estimize's contributors can more accurately forecast actual earnings than traditional sell-side analysts (Wang et al., 2014). An example strategy using Estimize's data is discussed in Deltix (2014). Short interest data are available from Compustat and

SunGard's Astec database. SunGard's data have a lot more details culled from stock lenders and prime brokers around the Street than a simple short interest number. In addition, their data are available on an intraday basis as a live feed, though the historical data do not have historical time stamps.

News data is another type of data that is becoming fashionable. Many vendors sell elementized news feeds (i.e., news that is machine-readable, which makes it easier to capture keywords, categories, and the like), including Bloomberg, Dow Jones, and Thomson Reuters. If it is too much trouble for your strategy to generate trading signals from raw news data, you can also buy news sentiment data from Ravenpack, Thomson Reuters News Analytics, MarketPsych, or Accern. (AcquireMedia's NewsEdge database is similar, but they provide only impact scores. This is a kind of unsigned sentiment score that doesn't tell you which way the stock will move, only that it will move, which may be suitable for options traders.) However, there is one problem for sentiment data: Different vendors have different ways to compute sentiment scores from the raw news. So a trading model depends to some extent on which vendors' sentiment scores are most predictive.

We will leave the topic of buying or renting intraday data to Chapter 6 on Intraday Trading, because the features associated with intraday data are intimately tied to the market microstructure. Here, we will just note that some of the historical intraday data vendors include tickdata.com, nanex.net, CQG, QuantGo.com, kibot, and of course, the various exchanges themselves.

Finding, buying, or renting data is both expensive and time-consuming, though consolidators like Quandl and QuantGo have made it much less so. Another way to avoid dealing with acquiring data directly is to adopt a trading platform that comes integrated with data (though you may have to pay for the data separately). A good example is Quantopian.com, which provides free US stock trades data with one-minute bars, together with many other forms of fundamental and news data at lower frequency. (I have been told that futures data will be available soon.) We will talk more about platforms like these in the section "Backtesting and Trading Platforms."

Live Market Data

Most if not all brokerages provide live market data to their clients, and if you are trading a daily strategy (i.e., you trade only at the market open or close), such data are usually more than sufficient. However, if you engage in intraday trading, then the quality of data becomes a bigger issue. As we will discuss more thoroughly in Chapter 6, low latency market data can be quite expensive to obtain. Vendors that provide data suitable for intraday trading that can tolerate a latency of more than 25 ms (ms = millisecond) include eSignal, IQFeed, CQG, Interactive Data, Bloomberg, and many others. But vendors that provide data feed with latency of below 10 ms are far fewer: They include S&P Capital IQ (formerly QuantHouse), SR Labs, and Thomson Reuters. Of course, you can also subscribe to the direct feeds from the exchange, but that is strictly for high frequency traders who find the high expense justified by the high return. (That is true unless you are after currency data, where most FX exchanges will give their customer a free direct feed.)

As with historical market data, many trading platforms also include live market data feeds. These will be discussed in the following section.

Backtesting and Trading Platforms

Traditionally, we would backtest our trading strategy on one platform (e.g., R) and once successful, write a different program to automate execution of the strategy that utilizes a broker's API. However, this proves to be quite bug-prone: there is no way to ensure that the backtest and the live trading program encapsulate exactly the same trading logic. Fortunately, most backtest platforms nowadays have extended their ability to execute live as well; hence, we will combine the discussions on backtesting and trading platforms here.

As I mentioned in the Preface, MATLAB has been my favorite backtesting platform. It has a very comprehensive and user-friendly interface for developing and debugging programs, and it has a wide array of toolboxes that cover almost every arcane mathematical or computational technique you will likely encounter in trading strategy development. One of these toolboxes, the Trading Toolbox, enables a MATLAB program to connect to a number of brokerages' APIs to receive market data, submit orders, and receive order status notifications. If you prefer not to buy the Trading Toolbox, there are at least three adaptors developed by third-party vendors that enable you to do the same: exchangeapi.com's quant2ib, undocumentedmatlab.com's IB-Matlab, and Jev Kuznetsov's free MATLAB-to-IB API available at MATLAB's File Exchange. I have discussed these options in some depth in Chan (2013). Finally, MATLAB is fast. (See Chapter 6 for a comparison of performance speed among MATLAB, R, and Python.) The only drawback for this platform is that it isn't free, but the "Home" license costs only $150, with each additional toolbox costing an extra $45. If you plan to buy MATLAB's Toolboxes, here are the three I recommend (in decreasing order of importance): Statistics and Machine Learning, Econometrics, and Financial Instruments (for options traders).

For those who prefer free, open-source platforms, there are always R and Python.

R is very similar to MATLAB: It is an array-processing language, and it has a large variety of specialized "packages" (the analogue of MATLAB's toolboxes), many of them perhaps more sophisticated than MATLAB's due to the large number of academic researchers who use R. There is a GUI development platform called RStudio, but I find its user interface to be quite crude compared to that of MATLAB, and hence debugging productivity is lower. R is also the slowest among the three languages, and the slowness is all the more problematic because, unlike MATLAB or Python, it cannot be compiled into C or C++ code for speeding up. (You can, however, use the Rcpp package to access compiled C++ code from within R.) As for automating executions, you can connect an R program to Interactive Brokers through a package called "IBroker."

Python is a language in the ascendant, though I know of quants who used it for backtesting back in 1998. Aside from being a standalone language of choice for many quantitative traders, platforms such as Quantopian also use it as their strategy specification language. Native Python is not an array processing language (though one can use SciPy packages which do have this feature). While array processing is convenient for backtesting a large number of instruments simultaneously (e.g., portfolio of stocks), it is not useful for writing an automated execution program. Hence, if we were to insist on using the same program for both backtesting and live execution, we can disregard this feature altogether. One major advantage of Python is that its codes can be developed and debugged using Microsoft's Visual Studio, thus piggybacking on the full power of this well-polished development environment. Another integrated development environment[2] (IDE) for Python that received good reviews is PyCharm. Python's pandas library is a data analysis package similar to R, and the rpy2 package provides an interface to access all R packages. Python isn't as fast as MATLAB, though it is faster than R, and can be compiled into C or C++.[3] You can connect a Python trading program to Interactive Brokers for executions via IBPy or a number of other packages.

TABLE 1.1 Ranking of Three Programming Languages for Quant Trading (Ranked from 1 to 3 where 1 = best ranking and 3 = poorest ranking.)

Feature	MATLAB	R	Python
Ease of use	1	2	2
IDE polish	1	3	1
Speed	1	3	2
Toolboxes	2	1	1
Compilation to C/C++	1	N/A	1
Connectivity to brokers	1	2	2
Customer support	1	N/A	N/A
Price	2	1	1

In Table 1.1, I provide my personal, arguably subjective, ranking of the various features and aspects of the three scripting languages most widely used in trading strategy development.

You may be wondering why I have left out some of the most common programming languages such as C/C++, Java, or C#. The fact is, the most productive way to develop trading strategies is to quickly build prototype programs to test a lot of them, and to quickly discard them if they fail to live up to their promises. Scripting languages (also called REPL[4] languages) like MATLAB, R, or Python allow us to shorten this research cycle. However, productivity in research is not the same as productivity in building an automated trading system. The latter usually involves the usual bells and whistles of software development such as object-oriented design, exception handling, version control, memory and speed optimization, and so forth. Such bells and whistles are actually quite cumbersome to implement in a scripting language, and, furthermore, it is quite easy to introduce bugs without a robust and extensible software architecture. Typically, once object-oriented design is imposed on a scripting language, it will run too slowly to be useful as an execution system.

To benefit from the best of both worlds, in our firm we do our initial research mostly in MATLAB or Python (though I often ask our research associates to test their strategies on Quantopian first, just to make sure their codes do not have look-ahead bias). After we settle on a strategy, our CTO, Roger, will then independently build a system in C# that can both backtest and execute live the same strategy, as a way to confirm the correctness of the initial backtest. Once it is confirmed, a figurative turn of the key will allow us to trade live, with much lower latency than if we were to execute using a scripting language. In building the execution system, we can often reuse existing classes that we have written for other strategies. This way, we have compressed the research life cycle without sacrificing software correctness, component reuse, or execution efficiency.

There are now many backtesting and automated execution platforms available that purport to make it easier to develop and deploy automated trading strategies both quickly and robustly, just like what I described in the last paragraph, but without using two different languages. I have written extensively about this in Chan (2013), so here I will restrict myself to those platforms that fit the following criteria:

1. It has integrated historical and live market data, or provides adaptors for popular data vendors.
2. It allows maximum flexibility in strategy design by relying on generic programming languages such as Python or Java.
3. It allows connection to popular broker APIs.
4. It allows backtesting and live trading in US equities, among other instruments.

The platforms that satisfy these criteria are Quantopian, QuantConnect, Ninjatrader, Marketcetera, AlgoTrader, OpenQuant, Deltix, and QuantHouse. (This is, of course, not an exhaustive list.) Some of these platforms, such as Quantopian, are free, while others, such as QuantHouse, have a price tag suitable for institutional traders.

If you are trading a high frequency strategy, it is possible that many of these platforms will not be adequate: either because they may be too slow, or because they are missing level 2 quotes. But there are platforms such as Lime Brokerage's Strategy Studio that are designed specifically for such demanding tasks. More about this will be discussed in Chapter 6.

Though these platforms have certainly made it easier to backtest and automate trading strategies, they usually come with some constraints on the exact type of strategies, data, or instruments that we are allowed to test. Not surprisingly, the more expensive a platform is, the more flexible it is. But if absolute flexibility coupled with low development cost is required, you will probably have to do what we do in our firm.

Brokers

In this day and age, practically every broker will offer customers an API where they can subscribe to market data, submit orders, and receive order status notifications: See the last two blocks on the right of Figure 1.1. Of course, the ease of use and comprehensiveness of their APIs differ widely. If you would rather not deal directly with the vagaries and low-level details of each broker's API, you can use one of the automated execution platforms that I described in the previous section.

Meanwhile, commissions are generally so low that it also isn't a crucial factor in deciding who to trade with. Brokers have other ways to make money from you besides commissions. One popular way, for some stockbrokers, is "payment for order flow." Essentially, when you send your order to this broker, it will forward your order to a particular market maker or a specific exchange for a rebate (e.g., a penny per share), and let them execute this order. Brokers who do this must inform their customers of this practice when they open their accounts. If you prefer not to let your broker earn this rebate, and instead want to pocket it yourself, you can use brokers with Direct Market Access (e.g., Interactive Brokers or Lime Brokerage). For some FX brokers, a popular way to earn money is to widen the bid-offer spread on a currency pair. This way, they earn the difference between the spread they offer you and the spread they have to pay in the interbank market where they execute your trade. This can make it hard to compare costs among different FX brokers, since this extra spread may change over time, but of course this is precisely the reason why some brokers adopt the practice. If you prefer transparency, you can restrict your search to FX brokers that only charge commissions, not spread.

If you are a futures or currency trader, there is one more item about your broker that you have to worry about: financial stability. For US securities (i.e., stocks trading) accounts, many traders know that their cash[5] is insured up to $250,000 by the Securities Investor Protection Corporation (SIPC). Many brokers also provide additional insurance through a private insurance company such as Lloyd's of London. However, none of this is applicable to commodities futures trading accounts—hence the furor in wake of the MF Global and PFGBest bankruptcies (MarketWatch, 2012). It would be pointless to advise you to ascertain the financial strength of a commodities broker before opening an account: If the National Futures Association (NFA) couldn't detect that some of these large brokers (called Futures Commission Merchants, or FCM) are not meeting capital requirement or are committing fraud, what chance do we have? However, there is one way out of this conundrum: If a securities broker is also an FCM, it might offer a way to automatically sweep the excess cash[6] from an uninsured commodities account into an insured securities account. (For example, Interactive Brokers offers such a cash sweep service.)

Currency traders may have heard of *Herstatt risk,* or settlement risk (Galati, 2002). To illustrate, let's say we have sold 1 million EURUSD to a bank, and have delivered 1 million EUR to it. But before this bank can send us the corresponding amount of USD, it collapses (as was the case with Bankhaus Herstatt in Germany, 1974). We won't be getting our USD any time soon, and have lost 1 million EUR. It is a risk that is not solved by having an account at a reputable FX broker, because your counterparty may be some bank in a faraway country, and your broker isn't liable for your loss. This scenario is often used by some uninformed financial advisors to scare customers off investing in foreign currency strategies or funds. However, since the establishment of the CLS bank in 2002, an institution owned by some of the largest banks in the world, this risk has been largely eliminated. The CLS bank is a US financial institution regulated by the US Federal Reserve, and it facilitates simultaneous settlement of both legs of a currency transaction. It can do so because it maintains accounts with 18 central banks around the world. In our example above, we will receive the USD payment at the same time our counterparty receives our EUR payment, all via the CLS bank. It is almost like transacting on a stock exchange, where we are guaranteed that if we sold some shares, payment for those shares would be forthcoming, even if the trader who bought our shares went bankrupt. The 18 central banks whose currencies settle in CLS are listed at www.cls-group.com/About/Pages/Currencies.aspx, and these are the currencies that have little or no settlement risk.

We have been discussing the risks that other parties (brokers or counterparties) fail to pay us in a transaction. But what if we are the ones who fail? More specifically, what if in a levered transaction, we lost more money in the brokerage account than our account equity? Are we liable to the negative equity? Can we lose more than what we invested in the account? The answer is yes and yes, if we invested as individuals. In a particularly poignant example, on January 15, 2015, the Swiss National Bank (Switzerland's central bank) suddenly announced that the Swiss Franc would no longer be pegged to the euro (Economist, 2015). EURCHF plummeted by about 10 percent in seconds, and ultimately lost 29 percent in a day. Many FX traders' account equities went negative. Some smaller FX brokers failed because their customers wouldn't pay them back the losses. In a situation like this, how do we make sure we won't be liable? The way to protect ourselves is not to invest in our own personal or family's name, but through a limited liability vehicle that we fully own, such as a corporation (or S-corporation in the United States), limited liability company (in the United States), or limited partnership. Investing in someone else's limited partnership, such as a hedge fund, will also work. In case of negative equity, the limited liability vehicle will have to declare bankruptcy. This isn't great, but is not catastrophic.

Performance Metrics

What performance metrics should a backtest program generate? I am typically interested in only five of them: CAGR (compound annual growth rate), Sharpe ratio, Calmar ratio, maximum drawdown, and maximum drawdown duration. I have discussed most of these except the Calmar ratio in detail in my previous books, so I will just briefly highlight some of their usage here.

CAGR is a bit different from average annualized returns: It assumes we do not transfer cash into or out of an account each time period, while maintaining the same leverage throughout. To take an extreme example, if a strategy returns 1 percent per trading day, CAGR will be $1.01^{252} - 1 =$ 1127 percent. That's compounding at work. On the other hand, the average annualized return would be just $252 \times 0.01 = 252$ percent, and it is the return we would get if we withdraw profit or add cash to make up for losses each time period. But I emphasize that we must keep the leverage constant to achieve this compounded growth. In other words, your positions or orders must be resized each day based on the account equity and the leverage—something that an automated trading program should be able to do quite easily.

In a backtest, I recommend we set the leverage to one. Otherwise, the higher the leverage we use, the higher will be the CAGR, up to a point as determined by the Kelly formula below. So it is quite meaningless to pick an arbitrary leverage for a backtest. But to ensure that the leverage is one, one must make sure that the returns are measured by taking the Profit and Loss (P&L) and divide that by the total gross market value of the position(s). For example, if we are long $100 of stock A while short $100 of stock B, and the P&L is $1, the unlevered return is just 0.5 percent.

I have written a lot before about using the Kelly formula (Chan, 2009):

$$Optimal\ leverage = \frac{Mean\ of\ Excess\ Returns}{Variance\ of\ Excess\ Returns}$$

If we leverage our strategy or portfolio higher than this optimal leverage, CAGR may start to go down with increasing leverage, and is almost guaranteed to be −100 percent when the leverage is high enough. But often, it isn't safe even if the leverage is equal to the Kelly optimal. I have found that Kelly's leverage is typically too high to be of practical use. The Kelly formula shown above assumes Gaussian distribution of returns: Risk is measured only by the second moment of returns. So let's consider a simulated excess returns series with a mean of about 0.05 percent and standard deviation of about 1 percent. This is not too different from the actual daily returns statistics of SPY minus the risk-free rate. Kelly formula would therefore recommend a leverage of 5. But suppose one of the days has a return of −20 percent, which is also close to the actual return of SPY on Black Monday, October 19, 1987. If we are long SPY with a leverage of 5, our equity would have been wiped out on that day, no thanks to Kelly. As a practical matter, I would recommend lowering the leverage until you are comfortable with the maximum drawdown in the backtest over a period that includes several financial crises.

Sharpe ratio is a risk-adjusted return measure that everybody uses, but its utility is limited because it also implicitly assumes that the returns distribution is Gaussian. Risk is again measured only by the standard deviation (volatility) of returns. But as everyone knows, returns distribution have "fat tails": abnormally large returns of either sign occur far more frequently than is predicted by a Gaussian distribution. Maximum drawdown is a much better measure of tail risks, as it does not rely on measuring just the second moment of returns distribution. (Maximum drawdown is also asymmetric: We are not concerned about periods with extremely positive returns.) Hence, I have been in favor of using the Calmar ratio instead: it is defined as the CAGR divided by the absolute value of the maximum drawdown over the most recent three years. Some people prefer to use the MAR ratio instead, which is the same as the Calmar ratio except that the maximum drawdown is over the entire history of the backtest (or live track record). One can see that Calmar ratio is better defined than the MAR ratio: The longer the backtest, the higher the absolute value of the maximum drawdown. So it doesn't quite make sense to have a measure that depends sensitively on the length of a backtest or a track record. Three years is a way of normalizing this measure. I prefer to trade strategies that have a backtest Calmar ratio of at least 1.

Portfolio Optimization

When we are trading multiple strategies, or holding positions in multiple instruments in a portfolio, how we allocate capital among them can be as important to our total return as how these strategies perform individually. This issue of portfolio optimization has been well-studied in academic finance research, although there are some subtleties that are worth highlighting.

Before we get into the details, we should differentiate between maximizing the return of a portfolio over one period (e.g., a day, a month, or a year) versus maximizing the compound return (CAGR) of the portfolio over an infinite horizon. The former is dealt with by the familiar Markowitz portfolio optimization method. Its objective is to maximize the expected return subject to a constant variance of returns constraint; or equivalently and more conventionally, to minimize the variance of returns subject to a constant expected return constraint.

In order to compute the expected return and variance of returns over one period, let's assume our portfolio has N instruments (stocks, bonds, futures, etc.) or strategies (mean-reverting, momentum, event-driven, options, etc.) From here on, we will use the generic term *instruments* to denote such components of a portfolio. Each instrument i has an expected return m_i. We assume that these returns have a covariance $C_{i,j}$. Note that by return here we mean net return, not log return. This distinction will become important later on. To clarify, net return in this context is calculated as

$$Net\ return(t) = \frac{Price(t)}{Price(t-1)} - 1,$$

while log return is calculated as

$$Log\ return(t) = \log(Price(t)) - \log(Price(t-1)).$$

Net returns can never have Gaussian distributions in principle (the "why" is left as an exercise), but log returns can. There is an interesting relationship between the mean log return μ and the mean net return m of a price series if the log returns have normal distribution:

$$\mu \approx m - \frac{s^2}{2} \tag{1.1}$$

where s is the standard deviation of the net return. This is also approximately equal to the standard deviation of the log return; hence, we can use the same symbol to represent both. The approximate equality in equation 1.1 will become exact as we subdivide the periods into smaller and smaller subperiods, so that we approach continuous time (see Box 1.1). It can be derived from Ito's Lemma, famous in continuous finance as a foundational formula for Black-Scholes options pricing formula. This equality will be useful when we try to maximize the expected compound growth rate later on.

Box 1.1: The mean of net vs. log returns

In this example, we will demonstrate numerically that equation 1.1 is approximately true when log returns have a Gaussian distribution, and that as we subdivide a time period into more and more subperiods, the approximation becomes exact.

Let's say that the log return over some time period has a mean of 100 percent and a standard deviation of 200 percent. We will use the *randn* function to simulate N subperiod log returns r_i with a mean of $\mu = 100\%/N$ and a standard deviation of $s = 200\%/\sqrt{N}$. We will try N = 100, 10,000, and 1,000,000.

```
r=1/N+2/sqrt(N)*randn(N, 1);
```

Their corresponding net returns R_i are just $e^{r_i} - 1$:

```
R=exp(r)-1;
```

You can compute the sample mean and standard deviation of the log returns

```
mu=mean(r);
sigma=std(r);
```

TABLE 1.2 Mean of Net vs. Log Returns				
N	m	μ	s	$m - s^2/2$
100	2.00e-2	2.99e-4	2.00e-1	-6.41e-04
10,000	2.24e-4	2.30e-5	2.00e-2	2.28e-05
1,000,000	4.66e-6	**2.65e-6**	2.00e-3	**2.65e-06**

and compare these to sample mean and standard deviation of the net returns

```
m=mean(R);
s=std(R);
```

and you will find that $m - s^2/2 \rightarrow \mu$, as $N \rightarrow \infty$. This is shown in the Table 1.2, where I have boldfaced the two quantities that converged.

The complete code can be downloaded as netVsLogRet.m from epchan.com/book3. The userid and password are both calmar.

If we denote by F_i the capital (or leverage) allocated to an instrument i, then the expected return of the portfolio over one period in matrix notation is simply $F^T M$, where F is the column matrix of F_i and M is the column matrix of m_i. Similarly, the expected variance of returns for the portfolio is $F^T CF$, where C is the covariance matrix $C_{i,\,j}$. For each fixed level of the expected return of the portfolio, we can minimize the expected variance of returns by varying F using a numerical quadratic programming method as illustrated in Box 1.2. The result of this constrained optimization can be plotted on a chart (Figure 1.2) that shows the portfolio's expected return against its expected minimum variance. This curve has a famous name: the *efficient frontier*. But what is the best trade-off between the expected return and variance? Markowitz said we should choose the *tangency portfolio* that maximizes the Sharpe ratio: that is, the ratio between the expected return[7] and the variance of the return. The tangency portfolio is noted on Figure 1.2, and it is so-called because if we draw a line from the origin representing a riskless portfolio (which has an expected return equal to the risk-free rate assumed here to be zero, and a variance of zero) to the efficient frontier, this line intersects the efficient frontier at a tangent right at the

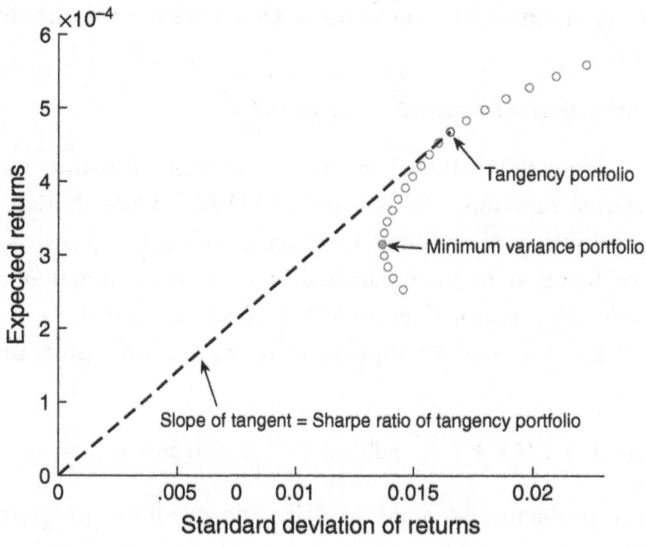

FIGURE 1.2 Efficient frontier

tangency portfolio. The slope of this line is the Sharpe ratio of the tangency portfolio.

Box 1.2: Calculating the efficient frontier using quadratic programming

In this example, we will numerically determine the efficient frontier of a portfolio of ETFs, with the constraint that no short position is allowed, and the weights of all the ETFs must add to 1 (i.e., no leverage on the portfolio is allowed). The set of ETF we use are EWC, EWG, EWJ, EWQ, EWU, and EWY. The efficient frontier is the set of minimum variances given a set of fixed expected returns. The first task in constructing the efficient frontier is to find the maximum and minimum expected returns possible. Given the no-leverage constraint, we know that the maximum (minimum) expected return is obtained when we have a weight of 1 on the ETF with the highest (lowest) expected return, and a weight of 0 on all other ETFs. If R is the array with each column representing the daily returns of one ETF over many days, we can compute the mean and the covariance of returns as

```
mi=mean(R, 1); % average return of each stock i.
C=cov(R); % covariance of returns
```

and the set of expected returns we want to consider for our efficient frontier is

```
m=[min(mi):(max(mi)-min(mi))/20:max(mi)];
```

These expected returns are the constraints for our variance minimization function. We will use MATLAB's Optimization Toolbox's quadratic programming function *quadprog* for this task. The objective function to be minimized is a quadratic function of the capital allocation vector *F*. From MATLAB's help manual, `x = quadprog(H,f,A,b,Aeq,beq)` attempts to solve the quadratic programming problem:

$$\min 0.5\, x' H\, x + f'\, x \quad \text{subject to: } Ax \leq \text{b and } Aeqx = beq.$$

In our problem, we want to solve the quadratic programming problem

$$\min F^T\ C\ F \text{ subject to: } F \geq 0 \text{ and } F^T\ M = m,$$

where *F*, *C*, and *M* are defined in the main text as the capital allocation vector, the covariance matrix, and the column matrix of each ETF's expected return, while *m* is the expected return of the portfolio. Hence, we have the mapping

$$x = F,\ H = 2\ C,\ f = 0,\ A = -I \text{ (negative of the identity matrix),}$$
$$b = 0,\ Aeq = M, \text{ and beq} = \text{m. In MATLAB,}$$

```
H=2*C;
f=zeros(1, length(mi));
A=-eye(length(mi));
b=zeros(length(mi), 1);
Aeq=[mi; ones(1, length(mi))];
beq=[m(i); 1];
```

Putting these in a loop over each $m(i)$ gives

```
for i=1:length(m)
    beq=[m(i); 1];
    [F, v(i)]=quadprog(H, f, A, b, Aeq, beq);
end
```

where the output *F* is the optimal allocation we desire, and $v(i)$ is the corresponding minimum variance. We have plotted the set of *F* and *v* results in Figure 1.2.

The tangency portfolio is found by maximizing the Sharpe ratio:

```
sd=sqrt(v);
sharpeRatio=m./sd;
[~, idx]=max(sharpeRatio);
beq=[m(idx); 1];
[F]=quadprog(H, f, A, b, Aeq, beq)
```

The resulting weights are $F = (0.45, 0.26, 0.00, 0.00, 0.00, 0.29)$. The minimum variance portfolio to be discussed in the main text is found by (what else?) minimizing the variance or standard deviation:

```
[~, idxMin]=min(sd);
scatter(sd(idxMin), m(idxMin), 'green', 'filled');


beq=[m(idxMin); 1];
[F]=quadprog(H, f, A, b, Aeq, beq)
```

The resulting allocations are $F = (0.38, 0.00, 0.60, 0.00, 0.01, 0.00)$.

You can see that both F's satisfy the constraints that their components are all non-negative and sum to 1. The complete code can be downloaded as ef.m.

Maximizing the Sharpe ratio may seem intuitively like a good thing, but actually what many investors (like myself) want is to maximize the expected compound growth rate of the portfolio over an infinite (or indefinite) time horizon. Fortunately, it turns out that maximizing the expected compound growth rate is equivalent to maximizing the Sharpe ratio. To prove this, we first recognize that the expected compound growth rate is just μ, the expected log return (see exercise 1.21 for proof). By equation 1.1, this is equal to $F^T M - \frac{1}{2} F^T CF$ for the portfolio. To maximize this, we take the partial derivative with respect to each F_i and setting it to zero. The solution is $F^* = C^{-1}M$, where F^* denotes the optimal allocation. But this is precisely the Kelly optimal allocation I wrote about in Chan (2009). To show that this allocation also maximizes the Sharpe ratio under the constraint of a finite, fixed, leverage, note that the Sharpe ratio of the portfolio is $F^T M/(F^T CF)^{1/2}$. We want to maximize this, subject to the constraint that the sum of F_i is 1, or $F^T 1 = 1$ (where 1 is a column vector of 1s, and it won't matter if we set $F^T 1$ to some other arbitrary constant that represents the leverage we apply). Using Lagrange multipliers, it is shown in Box 1.3 that $C^{-1}M/\mathbf{1}^T C^{-1}M$ is also a solution.

In other words, it is the same as the Kelly optimal allocation F^*, but in a normalized form such that the total leverage is 1. So F^* doesn't just maximize the compound growth rate, it also maximizes the Sharpe ratio and specifies the tangency portfolio (to within a constant factor). It turns out that maximizing 1-period return subject to a variance constraint has the same solution as maximizing compound growth over an infinite horizon. This maximum compound growth rate can be expressed in terms of the maximum Sharpe ratio: It is just $\frac{S^{*2}}{2}$.

Box 1.3: Maximizing the Sharpe ratio of a portfolio

(This exposition is based on my blog post "Kelly vs. Markowitz Portfolio Optimization": epchan.blogspot.com/2014/08/kelly-vs-markowitz-portfolio.html, which in turn was drawn from faculty.washington.edu/ezivot/econ424/portfolioTheoryMatrix.pdf.)

In Box 1.2, we have minimized the variance of a portfolio for a given level of expected return. We did this numerically, using quadratic programming techniques. However, if we simply want to find the capital allocation corresponding to the tangency portfolio, we can do this analytically by maximizing the Sharpe ratio of the portfolio, subject to a constant leverage constraint. (The constant leverage can be set to 1 without loss of generality.) In other words, we want to maximize the Sharpe ratio

$$F^T M/(F^T CF)^{1/2} \text{ subject to: } F^T\mathbf{1} = 1$$

where $\mathbf{1}$ is a column vector of 1s.

Using the Lagrange multiplier method, this is the same as an unconstrained maximization of

$$\frac{F^T M}{(F^T CF)^{\frac{1}{2}}} - \lambda(F^T\mathbf{1} - 1), \tag{1.2}$$

where λ is the Lagrange multiplier.

Normally, the next step would be to take the derivative of the expression 1.2 with respect to each F_i. But taking the partial derivatives of this fraction with a square root in the denominator is unwieldy. To make things easier, we can equivalently maximize the logarithm of the Sharpe ratio subject to the same constraint, resulting in

$$\log(F^T M) - \frac{1}{2}\log(F^T CF) - \lambda(F^T \mathbf{1} - 1). \tag{1.3}$$

Taking the partial derivatives of equation 1.3 with respect to F_i, and setting each partial derivative to zero gives

$$\frac{1}{(F^T M)} M - \frac{1}{F^T CF} CF = \lambda \mathbf{1}. \tag{1.4}$$

If we multiply this whole equation by F^T on the right, we get

$$\frac{1}{(F^T M)} F^T M - \frac{1}{F^T CF} F^T CF = \lambda F^T 1. \tag{1.5}$$

The left-hand side comes out to be exactly zero, while the right-hand side is just λ because $F^T \mathbf{1} = 1$ due to our constraint. Hence, λ must be zero. A Lagrange multiplier that turns out to be zero means that the constraint won't affect the solution of the optimization problem up to a proportionality constant. This makes sense because we know that if we apply an equal leverage on all the assets, the maximum Sharpe ratio shouldn't be affected. So equation 1.4 becomes

$$CF = \frac{(F^T CF)}{(F^T M)} M. \tag{1.6}$$

It is easy to see that $F = C^{-1}M$ is a solution to this equation, which is the Kelly optimal allocation formula I have described in Chan (2009), and which maximizes the Sharpe ratio of a portfolio of instruments.

All this classical financial mathematics is elegant and satisfying, but reality often intrudes. The main problem is simple to understand: Past returns are not a good predictor of future returns. So the optimal allocation for the past is not necessarily the optimal allocation for the future. On the other hand, covariances are easier to predict than returns. Also, while the estimates of expected returns do not improve with larger sample size, estimates of covariances do (Ang, 2014). If we don't have returns estimates but still have covariances estimates, we can construct a *minimum variance portfolio*—that is, an allocation that minimizes the variance of returns of the portfolio. This is also marked on Figure 1.2. A side benefit of the minimum variance portfolio is that research has shown that low volatility stocks consistently outperform high volatility stocks (Baker et al., 2011). In the last 20 years, investors have increasingly favored minimum variance over tangency portfolio, giving rise to such ETFs as SPLV, ACWV, EEMV, and USMV.

Some investors have gone even further: They distrust even the covariance of returns and rely solely on the volatilities of individual stocks in making their capital allocation. Such is the case with the so-called *risk parity portfolio*, where capital allocated to each asset is inversely proportional to its volatility (Asness, 2012). In essence, this is targeting the same risk for each asset in the portfolio, hence the name *risk parity*. The ETF SPLV is constituted using this principle, and so is the famous $70 billion Bridgewater Associates All Weather fund. However, many risk management strategies have backfired due to their penchant for creating contagion. In other words, if everybody is adopting the same risk management strategy, everybody's risk will increase instead. For example, let's say everybody follows Kelly formula's advice to keep the leverage of their portfolio constant, and everybody's portfolio contains similar stocks. Then a loss in value of this portfolio will cause everybody to liquidate holdings, driving the (net asset) value of this portfolio even lower, and forcing further liquidation. The same problem is present for risk parity portfolios. If the market suffers a meltdown, volatility tends to increase, forcing risk parity funds to liquidate. Well, you know the rest of the story. This happened in the fall of 2015, when a combination of Chinese economic woes and crashing oil prices caused a market panic. The All Weather fund lost 7 percent in 2015, and was blamed for starting just such a contagion (Copeland and Martin, 2015).

In addition to the contagious liquidation problem discussed above, targeting the same volatility for each component of a portfolio also relies on the implicit Gaussian assumption that volatility is bad. But volatility isn't what we should be afraid of—tail risk is. As discussed in the section "Performance Metrics," maximum drawdown is a good measure of tail risk. So I suggest we should target the same maximum drawdown for each component of a portfolio if you are into the risk parity allocation method.[8]

Summary

This chapter touches on all the basic components of building an algorithmic trading strategy, from data to software, brokers, performance metrics, and finally to ways of building and optimizing a portfolio of assets or strategies. These issues are relevant to all the strategies that we will be discussing in the following chapters.

Exercises

1.1. What is an API?
1.2. What is a good IDE for Python?
1.3. What is the most useful MATLAB toolbox for an algorithmic trader?
1.4. Can Python access all of R's packages? If so, how?
1.5. Among MATLAB, R, and Python, which one is the slowest?
1.6. How would you speed up a computationally intensive MATLAB or Python program? Can you do the same for R?
1.7. What is a possible platform you can use to backtest and automate a live trading strategy if you do not wish to learn the details of a broker's API?
1.8. What is the benefit of using the same program to backtest and live-trade a strategy?
1.9. Suppose you have a stock selection strategy on SPX stocks. What data would you need to ensure that your backtest is survivorship-bias-free? Would it be sufficient to have prices for all the stocks that were ever listed in the US exchanges?
1.10. What is the best kind of closing prices to use for testing daily strategies? What is the second best kind? How do these differ from the usual consolidated closing prices?
1.11. What are the implied volatility surfaces that options data vendors often provide? How are they computed?
1.12. What is a REPL language, and why is it convenient for backtesting or research in general?
1.13. How much is a MATLAB home license? How much is each of its toolboxes under this license?
1.14. What is the difference between Calmar ratio and MAR?
1.15. Do FX transactions suffer from settlement risks since 2002?

1.16. What is the CLS bank?

1.17. Are commodity futures trading accounts protected by SIPC insurance?

1.18. What is the benefit of opening a brokerage account in the name of an LLC or LP?

1.19. Why can't net returns ever have a Gaussian distribution in principle?

1.20. Prove that the expected market value at time t of a security that undergoes a geometric random walk from an initial value of \$1 is e^{mt}, with m is the expected net return over a unit time interval. (*Hint:* Divide a time interval into n segments, and express the market value as an exponential of the sum of log returns. Also, remember that if Z is a Gaussian random variable with mean μ and standard deviation s, then e^Z has mean $e^{\mu+s^2/2}$ and standard deviation e^s. Finally, make use of equation 1.1.)

1.21. Prove that the expected compound growth rate of a security that undergoes a geometric random walk is μ, its expected log return over a unit time interval. (*Hint:* The expected compound growth rate is defined as $E[\log(V(t)/V(0))]/t$, where $V(t)$ is the market value at time t. Express this expectation as a sum of log returns by dividing a time interval into n segments, and take the limit as $n \to \infty$.)

1.22. What is the formula for the Kelly optimal allocation? What does this allocation maximize? What's the name of the portfolio that uses Kelly optimal allocation?

1.23. Why is the minimum variance portfolio often favored over the tangency portfolio?

1.24. What is the difference between a minimum variance portfolio and a risk parity portfolio?

1.25. Why is it possible to generate a contagion in a financial crisis if everybody owns a risk 8 portfolio?

1.26. What is the drawback of measuring risk by computing volatility of returns? What are the alternatives?

Endnotes

1. If we are backtesting a portfolio strategy for stocks in a stock index, we will also need to know when the stock was added and/or removed from that index. Just having historical prices for delisted stocks won't be enough. Check out www.masteretfdata.com for historical index composition.

2. Integrated Development Environment, or IDE, is essentially an editor and debugger for programmers. It is crucial for software development productivity.
3. Numba is one of the Python packages that facilitates compilation to C/C++, and NumbaPro is the commercial version that allows parallel processing using a GPU (graphics processing unit).
4. REPL (Read-Eval-Print-Loop) languages do not require compilation; hence, debugging and modifications can be done much faster.
5. The maximum coverage for securities and cash combined is $500,000.
6. Excess cash means cash balance that exceeds the margin requirement for the existing futures positions.
7. Strictly speaking, we need to subtract the risk-free rate from the returns before taking the mean and variance. But since 2008, we can just assume the risk-free rate is zero.
8. For the financial sophisticates, there are also value-at-risk (VaR) and expected shortfall (ES) that one can use as stand-ins for volatility. These also do not rely on the Gaussian assumption. (See Ruppert, 2015.)

CHAPTER 2

Factor Models

If all we want is profit, we would not need to study quantitative finance or to trade at all. We just need to go and buy SPY and hold it for 30 to 40 years,[1] preferably longer. The reason some of us are reluctant to do so (at least, not for 100 percent of our net worth) is market risk: buying-and-holding the stock index has long periods of drawdowns. We may be forced to liquidate some of that holding to raise cash at a most inopportune time. What if we instead hold a long-short market-neutral portfolio? For example, we may hear that value stocks offer better long-term returns than growth stocks (after all, the value investor Warren Buffett is very rich). So why not just long value stocks and short growth stocks? That actually works quite well,[2] except during the dotcom bubble in the late 1990s, when this portfolio, too, came to grief. Just because this portfolio doesn't have market risk doesn't mean it doesn't have some other risk associated with long value and short growth. In fact, many of the strategies we will discuss in this book, whether they trade stocks or options, have such so-called factor risks. For example, many of the strategies in the options chapter are exposed to the volatility risk factor—they do poorly when volatility increases. They are by no means riskless arbitrage. In fact, their risks are unlike the random fluctuations of white noise—the factor risk of each stock is both *serially* and *cross-sectionally* correlated over a period of time. For our long-value short-growth portfolio, we are almost sure that it will lose money for long periods when we have "irrational exuberance." For our (short) options strategies, we are almost sure that they will lose in those periods when volatility increases, and that is true for practically any options you trade.

Traders and investors justifiably like to chase after "alphas"—returns that are not known to be associated with factor risks. Earning alpha is almost riskless arbitrage, because their risks can be reduced to zero by increasing diversification. The more stocks one includes in a portfolio with positive alpha, the smaller the (white noise) risk compared to its return. On the other hand, factor risk cannot be diversified away. No matter how many value stocks you add to the long side of a portfolio, and how many growth stocks you add to the short side, the factor risk remains unchanged. But because everybody loves alpha, it is especially hard to find. Every time someone finds alpha, they have to keep it a secret. And still, more and more people will discover it eventually, and the alpha diminishes. Even if nobody else finds it, alpha has limited capacity, so eventually it diminishes if too much capital has been applied to it. Factor risk is different. It is hardly a secret that investing in the market index will generate positive return in the long term, yet many people still shy away from the stock market because of the undiversifiable risk. It is hardly a secret that selling options will generate positive return in the long term (as the longevity of the insurance industry testifies), yet many people are still afraid of doing so because of the likely sharp drawdown in times of financial crises. Because of these risks, most factor returns remain alive and well, year after year. This is the reason why we will study factor models in this chapter, despite their relative lack of sex appeal compared to alpha generation. Also, trading factor models makes you a more sociable person, since you don't need to hide what you do for a living from your colleagues lest they steal your alphas.[3]

(It is true that some factor returns do decrease over time, such as the SMB factor we will discuss in the time-series factors section, or the put-call implied volatilities factor in the Using Option Prices section. Their returns decrease likely because investors perceive that the associated factor risks have decreased as well. In the SMB case, investors may believe that small-cap stocks are no more risky than large-cap stocks, as long as we are sufficiently diversified. After all, Enron and Lehman Brothers were both large-cap stocks.)

As I wrote above, many of the strategies I describe later in the book have implicit factor exposures, though one cannot call them *factor models*. This term is confined to simple linear models, where the predictors in the linear regression are our factors. This is also the reason why the regression coefficients for factors are sometimes called *smart betas,* a "dumb" beta being the regression coefficient between the return of a stock versus the return of the market index. I will describe the difference between time-series and cross-sectional factors, some of the new and interesting factors that researchers have discovered ranging from fundamental to option-implied, how surprisingly well you can do when all you have is price data, and the different ways to implement a factor model.

Time-series Factors

The two factors mentioned earlier in this chapter, the market return and the value-minus-growth return, are examples of time-series factors (Ruppert and Matteson, 2015). They are so-called because they vary from *time* to *time*, but they do not vary across different stocks or financial assets. The value-minus-growth factor is often called HML, because it is the returns of a basket of high book-to-market stocks minus that of a basket of low book-to-market stocks. Such a long-short portfolio whose returns represent a time-series factor is called a "hedge" portfolio.[4] What do vary across different stocks are their returns in response to this factor. This response is called the *factor loading* (or *factor exposure*), which is just a regression coefficient. Time-series factors usually (but not always) have dimensions of returns (i.e., dollar divided by time), but factor loadings are dimensionless. If we think that a stock's return is driven by multiple factors, we can write

$$Return(t, s) - r_F = \alpha(t, s) + \beta_1(s) * Factor_1(t) + \beta_2(s) * Factor_2(t) + \cdots + \varepsilon(t, s) \quad (2.1)$$

where each $Return(t, s)$ represents the return of a stock s over a period from $t - 1$ to t, r_F is the risk free rate over the same period, and the $\beta_i(s)$ are the factor loadings of that stock. The alpha α of a stock is included, in case we have some special arbitrage model that tells us why this stock will have a time-varying return not driven by common factors. In our modeling in this chapter, we won't have any such alpha models, hence α will be set as a constant in time: $\alpha(t, s) = \alpha(s)$.[5] Finally, a noise term ε is included to represent "white noise." This noisy return is a catchall term that captures anything that our factor or alpha models are unable to explain, and is supposed to be uncorrelated both serially (in time) and cross-sectionally (across stocks). These are the risks that can be diversified away by adding more stocks to our portfolio.

Since the time-series factors are observable (e.g., we can easily measure the market return) and known historically, all we need to do is use the usual least square fit to find the $\beta_i(s)$'s. But how do we use equation 2.1 for our investment decisions? Notice that the time index t is the same on both sides of the equation. This means that this factor model, as with most factor models you will read about in standard finance textbooks, are descriptive and explanatory, but not predictive. They *explain* the return of a stock that is *contemporaneous* with the returns of the market index, HML, SMB, and perhaps other factors. As such, this equation is not immediately useful for generating trading profits. All we could do is to assume that these factor returns will remain the same forever, with their future values equal to their past values, and buy the stocks that have the largest $Return(t, s)$ and short the stocks that have the smallest (perhaps negative) returns, according to equation 2.1. Apart from the effect of random noise, this is essentially buying the past winners, and shorting the past losers.

Alternatively, we can make things a little more interesting by turning equation 2.1 into a predictive equation. Just write

$$Return(t+1, s) - r_F = \alpha(s) + \beta_1(s) * Factor_1(t) + \beta_2(s) * Factor_2(t) + \cdots + \varepsilon(t, s) \quad (2.2)$$

and run a similar least square fit. Once we have obtained estimates of the α and β_i for each stock, we can use equation 2.2 for predicting the next period's return.

By replacing equation 2.1 with 2.2, I did not mean to imply that a descriptive factor model is useless for traders. Its use, however, is not in predicting returns—it is in risk management. If, for example, we know that a strategy or portfolio loads (regresses) positively to volatility change, we might want to trade another strategy or own another portfolio that loads negatively to volatility change as a hedge. This does not require us to predict whether volatility is going up or down, nor does it require us to predict the next day's return given today's volatility change. The two strategies or portfolios together will have minimum exposure to volatility risk, no matter which way volatility goes. Much of factor modeling practiced by large funds is not concerned with predicting returns, but with understanding and managing the factor risks, and for attributing returns of a strategy to different factors. Performance attribution is also important because some investors do not wish to pay incentive (performance-based) fees to the fund managers on returns that can be attributed to factor returns, since these returns can be easily obtained by buying smart-beta ETFs or other index funds. However, the use of factor models for risk management or performance attribution is not our focus in this chapter.

Besides the market return and HML, other popular time-series factors are SMB—the returns of a basket of small-market-capitalization stocks minus that of a basket of big-market-capitalization stocks, and UMD—the returns of a basket of stocks whose prices went up minus that of a basket of stocks that went down. (People also call this the WML factor: "Winners minus Losers.") The latter is, of course, a momentum factor. Interestingly, both the HML value factor and the UMD momentum factor have positive returns. As footnoted earlier, HML returned about 900 percent between 1965 and 2011, but UMD returned about 3000 percent over the same period (Ang, 2014)! There is no reason we have to choose one over the other: We can buy both hedge portfolios simultaneously. Other macroeconomic factors include economic growth (specifically, real quarterly GDP growth and quarterly real personal consumption expenditures growth), quarterly Consumer Price Index change, and volatility (VIX) change.

We show in Example 2.1 how the market return, HML, and SMB factors do in predicting daily returns of stocks.

Example 2.1: Using Fama-French factors to predict the next-day return

The three time-series factors we discussed in the main text, the excess market return (i.e., market return minus the risk free rate), the HML portfolio return, and the SMB portfolio return, are called the Fama–French factors (Fama and French, 1993). They are usually used as contemporaneous factors to account for the current returns of a stock. However, here we will see whether they can be used as predictor factors to predict the next day's returns of stocks in the S&P 500 Index.

For our backtest, we use mid-quotes at market close provided by the Center for Research of Security Prices (CRSP.com) survivorship-bias-free database from January 3, 2007, to December 31, 2013. We choose the midprice (half of the bid and ask prices) at the market close to represent the closing price in order to avoid effects of the widened bid-ask spread at the close. The daily market, HML, and SMB factors are from Professor French's website mba.tuck.dartmouth.edu/pages/faculty/ken.french/data_library.html#Research over the same period as the price data. We divide this data into two halves, and use the first half as a trainset to estimate the factor loadings for each stock separately (i.e., in a multivariate, multiple regression).[6] Using

MATLAB's Statistics and Machine Learning Toolbox (you can also use R's *lm* function), we can write

```
for s=1:length(syms)
     model=fitlm([mktRF(trainset) smb(trainset) hml(trainset)],
       retFut1(trainset, s), 'linear');
     retPred1(:, s)=predict(model, [mktRF smb hml]);
end
```

where *retFut1* is the excess return (return minus risk free rate) for the next trading day and *retPred1* is the predicted return for the next trading day. Note that *fitlm* will automatically supply a constant offset by default, so one does not need to augment the input variables with a column of ones as would be the case if we were to use the *regress* function in the same toolbox.

We then buy the top 50 stocks with the largest predicted returns and short the bottom 50 with the smallest.

```
positions=zeros(size(mid));
topN=50;

for t=1:length(tday)
    isGoodData=find(isfinite(retPred1(t, :)));
    [~, I]=sort(retPred1(t, isGoodData)); % ascending sort
    positions(t, isGoodData(I(1:topN)))=-1;
    positions(t, isGoodData(I(end-topN+1)))=1;
end
```

Since our data set is a survivorship-bias-free one, there are symbols that stopped trading as well as symbols that just started trading in the middle of the time period. Hence we can only make predictions for the subset of data *isGoodData* that has daily returns on a certain day.

Naturally, the model works very well in-sample: it has a CAGR of 242 percent and a Sharpe ratio of 3.7. However, it generated negative returns out-of-sample. Clearly, the Fama-French factors are not terribly useful for short-term predictions!

The complete code can be downloaded as FamaFrenchFactors_predict.m.

Cross-sectional Factors

Most of us are familiar with the notion that stock-specific factors such as price-to-earnings (P/E) ratio or gross margin would affect a stock's return. These are called cross-sectional factors, because they vary across different stocks. Actually, it is more accurate to call them factor loadings, in keeping with our convention that factors usually have dimension of returns and have the same value across different stocks but varying in time, while factor loadings are usually dimensionless and have the same value throughout time but vary across different stocks.

Time-series factors such as HML and SMB are directly observable as the returns of a well-defined hedge portfolio, while we have to run a regression fit to find out the value of the factor loading of each stock. In contrast, cross-sectional factor loadings such as P/E are obviously observable, and it is the time-series factors that have to be computed by regressing stock returns against these factor loadings.

Since practically every item in the financial statement of a company can be turned into a cross-sectional factor loading for its stock's return, it is hard to know what to include. As a start, you may try including everything you can easily get data on. In Example 2.2, we included 27 fundamental factor loadings in order to predict the quarterly returns of stocks, and the out-of-sample performance is quite respectable: the CAGR is 12 percent.

Despite the reasonable performance of applying factor model blindly to all the fundamental factors available, it is still useful to examine which individual factor loadings are particularly predictive and perhaps understand why they are so predictive. This has the benefit of avoiding overfitting to too many factor loadings, some of which may be just along for the ride. Also, we should look into innovative factor loadings that are not included in the financial statements of companies. We will explore these in the following sections.

Example 2.2: Fitting a cross-sectional factor model to predict the next-quarter return

We will attempt to use fundamental factor loadings extracted from the quarterly financial statements of companies to predict their next-quarter returns. The price data are midprice at market close provided by CRSP as in Example 2.1. The fundamental data are obtained from

Sharadar's Core U.S. Fundamentals database and delivered through Quandl.com. However, we avoid factor loadings that scale with the size of the company, such as total revenue or market capitalization. Any dependence of returns on size can be better captured by the time-series SMB factor instead. There are a total of 27 cross-sectional factor loadings that are company-size independent. These are listed as in Table 2.1.

TABLE 2.1 Input Factor Loadings that Are Size-Independent

Variable name	Explanation	Period
CURRENTRATIO		Quarterly
DE	Debt to Equity Ratio	Quarterly
DILUTIONRATIO	Share Dilution Ratio	Quarterly
PB	Price to Book Value	Quarterly
TBVPS	Tangible Asset Book Value per Share	Quarterly
ASSETTURNOVER		Trailing 1 year
EBITDAMARGIN		Trailing 1 year
EPSGROWTH1YR		Trailing 1 year
EQUITYAVG	Average Equity	Trailing 1 year
EVEBIT	Enterprise Value over EBIT	Trailing 1 year
EVEBITDA	Enterprise Value over EBITDA	Trailing 1 year
GROSSMARGIN		Trailing 1 year
INTERESTBURDEN	Financial Leverage	Trailing 1 year
LEVERAGERATIO		Trailing 1 year
NCFOGROWTH1YR		Trailing 1 year
NETINCGROWTH1YR	Net Income Growth	Trailing 1 year
NETMARGIN	Profit Margin	Trailing 1 year
PAYOUTRATIO		Trailing 1 year
PE	Price Earnings Damodaran Method	Trailing 1 year
PE1		Trailing 1 year
PS		Trailing 1 year
PS1	Price Sales Damodaran Method	Trailing 1 year
REVENUEGROWTH1YR		Trailing 1 year
ROA		Trailing 1 year
ROE		Trailing 1 year
ROS		Trailing 1 year
TAXEFFICIENCY		Trailing 1 year

These variables are stored as $T \times S$ matrices, where T is the number of historical days in the data, and S is the number of stocks (actually greater than 500, since we need to include stocks that were historically in the SPX index but were delisted on or before the last day in the dataset). We want to predict the returns of these stocks using a factor model similar to equation 2.2, with $\alpha(s)$ replaced by $\alpha(t)$ since this is now a cross-sectional model. In principle, fitting such a cross-sectional model means that at every time (calendar quarter) t, we will have a different set of regression coefficients $Factor_i(t)$. But due to the limited number of data points (about 500 for SPX stocks) at any one time, this regression won't be very robust. Furthermore, there is no reason to believe that the factors should change from quarter to quarter (though of course the factor loadings such as PE ratio do change). To increase robustness, we will combine all the data throughout the trainset for many quarters. In programming terms, we combine all the columns of data belonging to different stocks into one single vector with $T \times S$ rows, using the *reshape* function. Below, we show how to reshape the dependent variable (quarterly returns from the next day's close, which is the first closing price with which we could enter into positions):


```
retQ=calculateReturns(mid, holdingDays); % quarterly return
retFut=fwdshift(holdingDays+1, retQ);
trainset=1:floor(length(tday)/2);
Y=reshape(retFut(trainset, :), [length(trainset)*length(syms) 1]);
  % dependent variable
```

We can apply the same *reshape* function to the input factor loadings (the independent variables) as well. Notice we use only the first half of the data as train data to fit the regression model. Once the data are laid out in the proper dimension, we can use the *fitlm* function as in Example 2.1 for the regression fit:

```
model=fitlm(X, Y,  'linear')
```

The beauty of the *fitlm* function is that it will automatically ignore any rows (days) that contain a NaN value. In our case, this means that it will only regress on those days for a stock with an earnings announcement that makes available all the financial variables. So for each stock, only one day per quarter will actually be used as input data. This fit produces a very weak model: the R^2 is only 0.015. Nevertheless, predictive models in finance often are very weak, but that doesn't mean we cannot generate profits. To make predictions, we need to use the *predict* function and then unpack the vector containing the predicted returns back to a $T \times S$ matrix before we can compute our usual performance measures:

```
retPred=reshape(predict(model, X), [length(trainset)
   length(syms)]);
```

Our trading strategy uses these predicted quarterly returns by entering into a long position in a stock on the following trading day's market close whenever its predicted return is positive, and holding for a quarter (or more precisely, 63 trading days), and similarly for the short positions.

```
longs=backshift(1, retPred>0); %1 day later
shorts=backshift(1, retPred<0);

longs(1, :)=false;
shorts(1, :)=false;

positions=zeros(size(retPred));

for h=0:holdingDays-1
    long_lag=backshift(h, longs);
    long_lag(isnan(long_lag))=false;
    long_lag=logical(long_lag);

    short_lag=backshift(h, shorts);
    short_lag(isnan(short_lag))=false;
    short_lag=logical(short_lag);

    positions(long_lag)=positions(long_lag)+1;
    positions(short_lag)=positions(short_lag)-1;
end
```

Despite the weak regression fit, this strategy generates a CAGR of 12.3 percent out-of-sample, with a Sharpe ratio of 1.7, and a maximum drawdown of 7.6 percent. The equity curve is shown on Figure 2.1.

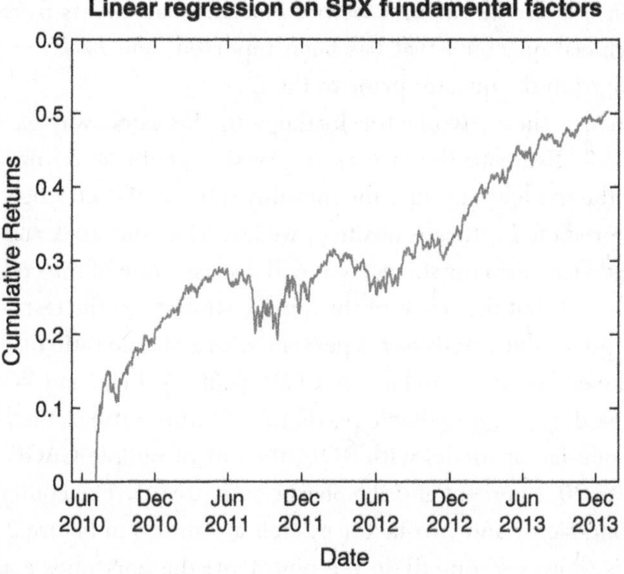

FIGURE 2.1 Fundamental cross-sectional factor model on SPX component stocks

The complete code can be downloaded as crossSectional_SPX.m.

You may be curious whether just throwing in the whole lot of fundamental factors, including those that scale with company size, will generate comparable returns. There are 112 such factors in total, and the R^2 on the trainset is greatly improved to 0.961 (even the adjusted R^2, which supposedly adjusts for the larger number of factors, is a very respectable 0.671.) Indeed, the CAGR of the training set is very high: 48 percent. However, this model fell apart completely on the test set, generating a negative CAGR. Clearly, the larger number of factors result in severe overfitting.

A Two-Factor Model

A paper by Chattopadhyay, Lyle, and Wang (2015) presented an exceedingly simple cross-sectional two-factor model that is derived from fundamental financial principles. The two-factor loadings are the log of return-on-equity (ROE) and the log of book-to-market ratio (BM). ROE is defined as

$$ROE(i, s) = 1 + X(i, s)/Book(i - 1, s)$$

where $X(i, s)$ is the net income before extraordinary items from the most recent financial quarter i that has been reported, and $Book(i-1, s)$ is the book value from the quarter prior to the ith.

We can use these two-factor loadings in the same way as we did in Example 2.2: Estimate the factors (regression coefficients) on a trainset, and apply the model to predict the monthly returns of each stock in the test set. If the predicted return is positive, we buy \$1 of the stock and hold for a month, and vice versa for shorts. We will discuss some of the coding details in Example 2.3, but the result of this simple strategy on the test set is seemingly very good: the CAGR is 9.3 percent with a Sharpe ratio of 1 from July 2010 to the end of 2013. In fact, as Chattopadhyay, Lyle, and Wang (2015) asserted, ROE is a more reliable predictor of future returns than BM. If we use just a one-factor model with ROE, the out-of-sample CAGR is actually increased to 20.2 percent and the Sharpe ratio to 1.3. The equity curves of both the one-factor and two-factor models are shown in Figure 2.2.

There is, however, one fly in the ointment: the portfolios generated by these trading strategies are usually net long. That is, they have more long

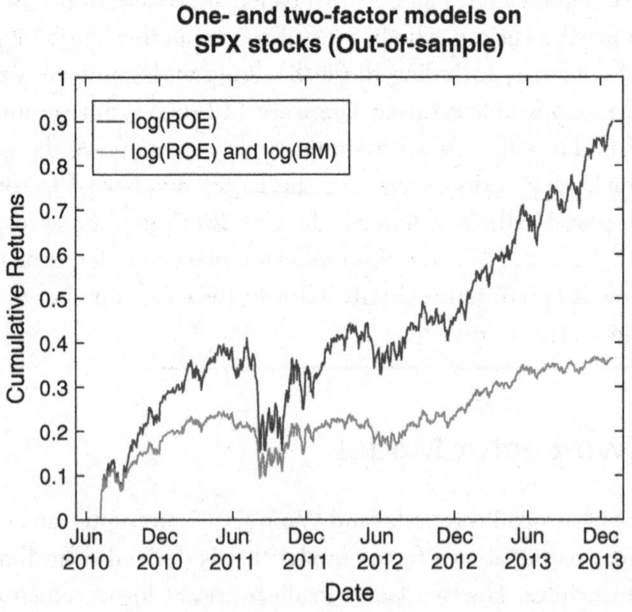

FIGURE 2.2 One- and two-factor models on SPX component stocks

than short positions. Since we enjoyed a fabulous bull market from 2010 to 2013, it is no surprise that these strategies produced a good return. If we use SPY to hedge the net exposure of the portfolio (whether long or the rare short net exposure), then the out-of-sample CAGR for either one or two factors is about zero.

There is another way to produce a market neutral portfolio other than hedging with SPY. On any given day, we can rank the predicted returns, and long the stocks in the top quintile of predicted returns, and short those in the bottom quintile (provided that there are five or more stocks that have earnings announcements in the previous day). Unfortunately, this technique generates negative returns on the test set for either one or two factors.

There is one reason why our market-neutral results here seem to pale beside that of Chattopadhyay, Lyle, and Wang (2015), who obtained out-of-sample CAGR of 4.3 percent for a market-neutral portfolio of US stocks. They included all stocks in the United States that are in the top 98th-percentile in market capitalization and liquidity,[7] while we included only large-cap (SPX) stocks. If we apply the ROE one-factor model to small-cap (SML) stocks only, we generate a CAGR of over 5 percent, which is a lot closer to the published results. This difference of factor model performance between large- and small-cap stocks is corroborated by the research of Kaplan (2014), who found that value factors are useless for predicting returns of SPX stocks.

Aside from its rigorous theoretical derivation from first principles, the ROE factor is actually quite similar to the return-on-capital and the earnings yield factors made popular by the author Joel Greenblatt in his *The Little Book That Still Beats the Market* (Greenblatt, 2010).

Example 2.3: Fitting the ROE and BM factor model to predict the next-month return

To validate the results of Chattopadhyay, Lyle, and Wang (2015), we use the same price and fundamental data set described in Example 2.2. For the variable *X* (Net Income before Extraordinary Items), we use the variable ARQ_EPS (Earnings per Basic Share) from Sharadar, whereas for the variable *book* (book value per share), we use ARQ_BVPS. To compute ROE, we divide ARQ_EPS of the most recent quarter by the book value per share of the prior quarter.

```
earningsInc=ARQ_EPS; % Earnings (net income) per Basic Share

bvpershr=ARQ_BVPS;
bvpershr_lag=backshift(1, fillMissingData(bvpershr));

ROE=1+earningsInc./bvpershr_lag;
```

To compute BM, we take the reciprocal of ARQ_PB (price-to-book ratio):

```
BM=1./ARQ_PB;
```

There are stocks with negative earnings (net income), and there are even stocks with negative book value. We effectively remove[8] such data from the input by setting them to NaN:

```
ROE(ROE <= 0)=NaN;
BM(BM <= 0)=NaN;
```


As in Example 2.2, we need to aggregate data from different stocks before running our regression fit:

```
X(:, 1)=reshape(log(BM(trainset, :)), [length(trainset)*
  length(syms) 1]);
X(:, 2)=reshape(log(ROE(trainset, :)), [length(trainset)*
  length(syms) 1]);
```

The rest of the code is identical to that in Example 2.2, and it can be downloaded as twoFundamentalFactors.m. This produces an out-of-sample CAGR of 9.3 percent.

If we want to test the market-neutral strategy mentioned in the main text, where we rank the predicted returns, long the stocks in the top quintile of predicted returns, and short those in the bottom quintile when there are five or more stocks that have earnings announcements in the previous day, we can write

```
[retPredSorted, idx]=sort(retPred, 2);

longs=false(size(retPred));
shorts=longs;
```

```
for t=2:size(longs, 1)
    idxFinite=find(isfinite(retPredSorted(t-1, :))); %1 day later
    if (length(idxFinite) >= 5)
        longs(t, idx(t-1, idxFinite(end-floor(length(idxFinite)/5)
          +1:end)))=true;
        shorts(t, idx(t-1, idxFinite(1:floor(length
          (idxFinite)/5))))=true;
    end
end
```

Once the *longs* and *shorts* arrays are thus determined, the rest of the code is again the same as in Example 2.2. This produces a CAGR of −9.2 percent.

Using Option Prices to Predict Stock Returns

Market folklore has it that options traders are smarter and better informed than mere stock traders. (One can frequently observe option traders with lifted chins looking down their noses at stock traders.) Therefore, one would think that we could predict stock returns using options price information. This intuition is borne out by a shocking number of academic studies. We can summarize the predictive options information in the form of factors. For those readers who may be unfamiliar with options terminology, you can first read Chapter 5 on options before reading this section.

1) Implied Moments

In a paper by Bali, Hu, and Murray (2015), implied volatility is defined as the average of the at-the-money (ATM) call and put options implied volatilities, while the implied skewness is measured by the difference between the out-of-the-money (OTM) calls and puts implied volatilities. Here, a call or put option is regarded as ATM if it has a delta of about 0.5 or −0.5, respectively, and OTM if it has a delta of about 0.25 or −0.25, respectively. Finally, implied kurtosis is measured by the difference between the sum of the implied volatilities of OTM calls and puts versus the sum of the implied volatilities of ATM calls and puts. We also specify that all these options should have a "tenor" of 30 days. That is, they all have 30 days until expiration. (We shall see how we can enforce this requirement in practice.) In summary,

$$Vol = \frac{CIV(0.5) + PIV(-0.5)}{2}$$
$$Skew = CIV(0.25) - PIV(-0.25)$$
$$Kurt = CIV(0.25) + PIV(-0.25) - CIV(0.5) - PIV(-0.5)$$

where CIV and PIV indicate call and put implied volatility respectively, and the number in the parentheses indicates the delta of the option. Why all these definitions? The researchers found that the underlying stock's expected return is strongly positively related to each of these implied moments.

We can construct a long-short portfolio that has a high expected return by following this recipe. First, sort the stocks by their implied skewness, take the top 30 percent, then sort this subset by their implied kurtosis, take the top 30 percent, then finally sort this sub-subset by their implied volatility, and again take the top 30 percent. This constitutes the long side of the portfolio. The short side is similarly constructed, except that we take the bottom 30 percent at each sorting step. We will perform the sorting every month and hold such a portfolio for a month. This long-short strategy returns an unlevered 9.68 percent per annum (i.e., if one is long $0.5 million and short $0.5 million of stocks, one should expect an annual profit of $96,800).

The reason why stocks with high implied volatilities have higher expected returns basically follows from the well-known dictum: Higher risks have to be compensated by higher returns. This is just the capital asset pricing model (CAPM) fondly studied by generations of finance students (Sharpe, 1964). Similarly, investors are averse to *kurtosis,* which is another word for *tail risks,* and thus they also need to be compensated by higher future returns if such risks are high. When expected risks are high, investors would pay more to buy options. In particular, they pay relatively more for OTM options than ATM options when expected tail risks are high. Bali, Hu, and Murray (2015), explain that stocks with high implied skewness have higher expected returns because investors with positive expectations about future returns buy OTM calls and/or sell OTM puts, thereby increasing the implied skewness.

This research was performed on all US stocks that have listed options from 1999 to 2012. The researchers used numerical techniques to construct a volatility surface and to back out the implied volatilities of call and put options that have the required deltas and tenor of 30 days. In Example 2.4, we will try this strategy on SPX stocks from 2007 to 2013.

One side note: Is it important that the authors chose tenor of 30 days? The answer seems to be no. The ratio of implied volatilities as a function of delta is independent of tenor, according to Sinclair (2016).

Example 2.4: Long (short) stocks with high (low) implied moments

Instead of applying the strategy described in Bali, Hu, and Murray (2015) to all US stocks with listed options, we apply it only to SPX stocks with listed options. As in the original paper, our stock price data come from CRSP, while options data come from OptionMetrics' implied volatility surface. Following the paper, we also picked the implied volatilities of those options that have a tenor of 30 days, and with a delta of ±0.5 for ATM options and ±0.25 for OTM options. These implied volatilities are stored in the arrays *impVolC_ATM* (for calls), *impVolP_ATM* (for puts), *impVolC_OTM*, and *impVolP_OTM*, which have the same $T \times S$ dimension as the closing price array *cl*, where T is the number of days in the data set, and S is the number of stocks. Our data runs from January 3, 2007, to December 31, 2013, and there are 743 stock symbols in our survivorship-bias-free database. To compute the variables *Vol*, *Skew*, and *Kurt* as described in the main text, we go through each day in a for loop, and

```
impVol=(impVolC_ATM(t, :)+impVolP_ATM(t, :))/2;
impSkew=impVolC_OTM(t, :)-impVolP_OTM(t, :);
impKurtosis=impVolC_OTM(t, :)+impVolP_OTM(t, :)-impVolC_ATM(t, :)
  -impVolP_ATM(t, :);
```

Next, we first sort by *Skew*, taking care to ensure that we choose only those stocks with finite implied skewness, and take the top 30 percent as long candidates, and the bottom 30 percent as short candidates:

```
goodData=find(isfinite(impSkew));
[~, idx1]=sort(impSkew(goodData), 'ascend');

topPct=0.3;

topN1=round(length(goodData)*topPct);
shortCandidates=goodData(idx1(1:topN1)); % Short low Skew
longCandidates=goodData(idx1(end-topN1+1:end)); % Buy high Skew
```

Then we sort the long candidates by *Kurt*, again taking the top 30 percent as the new long candidates:

```
[~, idx2L]=sort(impKurtosis(longCandidates), 'descend');
topN2L=round(length(longCandidates)*topPct);
longCandidates2=longCandidates(idx2L(1:topN2L)); % Buy high
  kurtosis
```

Similarly, we sort the short candidates by *Kurt*, taking the bottom 30 percent as the new short candidates:

```
[~, idx2S]=sort(impKurtosis(shortCandidates), 'ascend');
topN2S=round(length(shortCandidates)*topPct);
shortCandidates2=shortCandidates(idx2S(1:topN2S)); % Short low
  kurtosis
```

Finally, we sort the new long candidates by *Vol*, taking the top 30 percent as the final long candidates:

```
[~, idx3L]=sort(impVol(longCandidates2), 'descend');
topN3L=round(length(longCandidates2)*topPct);
longCandidates3=longCandidates2(idx3L(1:topN3L)); % Buy high IV
```


We similarly sort the new short candidates by *Vol*, taking the bottom 30 percent as the final short candidates:


```
[~, idx3S]=sort(impVol(shortCandidates2), 'ascend');
topN3S=round(length(shortCandidates2)*topPct);
shortCandidates3=shortCandidates2(idx3S(1:topN3S)); % Short low IV
```

Naturally, we will buy the long candidates, short the short candidates, and hold the portfolio for 21 days (1 month).

```
pos0(t, shortCandidates3)=-1;
pos0(t, longCandidates3)=1;

pos=zeros(size(pos0));

for h=0:holddays-1
    pos_lag=backshift(h, pos0);
    pos_lag(isnan(pos_lag))=0;
    pos=pos+pos_lag;
end
```

Note that instead of only entering into new positions at the beginning of the month, we do this sorting every day, and enter into a new portfolio every day. So there are a total of 21 portfolios that we hold simultaneously on each day, and we have to divide the P&L by the total gross market value of these portfolios to generate the unlevered return each day.

In contrast to Bali (2015), who obtained a CAGR of 9.68 percent, we obtain almost exactly zero return. Just like the model discussed in the section on "A Two-Factor Model," these factors have no predictive power on large-cap stocks at all! If you want to implement this trading strategy, I recommend trying it on all optionable stocks instead.

---

2) Monthly Change in Implied Volatilities

"Stocks with large increases in call (put) implied volatilities over the previous month tend to have high (low) future returns. Sorting stocks ranked into decile portfolios by past call implied volatilities produces spreads in average returns of approximately 1 percent per month ...," so wrote An et al. (2013). This means we can expect an unlevered CAGR of over 6 percent from buying those stocks in the top decile of predicted returns and shorting those in the bottom decile, and hold these for a month before rebalancing.

This may be the most intuitive of all the results in this section: when option traders expect a stock's price to increase, they will pay more for a call option which gives them the right to buy it at a pre-specified price. So this result just tells us that these option traders are correct in their expectation. The opposite result, of course, applies to put options.

This research was performed on about 1,000 to 2,300 US stocks from 1996 to 2011. The researchers used numerical techniques to construct a volatility surface as in Example 2.4 and to back out the implied volatilities of call and put options that have a delta of 0.5 (i.e., at-the-money, or ATM, options) with tenor of 30 days.

3) Put-call Implied Volatilities

Put-call parity (Sinclair, 2010) is only exactly true for European options, and small deviation from it is permitted for American options. Cremers and Weinbaum (2010), found that deviation from put-call parity is useful for predicting future stock returns. The deviation from put-call parity is simply the difference between the weighted implied volatilities from calls and puts:

$$VS(t,s) = \sum_j w_j(t,s)\left[IV_j^{call}(t,s) - IV_j^{put}(t,s)\right]$$

where t is a trading day, s is a stock in the universe, j runs over all strike prices and expirations, and $w_j(t, s)$ are the weights measured as the average open interest of the jth option pair. We can use the same long-short technique we applied above to capture this outperformance: if we buy stocks in the top quintile of *VS* and short those in the bottom quintile at the market close on day t, and hold these for a week before rebalancing, we can expect an unlevered CAGR of about 12.4 percent.

Why can the difference of call and put prices foretell a stock's return? The intuition is simple: if option traders believe stock price will increase, they would buy calls or short puts. Both actions increase call prices and decrease put prices, thus increasing *VS*, and vice versa if they believe stock price would decrease. Since option traders are on average correct in their predictions, we can use *VS* as a factor to predict stock returns.

The research was performed on 1,500 to 2,300 US stocks from 1996 to 2005, and a numerical (binomial tree) technique was again used to back out the implied volatilities of the options with various strikes and expirations. However, as with many informative factors, the power of this factor to predict expected returns has gradually diminished over time. Indeed, the CAGR in the last three years of this data set became 3.7 percent.

4) OTM Put–ATM Call Implied Volatilities

The difference between OTM put and ATM call implied volatilities is called the volatility smirk, or the skew, by Zhang, Zhao, and Xing (2008), who found that stocks in the top quintile of skew *under*perform those in the bottom quintile by 16 basis points per week (i.e., the factor is *negative* for this skew factor loading). So the unlevered CAGR would be 4.2 percent if we form a short-long portfolio weekly based on sorting on their skew.

The justification of this phenomenon is that informed traders who predict that a stock will suffer a price drop tend to purchase OTM puts to express their views, causing these puts to increase in implied volatility, and their predictions are correct on average. The ATM calls are just used as a benchmark for implied volatility because they are the most liquid.

Just like all the other options factors, this research was performed on all listed US stock options from 1996 to 2005, with implied volatilities backed out by binomial trees as above. A put option with ratio of strike price to the stock price (this ratio is called "moneyness") lower than 0.95 but higher than 0.8 is selected as OTM, while a call option is defined as ATM when the ratio of strike price to the stock price is between 0.95 and 1.05. Only options with tenor between 10 to 60 days are included, and a weekly skew is computed by averaging daily skew over a week (from Tuesday close to Tuesday close). When there are multiple ATM and OTM options for one stock on one particular day, the researchers further select options by choosing the call option with moneyness closest to 1, and the put option with moneyness closest to 0.95.

5) Daily Change in Implied *Market* Volatility

Instead of using the change in stock return implied volatility as cross-sectional factors as in (2), Chang (2009), used the daily change in SPX *market* index option implied volatility as a *time-series* factor to predict stock returns. They found that stocks with high sensitivities (factor loadings) to daily change in implied *market* volatility exhibit low returns on average. At the end of each month, if we buy stocks that are in the lowest quintile of the factor loading and short those that are in the highest quintile, weighing each stock by its market value within that quintile and holding the long-short portfolio for a month, we obtain an unlevered CAGR of 3.6 percent.

The reason stocks that react positively to increase in market volatilities tend to have lower returns is because they are a good hedge against market risk. Investors like such hedges and are willing to pay dearly for them, causing them to be overpriced and resulting in lower expected return.

The researchers tested this strategy on all listed US stocks from 1996 to 2007, using the VIX index as a proxy for implied volatility of the market index. The expected returns, as usual, are lower for the second half of the data. They have also used daily change in implied market skewness as another time-series factor, and the analogous strategy is found to have a higher return. But there are quite a few technical complications in implementing this, so we won't discuss that here.

Short Interest

The number of shares of a stock that have been borrowed for shorting is called the short interest. One may think that short sellers should be better informed than the average investor, since short sellers are exposed to theoretically unlimited risk. Therefore, short interest as a cross-sectional factor loading should have a negative factor with respect to future return.

To test this hypothesis, let's define short interest ratio (SIR) as the number of shares borrowed for shorting divided by the total shares outstanding.[9] If we sort SPX stocks from January 12, 2007, to December 31, 2013, based on their daily SIR, and buy the bottom decile (with the lowest SIR) while short the top decile, and rebalance daily, we actually find that the return is negative. (If we do the opposite and short the bottom decile and long the top decile instead, the CAGR is 2.2 percent.) So based on this measure of short interest, short sellers are actually wrong: The most shorted stocks actually have positive future returns.

However, SIR is not the only way to capture short interest. We can also compute a quantity often called days to cover, or DTC, which is the number of shares borrowed for shorting divided by the average daily trading volume.[10] In our backtest, we use the 20-day moving average as a proxy for the average daily trading volume. Constructing the long-short portfolio exactly the same way as above except now using DTC to sort stocks, we find that the unlevered CAGR over the same period is 5.8 percent, with the Sharpe ratio a respectable 1.1. So apparently DTC is a better short interest factor than SIR, and its factor with respect to future returns is indeed negative (i.e., short sellers are right after all!) Unfortunately, just as for many of the factors we have discussed so far, the predictive power of this factor is growing weaker in recent years. In fact, since 2012, the sign of its factor loading seems to have reversed (Zerohedge, 2014).

Liquidity

In a famous paper by Ibbotson (2014), it was found that the less liquid a stock, the higher its future return. The researchers measured liquidity of a stock as the sum of the 12 monthly trading volumes divided by each month's total shares outstanding. They then sorted the top 3,500 largest (by market cap) stocks by their liquidity and bought the first quartile (the least liquid) and shorted the fourth quartile. Each stock is allocated equal dollar weight. This long-short portfolio was rebalanced only once a year to minimize the potential transactions costs of trading illiquid stocks. This strategy generated a CAGR of 7.27 percent from 1972 to 2013.

This strategy may be suitable for long-term investors, but for traders with shorter horizon and who desire higher Sharpe ratio, I investigated a variation

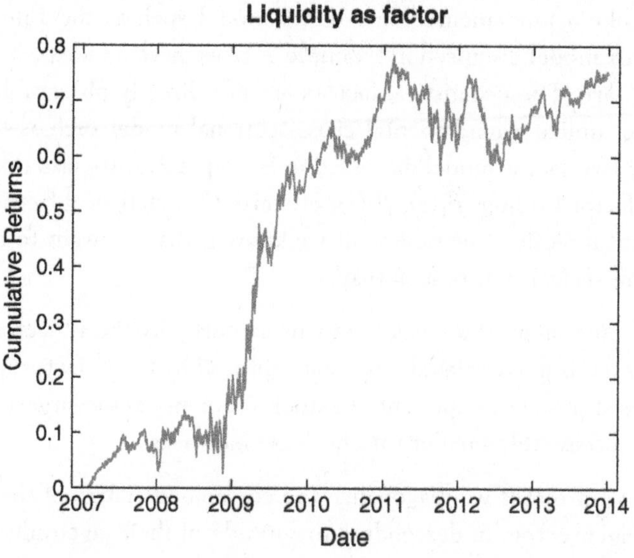

FIGURE 2.3 Liquidity factor on SPX component stocks

that would rebalance daily. In other words, I computed liquidity daily using the average of the last 21 days' trading volume divided by the most recently reported total shares outstanding. I also limited myself to SPX stocks in order to minimize the transaction costs that may be incurred by trading smaller market cap stocks. Finally, instead of buying and shorting the first and fourth quintile of the liquidity-sorted stocks respectively, we buy and short the 50 least and most liquid stocks. When we ran this backtest from February 1, 2007, to December 31, 2013, we found negative return. Conversely, if we short the 50 least and buy the 50 most liquid stocks instead, we generated a CAGR of 8.4 percent. (See Figure 2.3 for the equity curve.) Our result on SPX stocks is thus completely opposite to that of Ibbotson and Kim (2014)!

Statistical Factors

Statistical factors are so-called because they are derived purely from the statistical properties of the stock returns—more specifically, their covariance matrix. Let's suppose we want to write a decomposition of a stock's return as a time-series factor model as shown in equation 2.1:

$$Return(t, s) - r_F = \alpha(t, s) + \beta_1(s) * Factor_1(t) + \beta_2(s) * Factor_2(t) + \cdots + \varepsilon(t, s).$$

But unlike a fundamental time-series model such as the Fama-French three-factor model discussed in Example 2.1, we have no idea what $Factor_1$, $Factor_2$, ... are. These statistical factors are not directly observable. At the same time, unlike a fundamental cross-sectional model such as the Chattopadhyay two-factor model discussed in Example 2.3, we also don't know what the factor loadings $\beta_1(s)$, $\beta_2(s)$, etc. are. Our statistical factor *loadings* are also not directly observable. All we know is that we want to construct these (time-series) factors such that

1. The component of a stock's returns captured by the ith factor, $\beta_i(s) * Factor_i(t)$, is uncorrelated with that captured by the jth factor; and
2. The first ($i = 1$) component of a stock's returns has the largest variance, with successively smaller variances as i increases.

It turns out that if we diagonalize the covariance matrix of the returns, sort the eigenvectors in descending magnitude of their eigenvalues (which must be non-negative since any covariance matrix is positive semi-definite), and use the ith eigenvector as the factor loadings $\beta_i(s)$, then the properties (1) and (2) are both satisfied. This is just the well-known principal component analysis, or PCA (Ruppert and Matteson, 2015). Since the factor loadings are now known, all we have to do is to use linear regression to find the $Factor_i$. Hence this statistical factor model can be considered a cross-sectional factor model, which means that actually $\alpha(t, s) = \alpha(t)$, as in Example 2.2.

As we discussed before, equation 2.1 (more precisely, its cross-sectional version reproduced above) is descriptive, not predictive. We need to make it predictive as in equation 2.2. In order to do that with statistical factors, we need to first find out what each $Factor_i$ is. Fortunately, MATLAB's Statistics and Machine Learning Toolbox's *pca* function provides us not only with the eigenvectors, but also these factors themselves (plus the variances of each component, which we don't actually need for predicting returns). Once the factors are found, we can go back and find out what the $\widehat{\beta}_i(s)$ are in equation 2.2 through linear regression. Note that these $\widehat{\beta}_i(s)$ won't be the eigenvectors $\beta_i(s)$ of the original covariance matrix anymore!

In Example 2.5, I demonstrate how to apply this to SPX stocks, generating a CAGR of 15.6 percent with a Sharpe ratio of 1.4 from January 3, 2007, to December 31, 2013. The equity curve is shown in Figure 2.4. In contrast to many of the fundamental factor models we described so far, the statistical factor model actually produced positive returns even for large-cap stocks!

Statistical factors are often more useful than fundamental factors for short-term, or even intraday, trading. In a short time frame, fundamental

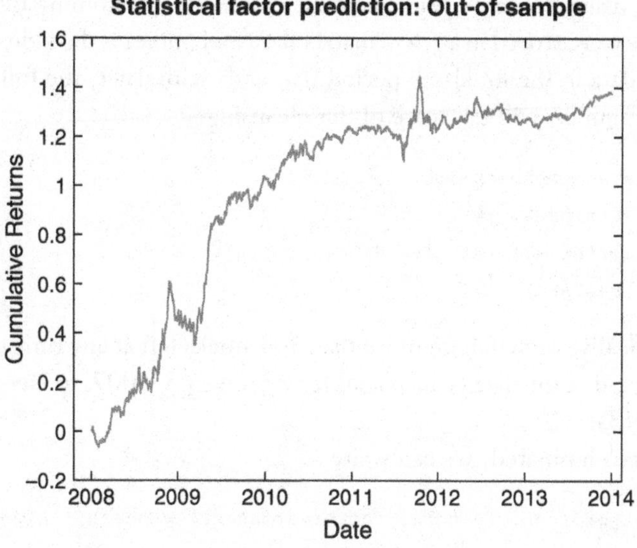

FIGURE 2.4 Statistical factor on SPX component stocks

factors do not change at all. Also, statistical factors can be more useful for trading in markets where fundamental factors are less important for predictive purposes. An example would be foreign currencies trading.

Example 2.5: Using PCA to find *predictive* statistical factors

As discussed in the main text, finding statistical factors that we can use for predicting the next day's return is a two-step process. The first step is the usual Principal Component Analysis, where the most important output to us is not the eigenvectors (i.e., the factor loadings), but the time-series factors themselves. Assume that we want the top five factors (the five factors that generate the largest variances), and that we use one year (252 days) of SPX stocks' daily returns data to construct the covariance matrix. These parameters, *numFactors* = 5, and *lookback* = 252, can, of course, be optimized in-sample, though we picked them arbitrarily. In order to apply the MATLAB Statistical and Machine Learning Toolbox's *pca* function to these returns, we need to eliminate any stocks that have *NaN* returns in the lookback period (i.e., stocks that have been listed or delisted in the middle of this period). This is similar to the data cleansing procedure used in Example 2.1, as we are using the same price database from CRSP. Assuming the daily returns were stored in a $T \times S$ matrix *ret1*, and *trainset* is the index array of the data in the lookback period that ends with day t, the following code fragment will take care of this cleansing:

```
trainset=t-lookback+1:t;
R=ret1(trainset, :);
hasData=find(all(isfinite(R), 1));
R=R(:, hasData);
```

Typically, we will have more than 300 stocks left at any time during the period of the data (which runs from January 3, 2007, to December 31, 2013).

Once eliminated, we can write

```
[factorLoadings, factors, factorVariances] = pca(R, 'Algorithm',
   'eig', 'NumComponents', numFactors);
```

If you are curious, you can examine the first column of the *factorLoadings* matrix, which corresponds to the eigenvector of the largest eigenvalue. You will see that all the values of this eigenvector are positive. The reason is that the first statistical (time-series) factor we have found is essentially the market return as in the Fama-French three-factor model, and there is no SPX stock that has a propensity to move in the opposite direction to the market (i.e., no stock has negative beta).

Though it is instructive to look at the factor loadings of this descriptive (contemporaneous) factor model, we don't actually have any use for them. We need to find the factor loadings for a predictive factor model. To do this, we regress the next day's returns against the factors that we have computed. To ensure that we only use data on or before day t within the lookback period in order to avoid look-ahead bias, we will only regress the future returns up to the second last day of the trainset. Just as in Example 2.1, we have to do this for each stock separately, in a multivariate, multiple linear regression:

```
for s=1:length(hasData)
    model=fitlm(factors(1:end-1, :), retFut1(trainset(1:end-1),
      hasData(s)), 'linear');
    retPred1(1, hasData(s))=predict(model, factors(end, :));
end
```

In the second line of the for-loop, we have also applied the fitted linear model to the factor of the last day of the trainset to predict the return for the following day. It is important to note that this last day wasn't used in the regression fit.

Finally, we will sort the predicted returns in ascending order, and buy $1 of each stock within the 50 highest predicted returns, and short $1 of each stock in the 50 lowest predicted returns.

```
isGoodData=find(isfinite(retPred1));
[~, I]=sort(retPred1(isGoodData)); % ascending sort
positions(t, isGoodData(I(1:topN)))=-1;
positions(t, isGoodData(I(end-topN+1:end)))=1;
```

Of course, *topN* = 50 is another parameter that can be optimized in-sample. This strategy generates a CAGR of 15.6 percent. The complete code can be downloaded as StatisticalFactors_predictive.m.

Putting Them All Together

One of the nice features of factor models is that we are not limited to this or that factor—we can put all the factors mentioned in this chapter together and use them in one predictive regression model. Of course, this is subject to the condition that none of these factors are collinear, and I am sure some of our factors are. But this is a minor technical snafu: a standard cure to collinearity is to systematically reduce the factors one by one based on the AIC or BIC criteria (Ruppert and Matteson, 2015). We will talk about that in the context of stepwise regression in Chapter 5.

While a regression model is often necessary to find out the factor loading(s) applicable to a specific stock, it is not necessary for predicting future returns. For example, as long as we are certain that stocks with higher ROE will have higher future return (see the section on "A Two-Factor Model"), we don't necessarily need to know the regression coefficient at a particular time (a time-series factor in this case) in order to construct a trading model. We merely need to rank the stocks based on their ROE and buy the top quantile while short the bottom one. This ranking methodology is simple and powerful: It often gives us a better trading model than using the precise predicted return of a regression model. The reason is that an outlier data point can easily bias the regression coefficients and thus the predicted returns. (These outliers are called "high-leverage points" in regression literature.) However, the ranking methodology is immune to such outliers. This is reminiscent of the situation with computing correlation coefficients. When two time series contain outlier data points, the estimate of correlation coefficient can be distorted. There, the usual remedy is to compute Spearman rank correlation instead of the usual Pearson correlation, analogous to ranking the factor loadings to determine trading signals.

When there are more than one-factor loadings, simple ranking or sorting becomes multisorting, just as univariate regression becomes multiple regression. We have seen this in action already with the implied volatility/skewness/kurtosis factor in the section "Using Option Prices to Predict Stock Returns." We just pick one-factor loading at a time to sort the stocks, pick the top and bottom quantiles, and sort those stocks within each of those quantiles with the next factor loading, and so on. Ultimately, we will only long the stocks in the top quantile of the last factor within the top quantile of the second last factor within the top quantile of the third last factor and so on, while we will short the opposite. Typically, we start sorting with the factor loading with the strongest predictive power, and then go down the list. The trading strategy does depend on the order of factor loadings we pick, and often, we may not know which factor loading has the strongest predictive power until we try them in a backtest. Of course, all these experiments and optimizations should be done in the trainset!

There is one other nuance when implementing a predictive factor model using the multi-sort method. The sign of the factor may very well depend on what universe of stocks we are applying the model to. For example, the liquidity factor we discussed earlier was found to have a negative factor for the top 3,500 stocks by Ibbotson (2014), but we found that the factor is positive for SPX stocks. The sign of a factor may also depend on the industry group to which a stock belongs. Hence, a more sophisticated version of the multisort algorithm might perform the sort only within a group (based on market cap, or industry group, or whether they are growth or value stocks, ...). This method is essentially sorting the stocks based on a time-series factor first (e.g., HML, industry group, SMB), before applying the cross-sectional factors (e.g., ROE, BM, liquidity) to each sorted quantile. This will result in a portfolio that is not only market neutral, but neutral to each of the time series factors we used for the groupings. (By being neutral to some factor, we ensure that the portfolio is unaffected by its associated risks.)

You might also wonder why we restrict ourselves to linear regression models when combining the factor loadings. In fact, we don't have to. But applying a nonlinear model to factor loadings is best left to Chapter 5 on

Artificial Intelligence techniques, where nonlinearity is the rule rather than the exception.

If you find it tiring to research and combine all these factors in an optimal way in order to predict stock returns, there are websites that will do it for you. For example, www.magicformulainvesting.com implements the simple two-factor model of Joel Greenblatt (Greenblatt, 2010), and www.Factorwave.com implements factor models created by options guru Euan Sinclair. Not surprisingly, the latter includes many factors derived from options prices.

Summary

Factor model is a central concept in modern investment finance. It is important for understanding what kind of systematic (as opposed to diversifiable idiosyncratic) risks a portfolio is subject to. Some of us are willing to take such risks (for example, the long-only investor is willing to take market risk), while others want to avoid them. However, our focus here is not risk management, but to predict returns based on specific factors. These factors may be time-series factors such as the market excess return, HML, SMB, UMD, the Daily Change in Implied Market Volatility, or even the unobservable statistical factors. Or they may be cross-sectional factor loadings such as log(ROE), log(BM), Implied Moments, Change in Implied Volatility, Call Minus Put Implied Volatility, Volatility Smirk/Skew, Short Interest, or Liquidity of a stock. Of course, we haven't cataloged all possible predictive factors in this chapter, and in fact we left out some factors that we discussed in Chan (2013), such as the mutual-funds-induced pressure, and news sentiment.[11]

Investors like factors because, unlike pure arbitrage, factor returns are not easily arbitraged away because they come with well-defined undiversifiable risks. Factor models also typically have much larger capacity than arbitrage models, since many factors do not change rapidly, making them suitable for longer holding periods. Nevertheless, some factor returns do diminish over time, mainly because their associated risks diminish over time. Examples of such factors would include SMB, Call Minus Put Implied Volatility, Daily Change in Implied Market Volatility, and the DTC Short Interest. Another limitation of some factors is that they do not work well on large cap stocks. For example, applying the log(ROE) and log(BM) two-factor model on large cap stocks result in returns indistinguishable from zero. The same holds for the Implied Moments factor. The problem with applying factor models to stocks outside of the large cap universe is of course that transaction costs are likely to be higher, so we must greet those reports of high returns with some skepticism. We are pleased to find, however, that some factor returns, such as that of liquidity, remain significant in recent times and are applicable to large-cap stocks. This last happy category includes the statistical factors, which, after all, are recomputed anew in a rolling window and never gets old.

Exercises

2.1. In Example 2.1, use a moving lookback window of 252 days instead of the static first half of the data as trainset for the regression estimate of the factor loadings. Does this improve the out-of-sample return of the model?

2.2. Compute the UMD factor yourself by creating a long-short hedge portfolio of SPX stocks that went up versus those that went down in the last 252 days. Add this as the fourth factor in Example 2.1. Does this improve the out-of-sample return?

2.3. In Example 2.1, use the factors to regress against monthly or quarterly instead of daily returns, and use the predictive factor loadings for a trading model that holds each position for a month (21 days) or a quarter (63 days). Do these changes improve the out-of-sample return? Also try this with the UMD factor you constructed in Exercise 2.2.

2.4. In Example 2.2, let the factor for each stock take different value every quarter. Does this improve the out-of-sample return of the model? Also, try to aggregate the returns of stocks within the same industry group, enforcing the same value for factors only within the same group.

2.5. In Example 2.2, what is the net exposure (net long-short market value divided by the gross long+short market value) of the strategy? If this net exposure is significant, adopt the two methods suggested in the Two-Factor Model section to turn the portfolio into a market-neutral one, and see how that affects the returns.

2.6. Modify twoFundamentalFactors.m to use only the ROE factor. Check that you get out-of-sample CAGR of 20 percent.

2.7. Modify twoFundamentalFactors.m so that the net exposure is hedged with SPY. Check that you get out-of-sample CAGR of 0 percent.

2.8. Referring to Chattopadhyay (2015), find the table and the entry that support our assertion that their out-of-sample CAGR is 4.3 percent for US stocks.

2.9. Using the data file inputData_SPX_200401_201312.mat from epchan.com/book3, and any one of the free databases from Quandl.com that contains total shares outstanding of each stock (just search for "total shares outstanding"), backtest the liquidity factor from 2007 to the end of 2013, and verify that you obtain a CAGR of about 8.4 percent.

2.10. Statistical factors are often more useful for intraday trading in markets that have few fundamental predictive factors. FX trading is one such example. Apply the code in Example 2.5 to intraday FX trading and see if you obtain good returns. Free intraday FX historical data are available from ratedata.gaincapital.com.

2.11. Try different numbers of statistical factors and different lookbacks in Example 2.5. Are five factors the optimal? Is a lookback of 252 days optimal?

2.12. In many of the example strategies discussed, we assume that we will invest an equal dollar amount to every stock that has a long or short signal. But we can instead invest a dollar amount proportional to the predicted return. Try this methodology to some of the examples and see if this improves returns and/or Sharpe ratio.

Endnotes

1. The *real* CAGR of SPX index was about 5.58 percent above inflation from 1987 to 2013, assuming a constant annual inflation rate of 2.3 percent.
2. Ang (2014), Figure 7.6 shows that such a market-neutral value portfolio returned about 900 percent between 1965 and 2011.
3. Many large pension funds such as the C$265 billion Canada Pension Plan proudly discuss what they use as factors. See, again, Ang (2014).
4. The daily returns of various time-series factors, or equivalently, the daily returns of such hedge portfolios, are listed on Prof. French's website at mba.tuck.dartmouth.edu/pages/faculty/ken.french/data_library.html.
5. If this were a cross-sectional factor model, α would have been set as a constant across all stocks instead; i.e., $\alpha(t, s) = \alpha(t)$.

6. A multiple regression involves multiple predictors but one dependent, or target, variable. A multivariate regression involves one or many predictors, but many dependent variables. A multivariate regression is essentially many independent multiple regressions run separately.
7. The authors applied two additional constraints: the stocks' prices must not be in the bottom 5th-percentile, and the prices must be greater than $1.
8. This is a common practice among financial researchers. See Brown, Lajbcygier, and Li (2007).
9. We obtained the historical data for short interest from Computat. Sungard also offers a more sophisticated data product called Astec Short Side with similar information.
10. Historical daily volume was obtained from CRSP database.
11. The mutual funds pressure factor return has become weaker in recent years, just like the other weakening factors discussed below.

CHAPTER 3

Time-Series Analysis

Economists and electrical engineers have long been trying to predict the next signal in a time series, which is exactly what traders try to do as well. This chapter is an introduction to the tools well known in econometrics and signal processing, and which have found wide acceptance in the quantitative investment community.

You may already have seen some time-series analysis techniques in action in my previous books (Chan, 2009 and 2013), as a way to test for stationarity or cointegration of price series. But these are just parts of a general package of linear modeling techniques with acronyms like ARIMA, VAR, or VEC. Likewise, almost every technical trader has tried moving averages as a way to filter out the noise in price series. But have they tried many of the advanced signal processing filters such as the Kalman filter?

Time-series techniques are most useful in markets where fundamental information and intuition are either lacking or not particularly useful for short-term predictions. Currencies and bitcoins fit this bill. Professor Lyons (2001) wrote that "... the proportion of monthly exchange rate changes our textbook models can explain is essentially zero." We will mention a few examples of using time-series techniques to predict currency returns in this chapter, and leave the bitcoin examples to Chapter 7. But just as technical analysis can be useful for stock trading despite the abundance of fundamental information there, we will describe examples where time-series analysis can be applied to stocks.

Unlike other books on time-series analysis, we will not be discussing the inner workings of these techniques, but focus solely on how we can use ready-made software packages to make predictions. Most of the examples are implemented using the MATLAB Econometrics Toolbox, but *R* users can find similar functions in the forecast, vars, and dlm packages.

AR(p)

The simplest model in time-series analysis is AR(1). It is just a linear regression model that relates the price in one bar to the next:

$$Y(t) - \mu = \phi(Y(t-1) - \mu) + \varepsilon(t) \tag{3.1}$$

where $Y(t)$ is the price at time t, ϕ is the (auto)regression coefficient, and ε is Gaussian noise with zero mean, sometimes called innovation. Hence, the name *auto-regressive* process. A time series is called weakly[1] stationary if its mean and variance are constant in time, and AR(1) is weakly stationary if $|\phi| < 1$ (the proof is left as an exercise). A weakly stationary time series is also mean reverting (Chan, 2013). If $|\phi| > 1$, the time series will trend. If $\phi = 1$, we have a random walk. To estimate ϕ, we use the *arima* and *estimate* functions in the Econometrics Toolbox.


```
model_ar1=arima(1, 0, 0) % assumes an AR(1) with unknown parameters
model_ar1_estimates=estimate(model_ar1, cl);
```


The function *arima*(p, d, q) reduces to an AR(1) model if we set $p = 1$ and $d = 0$ (We will discuss the more general version in the next section.) The *estimate* function just applies maximum likelihood estimation to find the parameters for the AR(1) model based on the input price series. Applying it to the one-minute midprice bars of AUD.USD from July 24, 2007 to August 3 2015 returns an estimate of $\phi = 0.99997$, with a standard error of 0.00001.[2] We conclude that though AUD.USD is very weakly stationary, it is very close to a random walk. Note that we tested on midprices instead of trade prices to reduce bid–ask bounce, which tends to produce phantom mean-reversion that cannot really be traded on.

Generalizing slightly from AR(1), we can consider AR(p), represented by

$$Y(t) = \mu + \phi_1 Y(t-1) + \phi_2 Y(t-2) + \cdots + \phi_p Y(t-p) + \varepsilon(t). \tag{3.2}$$

You can see that this is just a multiple regression model with the price at time t as the dependent (response) variable and past prices up to a lag of p bars as independent (predictor) variables. But introducing p as an additional parameter means that we can find the optimal p that gives the best fit of the AR(p) model to our data. As in many statistical models, we will use the

Bayesian information criterion (BIC) that is proportional to the negative log likelihood of the model but with an additional term that is proportional to p, which penalizes complexity. Our objective is to minimize BIC, and we do this by a brute-force exhaustive search:[3]

```
LOGL=zeros(60, 1); % log likelihood for up to 60 lags (1 hour)
P=zeros(size(LOGL)); % p values

for p=1:length(P)
    model=arima(p, 0, 0);
    [~,~,logL] = estimate(model, mid(trainset),'print',false);
    LOGL(p) = logL;
    P(p) = p;
end

% Has P+1 parameters, including constant
[~, bic]=aicbic(LOGL, P+1, length(mid(trainset)));

[~, pMin]=min(bic)

model=arima(pMin, 0, 0) % assumes an AR(pMin) with unknown
  parameters
```


In the above code fragment, *mid* is the array that contains the midprices.

Once we have decided on the best estimate of p, we can apply the *estimate* function to it to find the coefficients $\mu, \phi_1, \phi_2, \ldots, \phi_p$:

```
fit=estimate(model, mid);
```

Applying these functions to AUD.USD on one-minute midprice bars from July 24, 2007, to August 12, 2014, yields $p = 10$ as the optimal value, with the coefficients noted in Table 3.1.

We can now use this AR(10) model for prediction on the out-of-sample data set from August 12, 2014, to August 3, 2015.

```
yF=NaN(size(mid));
for t=testset(1):size(mid, 1)
    [y, ~]=forecast(fit, 1, 'Y0', mid(t-pMin+1:t)); % Need only
        most recent pMin data points for prediction
    yF(t)=y(end);
end
```

Note that $yF(t)$ is the forecast made with data up to time t; hence, it is actually the predicted price for time $t + 1$. Once the next bar prediction has

TABLE 3.1 Coefficients of an AR(10) Model Applied to AUD.USD		
Coefficient	**Value**	**Standard Error**
μ	1.37196e-06	8.65314e-07
ϕ_1	0.993434	0.000187164
ϕ_2	−0.00121205	0.000293356
ϕ_3	−0.000352717	0.000305831
ϕ_4	0.000753222	0.000354121
ϕ_5	0.00662641	0.000358673
ϕ_6	−0.00224118	0.000330092
ϕ_7	−0.00305157	0.000365348
ϕ_8	0.00351317	0.000394538
ϕ_9	−0.00154844	0.000398956
ϕ_{10}	0.00407798	0.000281821

been made, we can use it to generate trading signals: Simply buy when the predicted price is higher than the current price, and sell when it is lower:

```
deltaYF=yF-mid;

pos=zeros(size(mid));
pos(deltaYF > 0)=1;
pos(deltaYF < 0)=-1;
```


This strategy yields an annualized return of 158 percent on the out-of-sample set. See Figure 3.1 for its equity curve. To realize such amazing

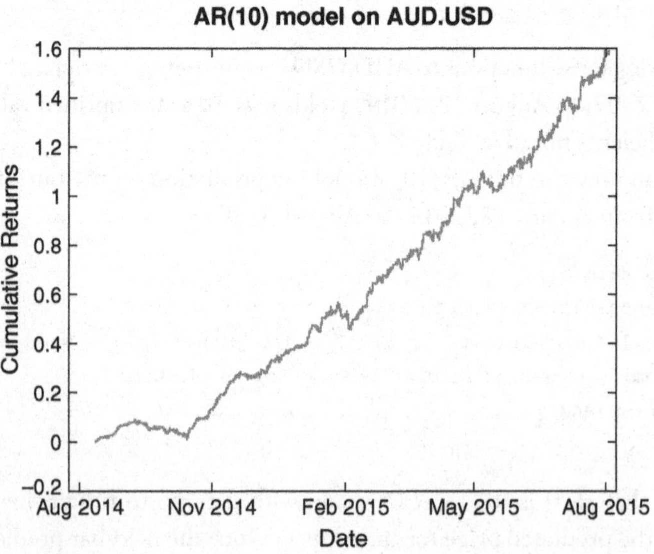

FIGURE 3.1 AR(10) trading strategy applied to AUD.USD

returns, one has to be able to execute at midprice; hence, a low latency execution program that manages limit orders is necessary.

ARMA(*p*, *q*)

From our application of AR(*p*) to AUD.USD, we see that the best fit requires 10 lags. This high number of lags is quite common for AR(*p*) models: They are trying to compensate for the simplicity of the model structure with a larger number of terms. A small extension of the AR model to include *q* lagged noise terms will often reduce the number of lags necessary. This is called the ARMA(*p*, *q*) model, or an auto-regressive moving average process, where the *q* lagged noise terms are described as a *moving average:*

$$Y(t) = \mu + \phi_1 Y(t-1) + \phi_2 Y(t-2) + \cdots + \phi_p Y(t-p) + \varepsilon(t) + \theta_1 \varepsilon(t-1) + \cdots + \theta_q \varepsilon(t-q) \tag{3.3}$$

Finding the best values of the *p* and *q* and the coefficient of each term in equation 3.3 is similar to the procedure we took for AR(*p*), but because we are now doing exhaustive search over two variables, we need nested for-loops:

```
LOGL=-Inf(10, 9); % log likelihood for up to 10 p and 9 q
  (10 minutes)
PQ=zeros(size(LOGL)); % p and q values

for p=1:size(PQ, 1)
    for q=1:size(PQ, 2)
        model=arima(p, 0, q);
        [~,~,logL] = estimate(model, mid(trainset),'print',false);
        LOGL(p, q) = logL;
        PQ(p, q) = p+q;
    end
end
```

For each *p* and *q*, we save the log likelihood in *LOGL*(*p*, *q*), and $p + q$ in *PQ* (*p*, *q*), the latter because it is used as a penalty term when minimizing BIC. How do we identify the optimal *p* and *q* that minimizes BIC from the *LOGL* and *PQ* matrices? We have to turn them into one-dimensional vectors, apply the *aicbic* function, and then use the *min* function:

```
% Has p+q+1 parameters, including constant
LOGL_vector = reshape(LOGL, size(LOGL, 1)*size(LOGL, 2), 1);
PQ_vector = reshape(PQ, size(LOGL, 1)*size(LOGL, 2), 1);
```

```
[~, bic]=aicbic(LOGL_vector, PQ_vector+1, length(mid(trainset)));
[bicMin, pMin]=min(bic)
```

Finally, we have to turn the one-dimensional BIC vector back into a two-dimensional array, but with only the cell corresponding to the minimum value populated, in order to facilitate easy visual identification of the row (corresponding to p) and column (corresponding to q) numbers of that cell:

```
bic(:)=NaN;
bic(pMin)=bicMin;
bic=reshape(bic,size(LOGL))
```

All these procedures are contained in the program *buildARMA_findPQ_AUDUSD.m*. The output for AUD.USD looks like the following:

```
bic =

   1.0e+07 *

  Columns 1 through 4

                 NaN               NaN               NaN               NaN
                 NaN               NaN               NaN               NaN
                 NaN               NaN               NaN               NaN
                 NaN               NaN               NaN               NaN
                 NaN               NaN               NaN               NaN
                 NaN               NaN               NaN               NaN
                 NaN               NaN               NaN               NaN
                 NaN               NaN               NaN               NaN
                 NaN               NaN               NaN               NaN
                 NaN               NaN               NaN               NaN

  Columns 5 through 8

                 NaN               NaN               NaN               NaN
  -3.469505397473728               NaN               NaN               NaN
                 NaN               NaN               NaN               NaN
                 NaN               NaN               NaN               NaN
                 NaN               NaN               NaN               NaN
                 NaN               NaN               NaN               NaN
                 NaN               NaN               NaN               NaN
                 NaN               NaN               NaN               NaN
                 NaN               NaN               NaN               NaN
                 NaN               NaN               NaN               NaN
```

```
Column 9

           NaN
           NaN
           NaN
           NaN
           NaN
           NaN
           NaN
           NaN
           NaN
           NaN
```

where we easily determine that the cell with the minimum BIC corresponds to $p = 2$ and $q = 5$. These are indeed shorter lags than the $p = 10$ we used in the AR(p) model. Plugging in these values to the *arima* function and then applying the *estimate* function on the ARMA(2, 5) model as we did in the section on AR(p) yields the coefficients shown in Table 3.2.

One should note that $|\phi_1|$ is now definitely smaller than 1, indicating strong mean reversion. However, using the *forecast* functions to generate trading signals as before actually decreases the out-of-sample annualized return from 158 percent to 60 percent. The added complexity of using moving average has not paid off in this case. The equity curve is shown in Figure 3.2. The backtest program is available as buildARMA_AUDUSD.m.

You may wonder why the function we used for the AR(p) and ARMA (p, q) models are called *arima*. You may also wonder why we focus on predicting prices rather than returns. The answer to both questions can be understood by studying the ARIMA(p, d, q) model.

TABLE 3.2 Coefficients of an ARMA(2, 5) Model Applied to AUD.USD

Coefficient	Value	Standard Error
μ	2.80383e-06	4.58975e-06
ϕ_1	0.649011	0.000249771
ϕ_2	0.350986	0.000249775
θ_1	0.345806	0.000499929
θ_2	−0.00906282	0.000874713
θ_3	−0.0106082	0.000896239
θ_4	−0.0102606	0.0010664
θ_5	−0.00251154	0.000910359

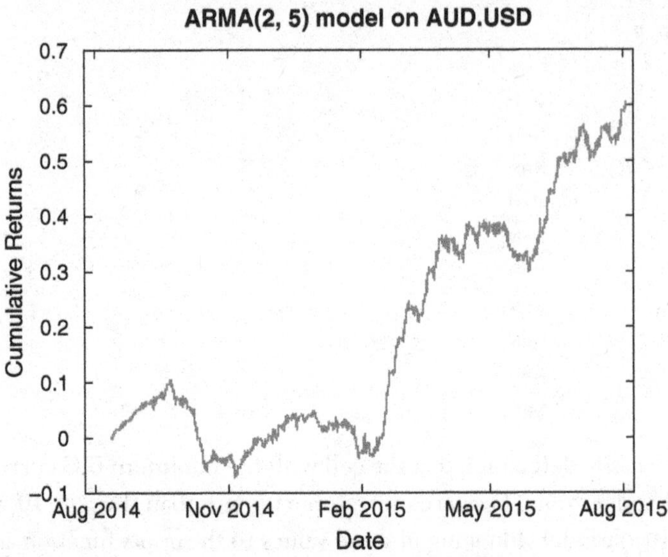

FIGURE 3.2 ARMA(2, 5) trading strategy applied to AUD.USD

ARIMA(p, d, q) stands for autoregressive *integrated* moving average. Let's just concern ourselves with $d = 1$, the simplest and the most common case in finance. If $Y(t)$ is an ARIMA(p, 1, q) model, it implies that $\Delta Y(t)$ is an ARMA(p, q), where $\Delta Y(t) = Y(t) - Y(t-1)$. We can understand this even better if $Y(t)$ represents log price instead of price. If this is the case, then using ARMA(p, q) to model the log returns is equivalent to using ARIMA (p, 1, q) to model the log prices.

Would it be advantageous to model log returns ΔY instead of Y using ARMA(p, q)? It would be, if we can further reduce the lags p and q from the ones obtained when modeling prices (or log prices) using ARMA(p, q). Unfortunately, I have never found that to be true. For example, modeling the log of AUD.USD time series using ARIMA(p, 1, q) gives $p = 1$, and $q = 9$.

The equivalence of an ARIMA(p, 1, q) model on log prices to an ARIMA(p, 0, q) model on log returns should not be confused with the statement that an ARMA(p, q) = ARIMA(p, 0, q) model on log prices is equivalent to some ARMA(p', q') model on log returns. The latter statement is false. An ARMA model in ΔY's can always be transformed into an ARMA model in Y's. But an ARMA model for Y cannot always be transformed into an ARMA model for ΔY. This is because an ARMA model for ΔY can only have ΔY as independent variables, whereas an ARMA model for Y can have both ΔY (which is just the difference of two Ys) and

Y as independent variables. Hence, a model for Y is more flexible and gives better results. If we want to have a model for ΔY that has both ΔYs and Ys as independent variables, we have to use a VEC(p) model, to be discussed at the end of the next section on VAR(p).

VAR(p)

The simple autoregressive model AR(p) in equation 3.2 can be easily generalized to m multivariate time series. This generalized model is called a *vector autoregressive* model, or VAR(p). All we need to do is to interpret the autoregressive coefficients ϕ as $m \times m$ matrices, and allow the noises $\varepsilon(t)$, which are m-vectors to have nonzero cross-sectional correlations but zero serial correlations. This means that $\varepsilon_i(t)$ is not correlated with $\varepsilon_j(s)$, for any $t \neq s$, but $\varepsilon_i(t)$ could be correlated with $\varepsilon_j(t)$. Since the autogressive coefficient matrices relate the current price of every time series to the lagged prices of all time series, VAR model is particularly suitable for modeling financial instruments that have correlated returns, such as a portfolio of stocks within the same industry group. We will focus on the computer hardware group within the S&P 500 Index on January 3, 2007, which consists of the tickers AAPL, EMC, HPQ, NTAP, and SNDK. To eliminate spurious mean-reversion effects due to bid-ask bounce, we will use midprices at market close provided by the Center for Research of Security Prices (CRSP) from January 3, 2007, to December 31, 2013.

As in the section on AR(p), we first need to determine the optimal lag p. We will use the first six years of data as training set for this determination. There are only minor differences in the codes required:[4]

```
for p=1:length(P)
    model=vgxset('n', size(mid, 2), 'nAR', p, 'Constant', true);
        % with additive offset
    [model,EstStdErrors,logL,W] = vgxvarx(model,mid(trainset, :));
    [NumParam,~] = vgxcount(model);
    LOGL(p) = logL;
    P(p) = NumParam;
end
```

It is gratifying that we find $p = 1$ minimizes BIC (simpler models are usually better), and this is a typical result for most industry groups. Once this is decided, the other parameters of the model can be determined by the function *vgxvarx*, which is the equivalent of the *estimate* function for ARIMA models. Using the same training set, the constant offsets, autoregressive coefficients, and the covariance of the noise terms are noted in Table 3.3. (In this table, in contrast to Table 3.1 or 3.2, the subscripts refer to the stocks instead of number of time lags.)

To make predictions using this model on the out-of-sample data in 2013, use the *vgxpred* function, which is similar to the *forecast* function for ARIMA.

```
pMin=1;
yF=NaN(size(mid));
for t=testset(1):size(mid, 1)
    FY = vgxpred(model,1, [], mid(t-pMin+1:t, :));
    yF(t, :)=FY;
end
```

In keeping with the linearity of the VAR models, we can construct a linear trading model as well. Furthermore, we can choose to make it

TABLE 3.3 Constant Offsets, Autoregressive Coefficients, and Covariance of a VAR(1) Model Applied to Computer Hardware Stocks

Constant Offsets	Value	Standard Error
μ_1	3.88363	1.15299
μ_2	0.669367	0.0970334
μ_3	1.75474	0.227636
μ_4	1.701	0.249767
μ_5	1.8752	0.282581

$\Phi_{i,j}$	AAPL	EMC	HPQ	NTAP	SNDK
AAPL	0.991815	0.0735881	−0.105676	0.0359698	−0.00619303
EMC	−7.15594e-05	0.970934	−0.0103416	0.00524778	0.00354032
HPQ	−0.00158962	−0.024093	0.965626	0.00898799	0.00190162
NTAP	−0.000771673	−0.0409408	−0.0284176	1.00662	0.00308001
SNDK	−0.000526824	−0.0579403	−0.0309631	0.01704	0.998657

$\langle \varepsilon_i \varepsilon_j \rangle$	AAPL	EMC	HPQ	NTAP	SNDK
AAPL	36.2559				
EMC	1.67571	0.256786			
HPQ	3.37592	0.449846	1.41323		
NTAP	3.78265	0.513747	1.20474	1.70138	
SNDK	4.39542	0.522437	1.26443	1.41357	2.17779

sector-neutral. We compute the mean predicted return $\langle r \rangle$ of all the stocks in the industry group every day, and set the target dollar allocation of a stock to be proportional to the difference between its predicted return and the industry group mean,

$$w_i = (r_i - \langle r \rangle) / \sum_j |r_j - \langle r \rangle|. \tag{3.4}$$

We have made sure that the initial gross market value of the portfolio is always \$1. You may notice that this formula looks similar to equation 4.1 in Chan (2013), but it is different. In the formula in my previous book, the returns used are the previous day's returns, and more importantly, we set the proportionality constant to -1 since we assumed mean reversion. The MATLAB code fragment[5] for computing the position (equivalently, dollar allocation) of each stock is

```
retF=(yF-mid)./mid;
sectorRetF=mean(retF, 2);
pos=zeros(size(retF));
pos=(retF-repmat(sectorRetF, [1 size(retF, 2)]))./repmat
  (smartsum(abs(retF-repmat(sectorRetF, [1 size(retF, 2)])), 2),
    [1, size(retF, 2)]);
```


This trading model yields an annualized return of 48 percent, with a Sharpe ratio of 0.9. See Figure 3.3 for its equity curve.

We often want to predict changes in price ΔY instead of price Y itself. So it is a bit awkward to use the VAR models, and the resulting AR coefficients do not make too much intuitive sense. Fortunately, VAR(p) can be transformed to a model with ΔY as the dependent variable, and various lagged ΔY's and Y's as the independent variables. This is called the VEC(q) (vector error correction) model, and is written as

$$\Delta Y(t) = M + CY(t-1) + A_1 \Delta Y(t-1) + \cdots + A_k \Delta Y(t-k) + \varepsilon(t). \tag{3.5}$$

The $m \times m$ matrix C in equation 3.5 is called the error correction matrix. To transform the coefficients of VAR(p) to VEC(q), first note that $q = p - 1$, and we can use the function *vartovec*. Applying this to the VAR model built above for computer hardware stocks:

```
[model_vec, C]=vartovec(model);
```

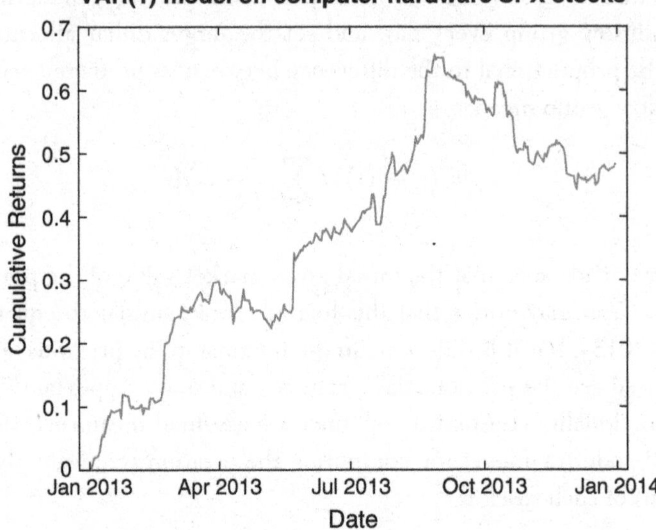

FIGURE 3.3 VAR(1) trading strategy applied to computer hardware stocks

we get Table 3.4, which displays the values of C:

TABLE 3.4 Error Correction Matrix of a VEC(0) Model Applied to Computer Hardware Stocks

$C_{i,j}$	AAPL	EMC	HPQ	NTAP	SNDK
AAPL	−0.0082	0.0736	−0.1057	0.0360	−0.0062
EMC	−0.0001	−0.0291	−0.0103	0.0052	0.0035
HPQ	−0.0016	−0.0241	−0.0344	0.0090	0.0019
NTAP	−0.0008	−0.0409	−0.0284	0.0066	0.0031
SNDK	−0.0005	−0.0579	−0.0310	0.0170	−0.0013

The values of C give us a more intuitive understanding of the relationships between the movements of the different stocks. You may notice that except for NTAP, all diagonal elements have negative values. This means that all but NTAP are serially mean reverting, albeit some very weakly.

Equation 3.5 is the same as equation 2.7 in Chan (2013), where it was discussed in connection with the Johansen test for cointegration. Indeed, if the portfolio of computer hardware stocks were cointegrating, C would give rise to a significantly negative eigenvalue in the Johansen test. But we do not need a cointegrating portfolio to use VEC(q) for prediction. Some of the stocks could be trending while others are mean reverting, as we saw in Table 3.4.

By the way, if you want to try VAR models on the entire SPX universe instead of just the computer hardware stocks, make sure your computer has an unusually large memory! Also, as mentioned before, these models may behave better if we use log prices instead of prices. (In any case, a log price representation will allow a better connection to the continuous version of VAR and VEC. See Cartea, Jaimungal, and Penalva, 2015, p. 285.)

State Space Models

The AR, ARMA, VAR, and VEC models we have considered so far all use observable variables (prices of various lags) to predict their future values. However, econometricians have also concocted a class of models with hidden variables, called *states,* which can determine the values of observed variables (though subject to observation noise). These models are called *state space models* (SSM), a linear example of which is the Kalman filter, discussed in Chapter 3 of Chan (2013) and used in Chapter 5 in this book. Though there can be nonlinear state space models, we will discuss only the linear version in this section.

A state space model starts with a linear relationship that specifies the time-evolution of the hidden state variable, usually denoted by x:

$$x(t) = A(t) * x(t-1) + B(t) * u(t) \tag{3.6}$$

where x is an m-dimensional vector, $A(t)$ and $B(t)$ are possibly time-dependent but observable matrices (A is $m \times m$, while B is $m \times k$), and $u(t)$ is k-dimensional Gaussian white noise with zero mean, unit variances, and zero serial and cross correlations. Equation 3.6 is often called the *state transition* equation. The observable variables (also called *measurements*) are related to the hidden variables by another linear equation

$$y(t) = C(t) * x(t) + D(t) * \varepsilon(t) \tag{3.7}$$

where y is an n-vector, $C(t)$ and $D(t)$ are possibly time-dependent but observable matrices (C is $n \times m$, while D is $n \times h$), and $\varepsilon(t)$ is h-dimensional Gaussian white noise, also with zero mean, unit variances, and zero serial and cross correlations. Equation 3.7 is often called the *measurement equation*.

What are these hidden variables, and why do we want to hypothesize their existence? An example of a hidden variable is the familiar moving average. Though we usually compute a moving average of prices using a fixed number of lagged prices and thus making it apparently an observable variable, we can argue that this fixed number of lags is an artificial construction. Also, why not use exponential moving average instead of moving average? The fact that no one can agree on a standard, unique *moving average* variable suggests that it may be treated as a hidden variable. We can give some structure to this hidden variable x by requiring that it evolves in a particularly simple way:

$$x(t) = x(t-1) + B * u(t) \tag{3.8}$$

We have assumed $A(t)$ is the identity matrix, which is of course invariant in time, and B is an unknown but also time-invariant matrix that determines the covariance of the estimation errors for the moving average x. (Remember that u itself has a covariance matrix that is the identity matrix.) Though we had said that B is supposed to be observable, it can be treated as an unknown parameter(s) to be estimated by applying maximum likelihood estimation on training data. (In other words, B is "observable" only to the extent that its values are not updated at each time step during Kalman filter updates.)

Given the moving average (plural if the time series is multivariate) of a time series, a trader may hypothesize that the prices are *trending*, and thus the best guess for the observed price at time t is just the estimated moving average at time t as well:

$$y(t) = x(t) + D * \varepsilon(t) \tag{3.9}$$

where D is another unknown and time-invariant matrix to be estimated by MLE.

Let's see this "moving average" model of equations 3.8 and 3.9 in action by applying it to the same computer hardware stocks' price series we studied in the section on VAR(p). We will assume that there are as many hidden state variables (five in total) as there are stocks in the computer hardware industry group. This is what a typical moving average model assumes as well—each price series has its own independent moving average. Furthermore, we assume also that the state noise of one moving average is uncorrelated with any other but each may have a different variance. Hence, B is a 5×5 diagonal matrix with unknown parameters. (Unknown parameters are denoted as NaN as an input to the MATLAB *estimate* function.) Similarly, we will assume the measurement noise of one stock's price is uncorrelated with another, but each may also have a different variance. Hence, D is also a 5 × 5 diagonal matrix with unkown parameters. We could have relaxed this zero-correlation constraint for the state and measurement noises, but this will mean many more variables to estimate, vastly increasing the time it takes for optimization and the danger of overfitting.

The code fragment for using the *estimate* function[6] to generate an estimate of the unknown variances of the state and measurement noises (the parameters in *B* and *D*) are as follows:

```
A=eye(size(y, 2)); % State transition matrix
B=diag(NaN(size(y, 2), 1))
C=eye(size(y, 2)); % Time-invariant measurement matrix
D=diag(NaN(size(y, 2), 1))


model=ssm(A, B, C, D);
param0=randn(2*size(B, 1)^2, 1); % 50 unknown parameters per bar.
model=estimate(model, y(trainset, :), param0);
```

which generates the values shown in Table 3.5.

In this case, the signs of the diagonal elements of the *B* and *D* matrices are immaterial, given that the noises $u(t)$ and $\varepsilon(t)$ are distributed symmetrically around a zero mean with no cross-correlations. One may also consider applying SSM on log prices instead, so that the Gaussian noise assumption is more reasonable.

TABLE 3.5 Estimated Values for *B* and *D* Matrices (Off-Diagonal Elements Are 0)

$B_{i,j}$	u_1	u_2	u_3	u_4	u_5
x_1	−3.74				
x_2		0.34			
x_3			−0.73		
x_4				−0.67	
x_5					−1.00

$D_{i,j}$	x_1	x_2	x_3	x_4	x_5
AAPL	−0.0000454				
EMC		−0.08			
HPQ			0.22		
NTAP				0.19	
SNDK					−0.15

Once the state transition and measurement equations are fixed, we can use the *filter* function to generate predictions of both the state and observation values.

```
[x, logL, output]=filter(model, y);
```

The $x(t)$ variable in the output of the *filter* function is the filtered price (moving average) at time t given observed prices up to time t. This model generates filtered prices that resemble the observed prices very closely, usually with less than 0.1 percent difference. Given equations (3.8) and (3.9), this also means that our prediction for next day's prices will also closely resemble today's prices. These predicted prices at t given observed prices can be extracted from *output(t).ForecastedObs*:

```
for t=1:length(output)
    yF(t, :)=output(t).ForecastedObs';
end
```

where we assign the predicted price for time t to $yF(t-1)$, using the same convention as we did previously. From these predicted prices, we can calculate the predicted returns


```
retF=(yF-y)./y;
```

Note that $retF(t)$ is the predicted return from $t-1$ to t, given the observed price y at time $t-1$. These predicted returns can be used in the same way as we did in the VAR model to create a sector-neutral trading strategy. We display in Figure 3.4 the cumulative returns of the model on the trainset, and Figure 3.5 displays the cumulative returns on the test set. The degree of overfitting is surprising, given that we merely use the training data to estimate the variances of the state and measurement noises.

Finding the moving average is not the only way the Kalman filter can be used to predict prices. If we assume trending behavior, we can also use it to find the *slope* of the recent trend in prices, leading to a prediction of the next price assuming the slope persists. This is left as an exercise for the reader.

Using the Kalman filter to make predictions on observations is not the only way to apply it to trading. Estimates of the hidden state itself may be useful—after all, it is supposed to be a moving average. Finding estimates of a hidden variable in the presence of noise is the original meaning of *filtering* and is a well-known concept in signal processing. Besides the Kalman filter, other well-known filters in finance and economics include the Hodrick-Prescott filter and the wavelet filter.

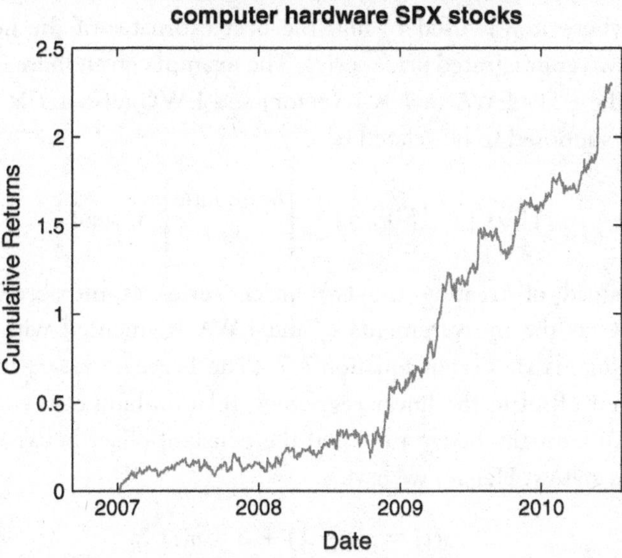

FIGURE 3.4 Kalman filter trading strategy applied to computer hardware stocks (in-sample)

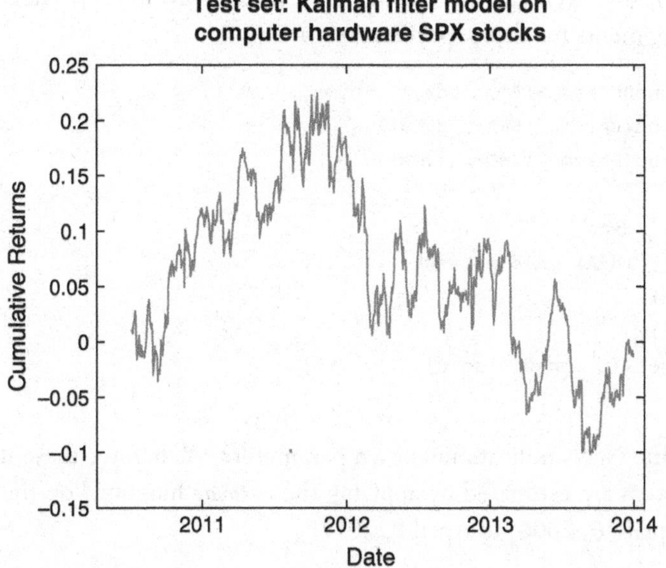

FIGURE 3.5 Kalman filter trading strategy applied to computer hardware stocks (out-of-sample)

Another application of Kalman filtering has been discussed in Chan (2013), where it was used to find the best estimates of the hedge ratio between two cointegrated price series. The example given there is the price series of the ETFs EWA (a $T \times 1$ vector) and EWC (also a $T \times 1$ vector), which are supposed to be related as

$$[EWC] = [EWA, 1] * \begin{bmatrix} hedge\ ratio \\ offset \end{bmatrix} + noise$$

But instead of treating the two price series as measurements, we treat EWC as the measurements y, and EWA augmented with 1s as the time-varying matrix $C(t)$ in equation 3.7. (The 1s are necessary to allow for the constant offset in the linear regression relationship between EWA and EWC.) We treat the hedge ratio and the constant offset between them as the hidden state x. Hence, we have

$$x(t) = x(t-1) + B * u(t) \tag{3.10}$$

$$y(t) = C(t) * x(t) + D * \varepsilon(t) \tag{3.11}$$

where x is a 2×1 time-varying vector $[hedge\ ratio, offset]'$, y is a scalar $[EWC(t)]$, and $C(t)$ is a time-varying 1×2 matrix $[EWA(t), 1]$. The MATLAB code fragments for these specifications are


```
load('inputData_ETF', 'tday', 'syms', 'cl');
idxA=find(strcmp('EWA', syms));
idxC=find(strcmp('EWC', syms));

y=cl(:, idxC);
C=[cl(:, idxA) ones(size(cl, 1), 1)];
A=eye(2);
B=NaN(2);
C=mat2cell(C, ones(size(cl, 1), 1));
D=NaN;
```

where the NaNs indicate unknown parameters. As before, these unknown parameters are estimated by applying the *estimate* function[7] on the trainset from April 26, 2006, to April 9, 2012:

```
trainset=1:1250;
model=ssm(A, B, C(trainset, :), D);
```

and the B matrix is displayed in Table 3.6, and the scalar D is estimated as -0.08. Unlike Table 3.5, we do not impose the constraint that the state noise has zero cross-correlations.

TABLE 3.6	Estimated Values for *B*	
$\mathbf{B_{i,j}}$	u_1	u_2
x_1	−0.01	0.02
x_2	0.41	−0.32

Note that these noise terms are markedly different than the ones we assumed in Box 3.1 of Chan (2013). There, we assumed that the state innovation noises $\omega_1(t)$ for the hedge ratio and $\omega_2(t)$ for the offset are uncorrelated, and each has a variance equal to about 0.0001. But here, we have estimated that $\omega_1(t) = -0.01 * u_1(t) + 0.02 * u_2(t)$ and $\omega_2(t) = 0.41 * u_1(t) - 0.32 * u_2(t)$, and given that $u_1(t)$ and $u_2(t)$ are assumed to be uncorrelated, the ω's have a covariance matrix

$$\begin{bmatrix} 0.00055 & -0.011 \\ -0.011 & 0.27 \end{bmatrix}.$$

Similarly, instead of arbitrarily setting the variance of the measurement noise $\varepsilon(t)$ to 0.001, we have now estimated that it is $D^2 = 0.0059$. Using these estimates and applying the function filter to the data generates estimates of the slope (Figure 3.6) and offset (Figure 3.7) that initially look quite different from Figures 3.5 and 3.6 in Chan (2013), but eventually settle into similar values. We can now apply the same trading strategy that we

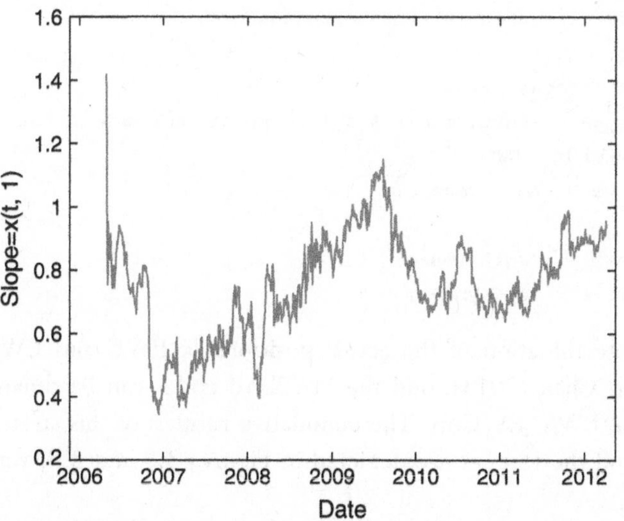

FIGURE 3.6 Kalman filter estimate of the slope between EWC and EWA

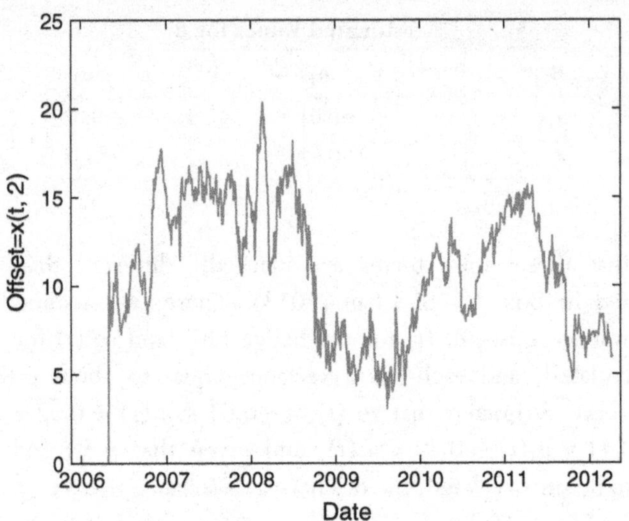

FIGURE 3.7 Kalman filter estimate of the offset between EWC and EWA

described in my previous treatment: buy EWC(y) if we find that the observed value of y is smaller than the forecasted value by more than the forecasted standard deviation of the observations, while simultaneously shorting EWA, and vice versa.


```
yF=NaN(size(y));
ymse=NaN(size(y));
for t=1:length(output)
    yF(t, :)=output(t).ForecastedObs';
    ymse(t, :)=output(t).ForecastedObsCov';
end
e=y-yF; % forecast error
longsEntry=e < -sqrt(ymse); % a long position means
   we should buy EWC
longsExit=e > -sqrt(ymse);

shortsEntry=e > sqrt(ymse);
shortsExit=e < sqrt(ymse);
```

The determination of the actual positions of EWC and EWA are the same as in Chan (2013), and the MATLAB codes can be downloaded as SSM_beta_EWA_EWC.m. The cumulative returns of this strategy on the trainset and the test set are depicted in Figures 3.8 and 3.9, respectively.

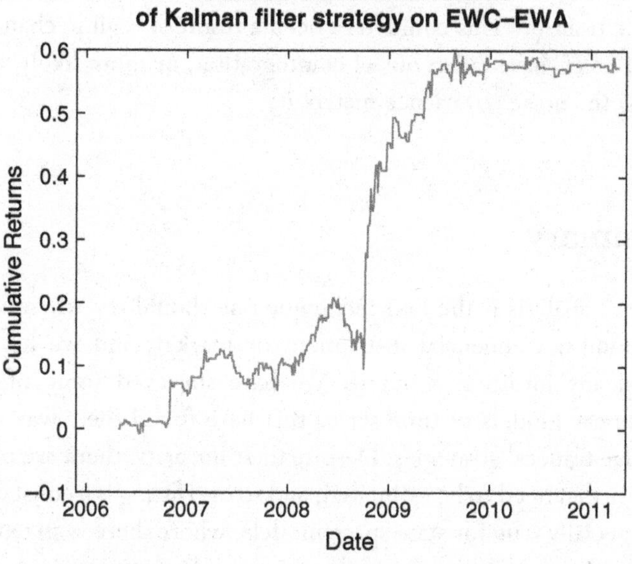

FIGURE 3.8 Kalman filter trading strategy applied to EWC–EWA (in-sample)

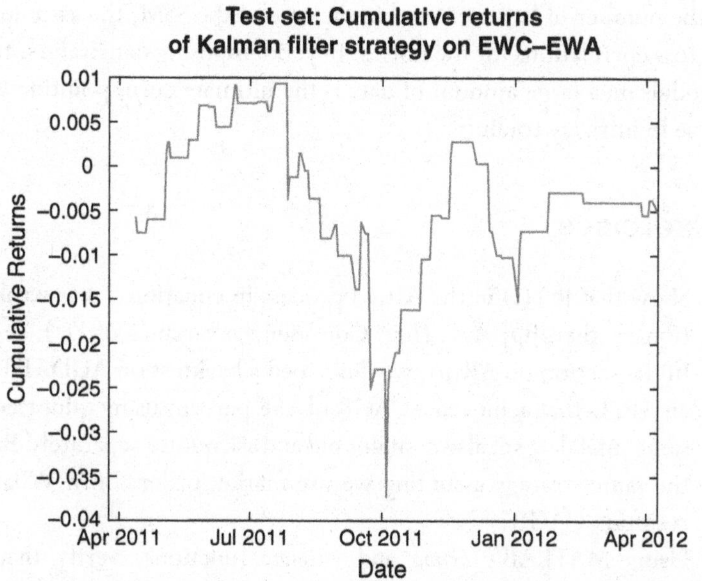

FIGURE 3.9 Kalman filter trading strategy applied to EWC–EWA (out-of-sample)

We can see that the equity curve has started to flatten even during the latter part of the trainset. This could have been a result of regime change, where EWA and EWC have fallen out of cointegration, or more likely, a result of overfitting the noise covariance matrix B.

Summary

Time-series analysis is the first technique one should try when confronted with a brand-new financial instrument or market, and we have not yet developed any intuition about it. We have surveyed some of the most popular linear models of time series that have found their way into many quantitative traders' strategies. Despite their linearity, there are often many parameters that need to be estimated, and so overfitting is a constant danger. This is especially true for state space models, where there is an extra hidden variable with its own dynamics that need to be estimated. A successful application of these methods to strategy building will involve imposing judicious constraints to reduce the number of unknown parameters. A popular constraint in the case of the ARMA or VAR models would be to limit the number of lags to 1, and in the case of the SSM, the assumption of zero cross correlations for the noises. Beyond imposing constraints, training the models on a large amount of data is the ultimate cure, pointing to their promise in intraday trading.

Exercises

3.1. Show that if $Y(t)$ in the AR(1) process in equation 3.1 is weakly stationary, then $|\phi| < 1$. *Hint*: Consider the variance of $Y(t)$.

3.2. In the section on AR(p), we described a backtest on AUD.USD using an AR(1) that achieved a CAGR of 158 percent using midprices. The same .mat data set also contains bid and ask quotes separately. Backtest the same strategy assuming we use market orders only. What is the resulting CAGR?

3.3. Using MATLAB's *arima* and *estimate* functions, verify that using ARIMA(p, 0, q) to model log returns of AUD.USD gives the same autoregressive coefficients as using ARIMA(p, 1, q) to model log prices. Show also that the best estimates for p and q are 1 and 9, respectively.

3.4. Apply the VAR model to EWA and EWC, and generate daily buy/sell trading signals when the predicted daily return is positive/negative. Assuming we always trade $1 per ETF, what is the CAGR and Sharpe ratio? Are there times when the trading signals for both ETFs have the same sign?

3.5. Comparing the *moving average* generated by equations (3.8) and (3.9) with an *N*-day exponential moving average (e.g., see en.wikipedia.org/wiki/Moving_average), what is the *N* that best fits our estimated state variable? What constraint(s) would you need to apply to the *B* or *D* matrices in equations 3.8 and 3.9 in order to enforce a larger *N*?

3.6. If you assume that *B* is diagonal in equation 3.9, are you able to backtest the Kalman filter trading strategy for EWC vs. EWA with a CAGR of 26.2 percent and a Sharpe ratio of 2.4 using data from April 26, 2006, to April 9, 2012? (These are the results we obtained in Chan, 2013.)

3.7. Apply VAR and VEC on computer hardware stocks as shown in the section on VAR(*p*) using log prices instead of prices. Do the out-of-sample returns and Sharpe ratio improve?

3.8. Instead of using the Kalman filter to find the *moving average* of prices, use it to find the slope of the recent price trend. Assuming that this slope persists into the future, backtest a trending strategy on, for example, the computer hardware stocks.

Endnotes

1. A time series is strictly stationary if all aspects of its behavior are unchanged by shifts in time (Ruppert and Matteson, 2015). A weakly stationary time series only requires that the mean and variance are unchanged. If this is a multivariate time series, the covariance also needs to be unchanged.
2. This complete program can be downloaded as buildAR1.m.
3. The complete code can be downloaded as buildARp_AUDUSD.m.
4. The complete code can be downloaded as buildVAR_findP_stocks.m.
5. The complete code can be downloaded as buildVAR1_sectorNeutral_computerHardware.m.
6. The complete code can be downloaded as SSM_MA_computerHardware_diag.m.
7. The complete code can be downloaded as SSM_beta_EWA_EWC.m.

CHAPTER 4

Artificial Intelligence Techniques

Most of the trading strategies in this book are developed based on the process a theoretical physicist would use. Where a theoretical physicist develops a hypothesis, designs an experiment to test that hypothesis, and confirms the hypothesis based on the test results, we quantitative traders develop a hunch about a possible inefficiency in the market (e.g., retail investors' herd-like behavior leading to stock momentum), devise a strategy to exploit that inefficiency, and use data to confirm whether that strategy actually works. The use of artificial intelligence (AI) or machine learning techniques is closer to the approach experimental physicists might take in their work: we don't have a preconceived theory of what the most important factors affecting the market are, and therefore, we need to explore as many factors and trading rules as possible with the help of efficient algorithms. Finance practitioners often derisively refer to this methodology as *data mining*. There is some justification of their derision: financial data are not only quite limited (unless we use tick data), they are also not very stationary in the statistical sense. That is, the probability distribution of returns does not stay constant forever. If we just turn our machine learning algorithms loose on these data, it is very easy to come up with trading rules that worked extremely well in certain past periods, but fail terribly going forward. Of course, even handcrafted trading models built with human intelligence can do that, too. But we can sometimes understand why it is that the model doesn't work anymore and take remedial actions. No such luck with machine-learned rules.

Despite our cautiousness toward AI techniques, keep in mind that this is a rapidly advancing field, where practitioners are developing techniques specifically designed to avoid the overfitting bias we alluded to. One may remember that neural networks were dismissed as quite impractical just a few years ago, but a breakthrough made in 2006 (Allen, 2015) revitalized the field, and neural net experts are now much sought-after in organizations such as Google and Facebook. More pertinent to trading, I remember a senior manager at the legendary quant fund Renaissance Technologies once remarked to the press that one of their most profitable trading strategies was also one that had no rational financial justification at all. That is also why it endured without being arbitraged away by other traders. These are the kind of trading rules that AI techniques can deliver to us. Another situation where AI techniques will be useful is when someone gives you a set of indicators, whether fundamental or technical, that you don't have any idea how to use and have no intuition about. Turning AI techniques loose on such indicators would be the easiest way to proceed. The results may even aid in gaining human understanding of the indicators. So let's not presume that our own minds and intuition have a monopoly on trading ideas and let AI surprise us!

The machine learning techniques we describe in this chapter are fairly basic and well-known. That's why they have been encapsulated in commercial software packages and are easily accessible to traders who do not wish to reinvent the wheel or to become a full-time AI researcher. The software packages that I use to demonstrate these techniques are MATLAB's Statistics and Machine Learning Toolbox and the Neural Network Toolbox, and in one instance, the Bayes Net Toolbox written by Dr. Kevin Murphy at Google. However, R programmers can easily find similar packages (Hothorn, 2014).

Though it may seem that we will be covering a hodgepodge of unrelated models, they can be categorized in several ways. Stepwise regression, regression tree, classification tree, support vector machine, and hidden Markov models can be considered linear models, or at least piecewise linear models, whereas a neural network is an explicitly nonlinear model. Stepwise regression, regression tree, and neural network typically try to predict response variables that are continuous, whereas classification tree and support vector machine try to predict responses that are discrete. (Hidden Markov models can work on either continuous or discrete data, but our example in this chapter is discrete.) All but the hidden Markov model use "supervised training" where we try to assign observable classes to data, whereas the hidden Markov model uses "unsupervised training" where we try to assign unobserved classes to the data.

All of these models can be improved by a number of common techniques. The first technique is called cross validation, where we train a lot of models on subsets of one training data set, and pick only the one that performs best out-of-sample. The second technique is called *bagging*. Here, we artificially create many training sets by resampling with replacement our original training set, and we train a model on each of these replicated training sets and average their predictions. The third technique is called random subspace, where instead of randomly sampling the training data as in bagging, we sample the predictors for each model that we create. The fourth technique, called random forest, is a hybrid between bagging and random subspace, and is especially designed for regression and classification trees. All four techniques are designed with the aim of reducing overfitting on the training set. There is a fifth technique that we will discuss, boosting, which is designed to force the learning algorithm to focus on its past prediction errors and improve on them.

To illustrate these models and techniques, we focus mostly on one simple example: the prediction of the ETF SPY's next-day return based on its past returns with various lookback. This allows us to compare the efficacy and nuances of different models and techniques without the distraction of understanding a new data set for each new technique. This doesn't mean that SPY is the most favorable instrument for AI methods, of course. You are encouraged to try them out on your own favorite market. In fact, most of these techniques work better if we have more predictors, and we can readily find more fundamental variables than (uncorrelated) technical variables as predictors. Hence, we include one important example at the end to illustrate the application of one of these techniques to identifying predictive fundamental stock factors for returns prediction.

Since this is a book on practical trading, and not on the theoretical foundation of finance, much less the theoretical foundation of machine learning, we will not dwell on the intricate details of the algorithms presented here. Trading strategies based on AI have earned a well-deserved reputation of being "black-box."[1] Even if one were to understand fully the mathematical justification of every AI learning algorithm, we would be no closer to intuiting why the algorithm generates a certain trading signal at a certain moment.

Stepwise Regression

One key utility of AI is that an algorithm can automatically select the most important independent variables (predictors) for the prediction of a dependent (response) variable based on a model that specifies the functional relationship between them. For example, if we want to predict the future one-day return of SPY, one predictor might be the previous one-day return, another might be its stochastic oscillator (for a technical analyst), the third one might be its P/E ratio (for a fundamental analyst), and so on. We don't usually know which predictor is important, so we should just throw everything but the kitchen sink at the AI algorithm, and hope for the best. The AI algorithm will perform what is called *feature selection*. The model that relates the predictor to the response variables need not be complicated. In fact, we will begin with one of the simplest models—linear regression—to illustrate the AI paradigm. The result of marrying feature selection to linear regression is stepwise regression.

Let's look at the example predicting SPY returns. Instead of using a mixture of technical and fundamental predictors, let's just use previous returns with various lookbacks (1-day, 2-day, 5-day, and 20-day) as predictors. In a usual multiple regression, we would fit the future one-day return to all the predictors simultaneously and find the regression coefficients of all the predictors (plus the y-intercept.) This can be accomplished using the *fitlm* function in MATLAB:

```
model_train=fitlm([ret1(trainset) ret2(trainset) ret5(trainset)
   ret20(trainset)], retFut1(trainset), 'linear')
```

The *ret1*, *ret2*, ... , *ret20* are $T \times 1$ arrays with previous returns of various lookback, and *retFut1* is a $T \times 1$ array with the future one-day return. By default, *fitlm* assumes there is a constant term, so we do not need to include a column of 1s in the predictors. The parameter "linear" indicates we don't want products of independent variables as predictors. We should not use the entire data set for fitting this regression model—we shall leave the second half of the data as the test set. Here *trainset* is an index array denoting the indices of the first half of the data. This separation between training and test sets is of course a procedure that we always follow in building any trading model, but especially important in building machine-learning models due to their propensity for overfitting. To see how this model does on the training set as a sanity check, we apply the *predict* function to *model* and the training data:

```
retPred1=predict(model, [ret1(trainset) ret2(trainset)
  ret5(trainset) ret20(trainset)]);
```

retPred1 is similar to *retFut1*, but contains the predicted future one-day returns instead of the actual future one-day returns contained in *retFut1*. If we build a simple trading strategy by buying $1 of SPY when *retPred1* is positive, and shorting $1 when it is negative, holding just one day:

```
positions(retPred1 > 0)=1;
positions(retPred1 < 0)=-1;
```

we find that the CAGR is 34.3 percent, with a Sharpe ratio of 1.4. So this model fits the training data from December 22, 2004, to September 15, 2009, quite well—so far, so good. We can repeat the same procedure on the test data from September 16, 2009, to June 2, 2014. Running

```
retPred1=predict(model, [ret1(testset) ret2(testset) ret5(testset)
  ret20(testset)]);
```


and applying the same simple trading strategy on the test set now yields a CAGR of 0.4 percent, with a Sharpe ratio of 0.1. This model[2] does no better than random on the test set. This establishes an easy benchmark for stepwise regression to beat.

Stepwise regression differs from multiple regression in that it starts with just one "best" predictor based on some common goodness of fit criterion such as the sum of squared error (the default for MATLAB's *stepwiselm* function), Akaike information criterion (AIC), or Bayesian information criterion (BIC). Then the algorithm will try to add other predictors one at a time until the goodness of fit does not improve. Then it goes in reverse and tries to remove predictors one at a time, again stopping when the goodness of fit does not improve. In practice, to switch from using multiple regression to stepwise regression in MATLAB is as simple as switching the name of the function from *lmfit* to *stepwiselm*.

```
model=stepwiselm([ret1(trainset) ret2(trainset) ret5(trainset)
  ret20(trainset)], retFut1(trainset), 'Upper', 'linear')
```

The input parameter name/value pair "Upper" with its value "linear" indicates that we only want linear functions of the independent variables as predictors, not products of them.

The algorithm picks just one predictor: *ret2*.[3] This one predictor causes the in-sample CAGR to go from 34.3 percent to 43.5 percent, and the Sharpe ratio from 1.4 to 1.6. This is unusually encouraging, because a simpler model with fewer predictors usually produces worse results than a complicated model in-sample. But more importantly, stepwise regression causes the out-of-sample CAGR to go from 0.4 percent to 10.6 percent, and the Sharpe ratio from 0.1 to 0.7, indicating the model is close to achieving statistical significance (the threshold for that is a Sharpe ratio of 1). The equity curve shown in Figure 4.1 suggests that most of the performance comes during the earlier period from 2009 to 2011, but that isn't the fault of the algorithm. To improve on this, we can always retrain the program at every step by adding the latest data point to the training set. Also, the model makes a prediction of returns, but we have only used the sign of the return as a trading signal. One way to use the magnitude of the predicted return is to buy or sell only when the magnitude exceeds a certain threshold. Another way is to buy or sell a dollar amount that is proportional to the return magnitude. We will leave all these variations as exercises.

One last detail we should notice: the regression coefficient of *ret2* is negative, meaning that this model predicts that future one-day return will

FIGURE 4.1 Out-of-sample performance of stepwise regression on SPY

revert from the past two-day return. Just because a model is generated by AI doesn't mean that we should not use it to improve our own understanding of the market!

Regression Tree

Using a regression tree (and its sibling classification tree for discrete dependent variables such as, "Will it be an up or down day tomorrow?") is another way one can select important predictors. However, unlike stepwise regression, where all the selected predictors are applied to all data jointly just as in a multiple regression, regression trees take a hierarchical approach. In fact, the regression tree algorithm has little to do with linear regression. Once the algorithm picks the "best" predictor based on some criterion, it will split the data into two subsets by applying an inequality condition on this predictor (such as "previous two-day return < 1.5%"). The original data form the *parent* node, and each subset is a *child* node. The algorithm will then be iteratively applied to each child node, until a stopping condition is met. The criterion that is used to pick the best predictor at each node is usually based on minimizing the variance of the response variable in each child node (Breiman et al., 1984). Minimizing the variance of the response variable in a node is another way of saying we want to minimize the mean squared error (MSE) of the predicted response compared to the true response, because the predicted response for a node is none other than the average of the response variables. The stopping condition is met when any of the following occur:

1. There is no reduction of variances compared to the variance of the parent node; or
2. There are too few observations in the parent node (*MinParentSize* is an input parameter); or
3. Splitting the parent node using any predictor would have resulted in a child node with too few observations (*MinLeafSize* is another input parameter); or
4. The maximum number of nodes have been reached (*MaxNumSplits*, a third input parameter, limits the total number of splits).

Note that due to the iterative nature of this algorithm, the same predictor can be reused at each child node for an unlimited number of times. Each "leaf" of a tree (a child node without children itself) can be summarized as a set of inequalities on the predictors (e.g., "previous two-day return < 1.5%" *and* "previous one-day return < −1.4%"). We can therefore pick those leaves (equivalently, the set of inequalities) that have the average response (e.g., high average future one-day return) we desire. When we have a new data point from the test set that satisfies all the inequalities that lead to a leaf with high average future return, we will predict that this data point will generate a high future return, too.

We can try our hands at the regression tree algorithm on the same set of data, predictors, and response variable (future one-day return of SPY) as we used in the stepwise regression example. The program rTree.m is practically the same as stepwiseLR.m: we just need to replace the function *stepwiselm* with *fitrtree*.

```
model=fitrtree([ret1(trainset) ret2(trainset) ret5(trainset)
  ret20(trainset)], retFut1(trainset), 'MinLeafSize', 100);
```

We choose to set *MinLeafSize* to 100, but you are free to experiment with other values and see what is optimal on the trainset. Generally speaking though, we don't want to have a leaf size that is too small in order to avoid overfitting. To see what the tree looks like, including the inequalities in each child node, apply the function *view* to the model:

```
view(model, 'mode', 'graph'); % see the tree visually
```


which produces Figure 4.2.

We can examine the numbers below the leaf nodes: they indicate the expected value of the response variable under the sequence of inequalities.

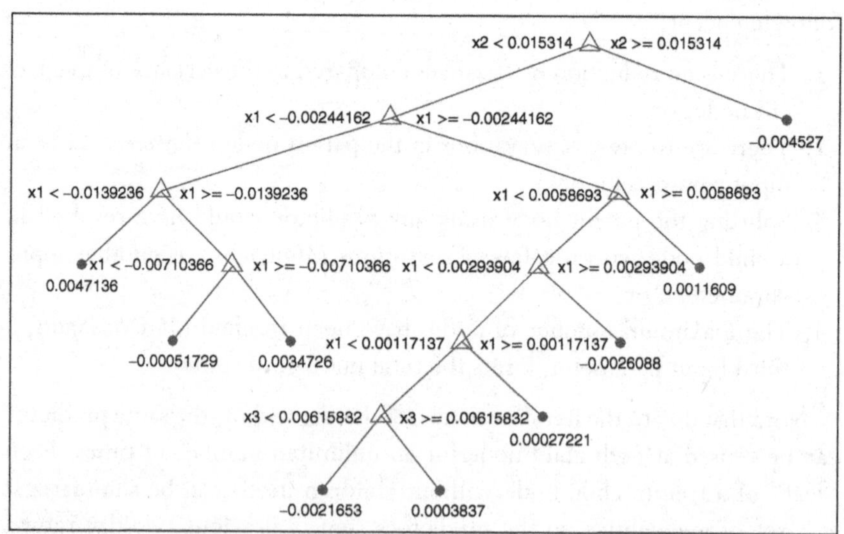

FIGURE 4.2 Regression tree on SPY

For example, if we want a leaf node with the highest expected value (0.0047136 for the left-most node), we see that the sequence is $x2 < 0.015314$, $x1 < -0.00244162$, $x1 < -0.0139236$, which we can paraphrase as ret2 < 1.53% and ret1 < −1.39%. This can be used as a ready-made trading rule for buying SPY. Similarly, we can look for a leaf node with the most negative expected value (−0.004527 for the right-most node). The single inequality that leads to that can be paraphrased as ret2 >= 1.53%. This can be used as a trading rule for shorting SPY. Both trading rules are mean-reverting, just as the trading model produced by stepwise regression. If we buy SPY at the close and hold it one day according to the long rule, and short SPY and hold it one day according to the short rule, we obtain a CAGR of 28.8 percent with a Sharpe ratio of 1.5 on the training set, and a CAGR of 3.9 percent with a Sharp ratio of 0.5 on the test set. This isn't as good as the stepwise regression result, and the equity curve in Figure 4.3 also shows that these mean reversion models worked only during the first half of the test set.

One may wonder why we limit ourselves to the two extreme leaves (extreme in terms of expected response), and do not generate a trading rule based on the expected response of every single leaf? If we try that

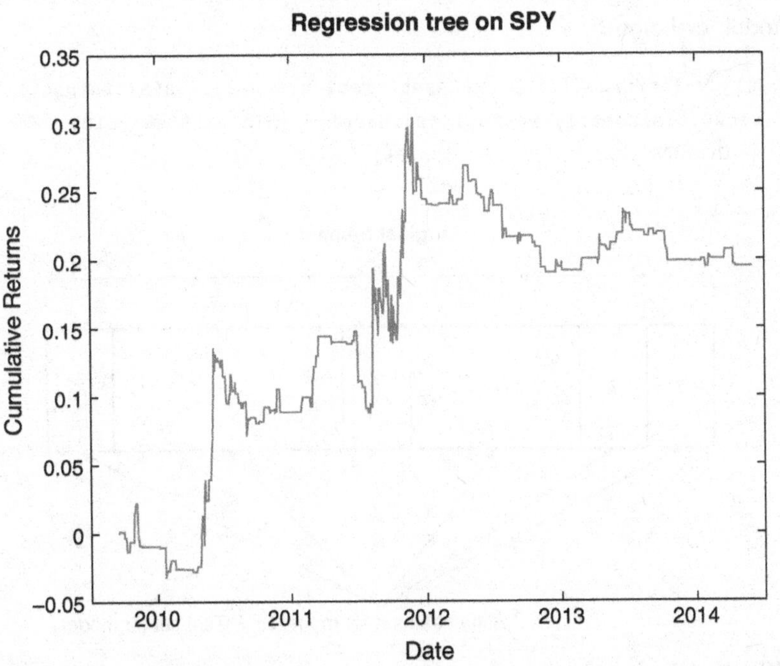

FIGURE 4.3 Trading model based on regression tree

(all we need to do is to use the *predict* function we have used before in stepwiseLR.m.), we will find that the in-sample CAGR will be boosted to 73 percent, but the out-of-sample CAGR will drop to −7.2 percent—a clear symptom of overfitting. But there is a way to have your cake and eat it, too. In the next three sections, we will explore some general techniques for reducing overfitting so that we can in fact use all leaves for prediction.

Cross Validation

Cross validation is a technique for reducing overfitting by testing for out-of-sample performance as part of model building. To do this, we randomly divide the training set into K roughly equal subsets. Model i will be built on the union of all subsets except the ith. We then test for the predictive accuracy of model i on the out-of-sample i^{th} part. (See Figure 4.4.) This is called the cross-validation accuracy. Finally, we will pick the model that has the highest cross-validation accuracy.

We can try this on the regression tree model we built in the previous section that uses every leaf for generating trading signals. We simply need to add the name/value pairs "CrossVal" and "On," "KFold" and 5, when using *fitrtree* for model building. This would generate $K = 5$ trees stored in model_cv below:


```
model_cv=fitrtree([ret1(trainset) ret2(trainset) ret5(trainset)
   ret20(trainset)], retFut1(trainset),  'MinLeafSize', 100,
     'CrossVal', 'On', 'KFold', 5);
```

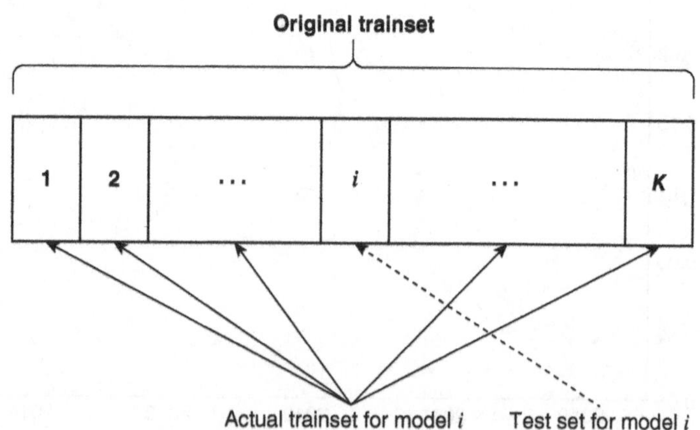

FIGURE 4.4 Leaving out a subset of training set for cross-validation test

To find the cross-validation accuracy (or its inverse, the loss or mean squared error of the predicted responses compared to the true responses) of each tree, we apply the *kfoldLoss* function to these trees and pick the tree with the minimum loss:

```
L= kfoldLoss(model_cv,'mode','individual'); % Find the loss
   (mean squared error) of the predicted responses in a fold
      when compared against predictions made with a tree trained
          on the out-of-fold data.
[~, minLidx]=min(L); % pick the tree with the minimum loss,
   i.e. with least overfitting error.
bestTree=model_cv.Trained{minLidx};
```

Running the predict function on the test set using *bestTree* as the model generates a CAGR of 0.6 percent with a Sharpe ratio of 0.11, which is definitely better than the previous result without using cross validation, but not as good as if we just pick the two extreme leaves. (If you run this program with a different random seed, you will get a different tree and different CAGR. This is because the cross-validation algorithm picks the subsets of training data for each tree randomly.) The code for this is part of rTree.m.

Some readers may wonder why we pick $K = 5$ instead of 10, which is the MATLAB default for the number of subsets used for cross validation. The reason is that while our training set from December 22, 2004, to September 15, 2009, may be a reasonable size for trading research, it is considered quite small by machine learning standards. If we divide this training set into 10 subsets, the out-of-sample subset will be so small that the cross-validation accuracy is subject to large statistical errors, and so the "best" tree produced won't necessarily be any good when applied to the test set. On the other hand, if we set K to be too small, say 2, then we don't have enough trained models to choose the best one from.

Bagging

In cross validation, we introduced the idea that it is often useful to present somewhat different training data sets to the learning algorithm so that it does not overfit to the statistical fluctuations in one single training set that won't be repeated in the test set. Bagging is another variation on this theme. Instead of randomly dividing the original training set of size N into subsets as we did in cross validation, we randomly sample N observations from the original training set *with replacement* to form a replica (a *bag*) of the original training set. Since we are sampling with replacement, some observations from the original training set will be repeated multiple times in the replica and other observations will be omitted (these will be called *out-of-bag* observations). We repeat this process *K* times, so that we form an ensemble of *K* such replicas, each with the original training set size *N*. Since this process essentially increases the training sample size, it is also called bootstrapping. Like cross validation, we will train a model (regression tree in our example) on each replica, and test its predictive accuracy on the corresponding out-of-bag (and, therefore, out-of-sample) observations. (See Figure 4.5.) But unlike cross validation, we do not just pick the tree with the most accurate out-of-bag prediction. We average the predicted response from *all* the trees built from all the replicas.

To apply bagging to the regression tree learner, use the *TreeBagger* instead of the *fitrtree* function in MATLAB:

```
model=TreeBagger(5, [ret1(trainset) ret2(trainset) ret5(trainset)
    ret20(trainset)], retFut1(trainset), 'Method', 'regression',
       'MinLeaf', 100);
```


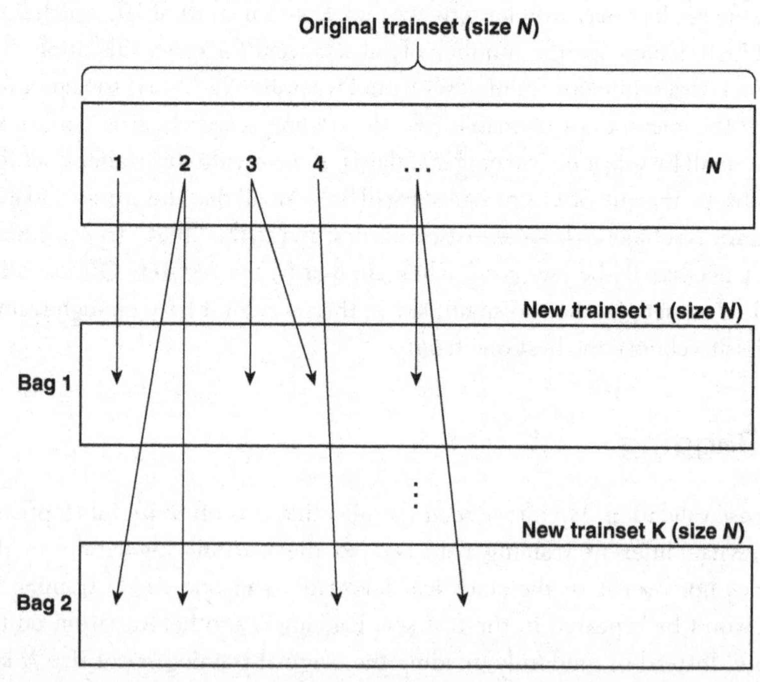

FIGURE 4.5 Bagging with *K* bags (In bag 1, data samples 2 and 4 will be part of test set 1. In bag *K*, data samples 1 and 3 will be part of test set K.)

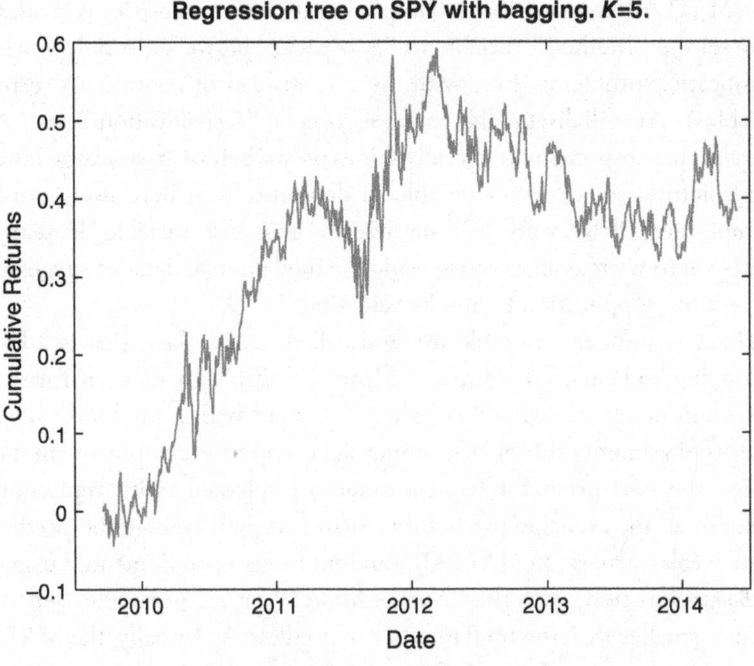

FIGURE 4.6 Trading model based on regression tree with bagging ($K = 5$)

We picked $K = 5$ (the first parameter in the *TreeBagger* function[4]) since this was the number of trees we built with cross validation as well. This yielded significantly better predictive performance than the cross validation model: CAGR is 7.2 percent with a Sharpe ratio of 0.5. The equity curve is displayed in Figure 4.6.

Increasing K will actually degrade out-of-sample performance, because the average result of a large ensemble of replicas will be very similar to that of using the original training set.

Random Subspace and Random Forest

With bagging, we randomly sample *data* with replacement to train multiple models. With random subspace, we randomly sample *predictors* with replacement (but with decreasing sampling probability for those that have been chosen previously) to train multiple models. In both cases, we will average the predictions of all these models (*weak learners*) so that the ensemble prediction is stronger. Any method that trains many weak learners to form a strong learner is called an "ensemble" method.

In MATLAB, the function that implements random subspace is *fitensemble*, if we set the "Method" variable to "Subspace." However, it only works on classification problems (i.e., with discrete instead of continuous response variables). We will discuss that in the section on "Classification Tree." Also, the random subspace method really shines only when we have a large number of predictors, so we won't be able to demonstrate it here using our SPY example even if we were to discretize the response variable. Instead, we invite you to try it as an exercise using the fundamental data set suggested in the section "Application to Stocks Selection."

There is another ensemble method called *random forest* that is a hybrid of bagging and random subspace. More specifically, a random forest is a regression or classification tree where we start with a randomly selected (with replacement) subset of training data, and at each split of the node, choose the best predictor from a randomly selected (with replacement) subset of all the available predictors. Again, we will average the prediction of the weak learners. In MATLAB, random forest is implemented using the *TreeBagger* function, with the "*NumPredictorsToSample*" parameter set to any number smaller than the total number of predictors. Actually, the MATLAB default is to have *NumPredictorsToSample* set to one-third of the total number of predictors, which is what we used in the bagging example in the previous section and in rTreeBagger.m. If we actually want to use all the predictors at every node for prediction, we can set *NumPredictorsToSample* to "all." This decreases the out-of-sample CAGR of the previous example from 7.2 percent to 1.5 percent, and the Sharpe ratio from 0.5 to 0.2.

Boosting

As humans, we pride ourselves on our ability to learn from our past mistakes. The best of us don't waste our time reminiscing on past triumphs. It turns out that we can teach our AI algorithms to do the same, and this method is called *boosting*.

Boosting involves applying a learning algorithm iteratively to the prediction errors of the model constructed in the previous iteration. As a first step in boosting, we apply a learning algorithm such as a regression tree to the training data as before. The first step is complete once the tree is constructed and predictions made for the training set. We begin the second step by creating a new training set where the responses are the differences between the actual responses and the predicted response from the first model. The objective of this second tree is to minimize the square of these differences. We will repeat this so as to create a total of *M* trees and take the predictions of the Mth tree as final. The hope is again to turn a weakly predictive algorithm into a stronger one.

We will apply this procedure to the regression tree model that we created before. We need to just replace *fitrtree* function with the *fitensemble* function in our code (rTreeLSBoost.m), just as in the case with the random subspace method. We need to specify "LSBoost" as the boosting algorithm, which is the gradient descent method (Friedman, 1999) for boosting regression or regression tree models. We also specify *M* as the number of iterations for boosting. Finally, we specify "Tree" as the learning algorithm.

```
model=fitensemble([ret1(trainset) ret2(trainset) ret5(trainset)
  ret20(trainset)], retFut1(trainset), 'LSBoost', M, 'Tree');
```

As opposed to cross validation and bagging, boosting does not seem to alleviate overfitting (although there are theoretical arguments on why it won't overfit). (See Kun, 2015.) We can see in Figure 4.7 the effect of boosting the previously constructed regression tree on the train versus

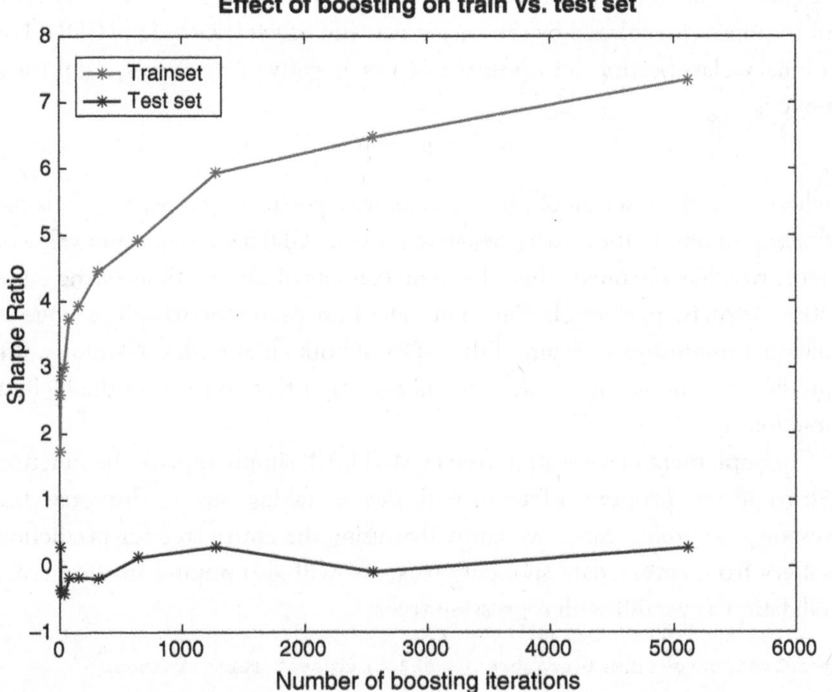

FIGURE 4.7 Effect of boosting a regression tree on train vs. test set Sharpe ratio

test set. With increasing number of iterations, the Sharpe ratio on the trainset increases rapidly, while the Sharpe ratio on the test set increases much more slowly. In fact, the Sharpe ratio for the test set remains insignificant at any reasonable number of iterations. Applying cross validation to the best tree at each iteration actually worsens performance.

Classification Tree

The core learning algorithms we have discussed so far assume that the response variable is continuous. This is natural because we are mostly interested in expected returns in trading. But there are some learning algorithms that are specifically designed for discrete (also called categorical) response variables. There is no reason why we should deprive ourselves of them—we just need to discretize our returns into, say, positive and negative returns. In this section, we will apply the classification tree to the SPY prediction task.

Classification tree is a close sibling of regression tree. With regression tree, the best predictor to split a node is one that minimizes variance of responses in the child nodes. With classification tree, the variance of responses is replaced by the analogous Gini's Diversity Index (GDI). For a binary classification into positive (+) or negative (−) classes, GDI for a node is

$$1 - p_+^2 - p_-^2$$

where p_+ is the fraction of observations with positive returns, and p_- is the fraction of observations with negative returns. GDI has a minimum value of zero, which is obtained when the node consists of observations of the same class—that is, perfect classification. The best predictor to split a node is one that minimizes the sum of the GDIs of both child nodes. Naturally, the predicted response of a node is the observation that constitutes the highest fraction.

To implement classification tree in MATLAB, simply replace the function *fitrtree* in our program rTree.m with *fitctree*, taking care to discretize the response variable.[5] Since we know that using the entire tree for prediction suffers from severe data snooping bias, we will also impose fivefold cross validation as we did with regression trees:

```
model=fitctree([ret1(trainset) ret2(trainset) ret5(trainset)
   ret20(trainset)], retFut1(trainset) >= 0, 'MinLeafSize', 100,
     'CrossVal', 'On', 'KFold', 5); % Response: True if >=0,
       False if < 0.
```

We can use this model in an obvious way to generate trading signal: just buy when the predicted response is positive, and short when it is negative. The complete program is in cTree.m. The resulting CAGR on the test set is 4.8 percent, with a Sharpe ratio of 0.4, which is better than the cross-validated regression tree results, but not as good as the regression tree with random forest. (Of course, you can apply the random forest algorithm to the classification tree as well. This is left as an exercise.)

One doesn't have to categorize the response as positive or negative returns. We can create a class for high positive returns (i.e., returns higher than some threshold) and another one for the complement, and generate buy signals only when we predict this high-return class. Similarly, we can create a class for low negative returns and generate short signals for predictions in this class. However, this doesn't seem to improve the performance of the trading strategy.

Support Vector Machine

The support vector machine (SVM) is another popular classification technique that works on discrete responses. The intuitive idea behind it is quite visually appealing: let's imagine each sample data point resides in an m-dimensional space, where m is the number of predictors (which are still continuous variables). Let's say some of these data points are labeled "plus" the remaining ones are labeled "minuses." (See Figure 4.8). These pluses and

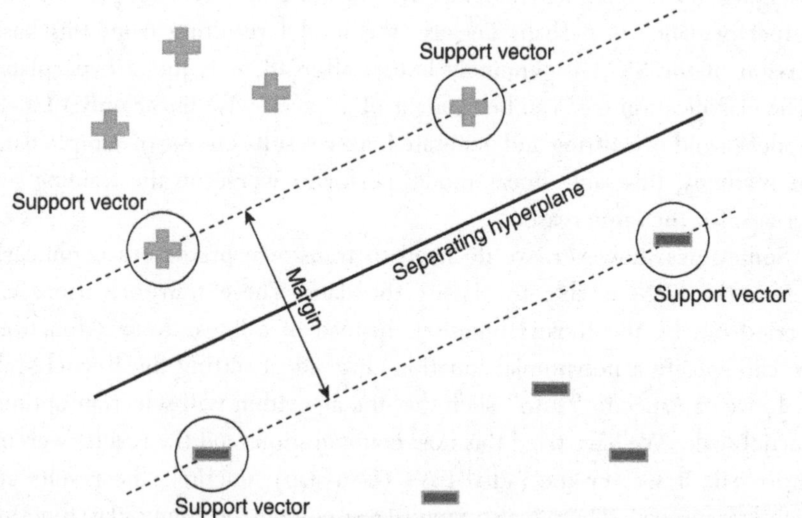

FIGURE 4.8 Support vector machine illustrated

minuses are our discrete responses. The SVM attempts to find a hyperplane in this *m*-dimensional space that can separate the pluses from the minuses. Furthermore, it wants to separate them with the largest possible margin. If that can be done, we have achieved our classification task: whenever a data point has coordinates on one side of this hyperplane, we will know exactly which response category it will have. In our 2-D illustration in Figure 4.8, the black line in the middle achieves such a clean separation: all the minuses are on the right side of the line, and all the pluses are on the left. The pluses that come closest to the separating hyperplane (line) form a set of "support vectors," and so do the minuses that come closest. The separation between the two sets of support vectors is the margin which we maximized with our SVM.

Of course, real data are rarely as obliging as our fantasy data set. Even with the "best" hyperplane, we will find pluses on the right side and minuses on the left. We can attempt to find the best hyperplane by maximizing the margin of separation while simultaneously minimizing a penalty term that penalizes misclassified data points. (The mathematical details can be found in Anonymous, 2015.) To use the SVM in MATLAB, simply substitute the function *fitcsvm* for *fitctree* and again apply fivefold cross validation.[6]

```
model=fitcsvm([ret1(trainset) ret2(trainset) ret5(trainset)
  ret20(trainset)], retFut1(trainset) >= 0, 'CrossVal', 'On',
    'KFold', 5); % Response: True if >=0, False if < 0.
```


The resulting CAGR of 13.3 percent with a Sharpe ratio of 0.8 on the test set is much superior to that of the classification tree. The equity curve in Figure 4.9 also shows no deterioration in the more recent period. This outperformance is perhaps because the model resulting from this basic version of the SVM is genuinely linear: after all, it is just a hyperplane. (The classification tree can be thought of as piece-wise linear only.) Linear models avoid overfitting and generate better results on out-of-sample data. Interestingly, this same linear model performs worse on the training set, perhaps for the same reason.

Sometimes, however, we do need to transform predictors nonlinearly before the SVM is able to classify the data. These transformations are carried out by the Kernel function. Instead of a linear Kernel function, we can specify a polynomial function. Instead of setting the Kernel scale to 1, we can specify "auto" such that the algorithm will select an optimal Kernel scale. We have tried this new configuration, and the results weren't improved. If we try the radial basis (Gaussian) function, the results are slightly improved. There is also a multilayer perceptron (sigmoidal) function

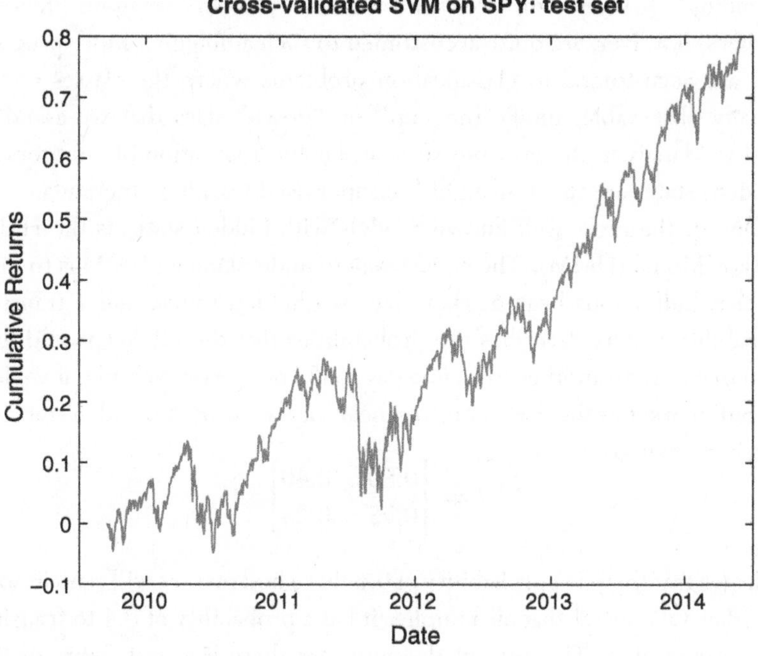

FIGURE 4.9 Support vector machine with cross validation

that we can apply, but it isn't part of the Statistics and Machine Learning Toolbox, so you would have to construct it yourself. (Interested readers can explore whether they can extract this function from the Neural Network Toolbox and apply that to the SVM.) Applying a nonlinear Kernel function to the predictors is effectively using a curved membrane instead of a plane to cut through the data. Another way of thinking about the Kernel transformation is that we are transforming the data into a higher dimensional space such that a hyperplane there can cleanly separate them. A reverse transformation of this hyperplane appears as a curve, not a line, in the original space. This allows for much more flexibility (and more room for overfitting).

Hidden Markov Model

It is common for traders to label a certain market moment "bull" or "bear." It isn't clear, though, what constitutes a bull or bear market, since we can certainly experience down days in a bull market and up days in a bear market. No two cable TV commentators are able to agree on the exact definition of a bull or bear market. The same goes for "mean-reverting" versus "trending" markets, or "risk-on" versus "risk-off" regimes. Machine learners, however, are quite accustomed to such ambiguity. More precisely, they are accustomed to classification problems where the classes are not actually observable, unlike the "up" or "down" days that we asked the SVM to classify in the previous section. Such classification of unobservable (hidden) states are the domain of "unsupervised learning" methods.

One of the most well-known models with hidden states is the Hidden Markov Model (HMM). The easiest way to understand an HMM is to imagine that bull versus bear markets are two hidden states, and a transition probability matrix describes the probabilities that the market would jump from one state to another from one day to the next. For example, if we label the bull market as the first state, and bear market as the second, a transition matrix T such as

$$T = \begin{bmatrix} 0.60 & 0.40 \\ 0.75 & 0.25 \end{bmatrix}$$

indicates that there is a probability of 0.6 that a bull market will remain so the next day. Of course, that also implies it has a probability of 0.4 to transition to a bear market. This matrix also indicates there is a probability of 0.25 that a bear market will remain so the next day, and a probability of 0.75 that it will transition to a bull market. Naturally, the probabilities on each row must add up to 1.

Besides the transition probabilities as tabulated in the transition matrix, we also need to know the probabilities that a bear state will "emit" a down day and an up day, respectively. The down and up days are called *emissions*, or observables. Similarly, we need to know the same for a bull state. These "emission" probabilities are tabulated in an emission probability matrix E such as

$$E = \begin{bmatrix} 0.19 & 0.81 \\ 0.97 & 0.03 \end{bmatrix}$$

where we label the down days as the first emission symbol and the up days as the second. So this emission matrix is telling us that there is a 19 percent chance that a bull state will emit a down day, and an 81 percent chance that it will emit an up day. There is a 97 percent chance that a bear state will emit a down day and a 3 percent chance that it will emit an up day. Again, the probabilities of each row must sum to one. Figure 4.10 illustrates the transition matrix.

Since bull and bear are unobservable, they are just names we give to the states. They can just as well be called "mean-reverting" and "trending,"

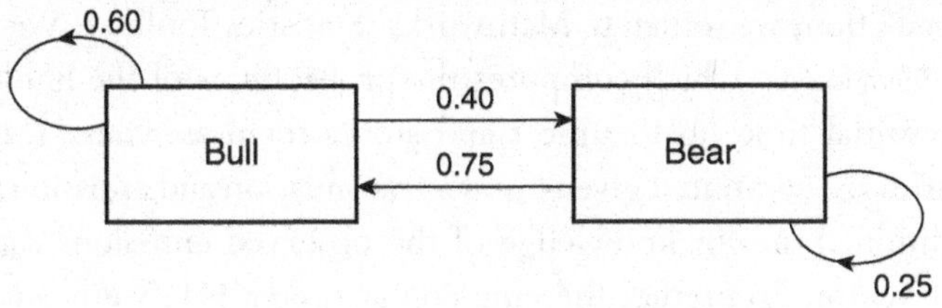

FIGURE 4.10 Hidden states transition probabilities of an HMM

or "risk-on" and "risk-off," or even "greed" and "fear," and the learning algorithm will be none the wiser. The only assumption we have made is that the down and up days are generated by two unobservable states, in order to account for the fact that the probabilities of observing the up and down days seem not to be described satisfactorily by a stationary probability distribution. In other words, we can regard HMM as just a more complicated time-series model than the ones we described in Chapter 3, with more parameters to estimate, and needless to say, more scope for data-snooping bias.

Just like other learning algorithms, the parameters (namely, the transmission matrix *T* and the emission matrix *E*, and possibly the prior probability distribution on the emissions) need to be estimated using the training set. One of the most famous unsupervised learning algorithms for an HMM, and indeed for any models with hidden states, is the EM algorithm (Murphy, 2012). Mathworks' Statistics and Machine Learning Toolbox does have the function *hmmtrain* that implements a version of the EM algorithm, but unfortunately, it often returns singular solutions for unbeknownst reasons. Instead, we used an open-source software called Bayes Net Toolbox for MATLAB (https://code.google.com/p/bnt/) for training. This is a complex piece of software, and quite difficult to use. We used their function called *learn_params_dbn_em* for training, as shown in our program hmm_train.m. The goal of training is, as usual, to find the parameters that generate the maximum log likelihood of the emissions. Since I expect there will be multiple local maxima, I run this training process 10 times, record the likelihood achieved for each maximum, and pick the model that has the highest likelihood among them. (Of course, if your computer is much faster than mine, or if you have much more patience than I did, you can run this many more times than 10.) Running this on SPY daily returns gives the *T* and *E* matrices that I used previously.

For prediction, we return to Mathworks' Statistics Toolbox. We need the function *hmmdecode*, which computes the probabilities of the hidden states from the initial time up to time t and stores them as *pstates*$(1{:}t)$. These probabilities are computed given known transmission and emission matrices and conditioned on our knowledge of the observed emissions *data* stored in a $t \times 1$ vector. To predict the emission at time $t + 1$, we need to know *pstates*$(t + 1)$, which is given by $T' \times$ *pstates*(t), where T' is the transpose of T. Then the probabilities of emissions are *pemis*$(t + 1) = E' \times$ *pstates* $(t + 1) = E' \times T' \times$ *pstates*(t). The MATLAB code fragment for this is

```
pemis=NaN(2, size(data, 1));
for t=1:size(data, 1)-1
    [pstates]=hmmdecode(data(1:t)', T, E);
    pemis(:, t+1)=E'*T'*pstates(:, end);
end
```

Note that this algorithm requires us to run *hmmdecode* with *all* previously observed data as input. It is not an "online" algorithm where we can just add the latest data point at time t and it would update *pstates*(t). In contrast, the continuous sibling of HMM is the Kalman filter, where we have indeed used an online algorithm to update our estimates of the hidden state variable and other parameters in our discussion in Chan (2013) and again mentioned in Chapter 3 of this book. We will leave the task of finding (or implementing one from scratch) an online decoding function for HMM as an exercise.

Given the emission probabilities for the next day, we can construct a simple trading strategy that buys SPY if the probability of "up" is higher than "down," and vice versa. We have created the program hmm_test.m to do just that. For the training set, it performed decently, giving a CAGR of 8.7 percent, but it gives a CAGR of 1 percent for the test set.

There are many variations to the way we builds an HMM to predict the next day return. Instead of estimating parameters using the first half of the data as training set, we can perform estimation with every new observed emission. Instead of discrete emissions (up or down days), we can model them as continuous variables with some parametric distributions such as Gaussian or Student-t (Dueker, 2006). Instead of the emissions depending only on the hidden state variables, they can depend on some observed input variables too (such as the predictors used in all the supervised models in this chapter so far).

There is a side benefit of using HMM, aside from using it to predict the next emission. Given the observed emissions, HMM can tell us what the most probable hidden state sequence is. We can use the *hmmviterbi* function for that (in honor of Prof. Andrew Viterbi, the inventor of the decoding algorithm and the cofounder of Qualcomm, Inc., which likely made the chip in your smartphone).

```
states=hmmviterbi(data, T, E);
```

What is the benefit of knowing the most probable state sequence? Next time, if someone asks you whether you think this is a bull or bear market, you can consult your HMM and give them a well-defined answer.[7]

Neural Network

Neural network may be the most well-known of the machine learning algorithms. Because of its long history, it has also evolved into many subspecies, architectures, and training algorithms. It is in fact so evolved that Mathworks decided to gather all neural network algorithms into a separate Neural Network Toolbox. We certainly won't be able to do justice to all its flavors in a few short paragraphs. Instead, we will highlight the most basic architecture that is suitable for our SPY returns prediction task.

We can understand neural network as simply a way to approximate any function of an arbitrary number of predictor variables by a linear function of sigmoid functions $S(x) = 1/(1 + e^{-x})$, or linear function of sigmoid functions of linear functions of sigmoid functions, and so on. How many iterations of these sigmoid functions to use, how much weight to put on each, how to connect the output of one such function to the input of another, can only be decided by experimentation and optimization on the training set. Determining the weight of each function based on the training data set is the job of the training algorithm, which is also an optimization problem on the training set.

The most basic architecture we can use is the feed forward network. A feed forward network consists of a number of hidden layers, each with a number of "neurons" that represent the sigmoid functions (with different weights), and a final output layer that represents a linear function. In the Neural Network Toolbox, the number of neurons in each layer can be specified as an input parameter *hiddenSizes* (a row vector) to the *feedforwardnet* function. For example, we can specify

```
hiddenSizes=[2 4 3];
```

which indicates the first layer has 2 neurons, the second 4 neurons, and the third 3. This means that our input vector x_i, which in the SPY example has a dimension of 4, plus the constant 1 just like the constant offset of a linear regression, is first summed into a scalar with different weights:

$$I_j = \sum_{i=1}^{4}(w_{j,i}x_i + w_{j,0})$$

where I_j is the input to the jth neuron, and $w_{j,i}$ is the weight (to be determined during the training phase of the network) for the ith component of the input vector for the jth neuron, and $w_{j,0}$ is its constant offset. The output of each of these two linear functions of the input is then fed into its corresponding sigmoid function.

If the sigmoid function *were* just the identity function $S(I_j) = I_j$, this neuron would be just our usual multiple linear regression fit discussed in the beginning of the section on stepwise regression. But instead, we believe a nonlinear function will fit better, and thus neural networks use the sigmoidal form shown before. The output of the two first layer neurons is a vector $S(I_j)$ with a dimension of 2, which is then fed as input into each of four neurons in the second layer, and so on. Finally, the output of the final three neurons in the third layer is then fed as a three-vector into the output layer with just one node, this time just a linear function. This assumes, as in our example, that the output is a scalar y. If the output is a vector, then there will be several nodes in the output layer corresponding to the dimension of the output vector. This sequence of iterated operations on an input vector: multiplication by weights (w), summation of different components (Σ), and transformation by the sigmoid function (S), is represented by the network diagram in Figure 4.11.

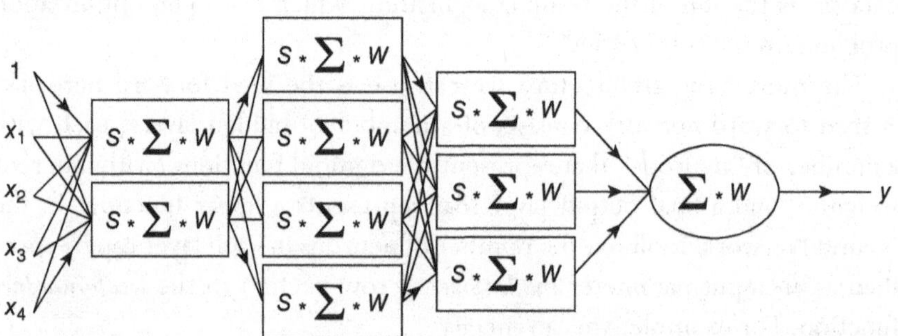

FIGURE 4.11 A feed forward neural network for our example

Instead of starting with all these hidden layers and multiple neurons for our SPY return prediction problem, let's just start with one hidden layer with one neuron (*hiddenSizes* = 1). Overfitting is a paramount concern, as always, and more hidden layers with more neurons make things worse. We will not discuss the training algorithm for the weights (w), except to note that there is randomness involving the initial guesses of the weights, and these different guesses will cause the final network to settle onto different local minima in network prediction error on the trainset. To minimize overfitting, the training algorithm utilizes a cross validation data set, whose size is specified by the user:

```
net.divideParam.trainRatio=0.6; % 0.6 (default is 0.7) Pick 4/5
   of trainset randomly to serve as train data
net.divideParam.valRatio=0.4; % 0.4 (default is 0.15) Pick 1/5
   of remaining trainset to serve as validation data for early
     stopping
net.divideParam.testRatio=0;
```

where trainRatio indicates the percentage of the training data set we will randomly pick for prediction error minimization, valRatio indicates the percentage of the validation set, and testRatio is the percentage of the test set. If during network training, the error on the validation set starts to increase, training will stop immediately. We set the test set to zero, because it actually isn't used during the training, and we have our own test set (which is half our data) for backtesting the trading strategy. You can verify that (using the same random number generator seed) the in-sample CAGR is 19 percent, but the out-of-sample CAGR is −4 percent.[8] We haven't solved the overfitting problem yet.

We can try more hidden layers with *hiddenSizes* = [1, 1]. This neither improves the in-sample nor the out-of-sample result. On the other hand, if we increase the number of nodes in each layer by setting *hiddenSizes* = [2, 2], we obtain an in-sample CAGR of 20 percent and an out-of-sample CAGR of 5 percent. This might look like a major improvement, but the result is very sensitive to what random seed we use. We need a way to reduce this sensitive dependence and increase the robustness of the resulting network.

There are two ways to reduce dependence on the initial guesses. One is called retraining, which is a lot like cross-validation. We will train, say, 100 different networks with different initial guesses for the weights and different selection of the data as trainset (60 percent of original trainset as before) and validation set (remaining 40 percent). We record the prediction error

TABLE 4.1 Performance Comparison for Different Network Architectures with Retraining

CAGR (100 networks)	1 Hidden Layer In-sample	1 Hidden Layer Out-of-sample	2 Hidden Layers In-sample	2 Hidden Layers Out-of-sample	3 Hidden Layers In-sample	3 Hidden Layers Out-of-sample
1 neuron	29%	3.2%	28%	−2.0%	31%	−3.9%
2 neurons	40%	−3.3%	27%	−3.4%	33%	−5.4%
3 neurons	28%	−10.0%	47%	1.4%	24%	−12.0%

on the validation set for each of these networks and pick the network with the lowest such error for testing. (Note that valRatio is set to zero for each network, since we have a separate validation set now.) We tried various hidden layers with various number of neurons per layer and recorded the results in Table 4.1.[9]

We can see that increasing the number of hidden layers or the number of neurons per layer often increases the in-sample performance, but to the detriment of the out-of-sample performance. The conclusion from this experiment is that, to avoid overfitting, we can only use one single neuron in one single layer for this problem.

The other way to reduce dependence on initial guesses is to again train 100 networks, but instead of picking the best, we average the predicted returns of all 100. This is a lot like bagging. The result of this experiment[10] is shown in Table 4.2.

The conclusion from surveying the two methods of training ensemble of neural networks is that only the simplest network with just one single node produces the best, consistent, result. But even that is a fairly weak result compared to that of the previously discussed methods.

This conclusion may create cognitive dissonance, as lately *deep learning* has been touted as a technique that can accomplish fantastic pattern

TABLE 4.2 Performance Comparison for Different Network Architectures with Averaging

CAGR (100 networks)	1 Hidden Layer In-sample	1 Hidden Layer Out-of-sample	2 Hidden Layers In-sample	2 Hidden Layers Out-of-sample	3 Hidden Layers In-sample	3 Hidden Layers Out-of-sample
1 neuron	26%	1.9%	28%	−0.57%	23%	−2.8%
2 neurons	52%	−6.2%	54%	−0.5%	62%	−2.5%
3 neurons	43%	−0.62%	55%	0.7%	79%	5.5%

recognition tasks. These are neural networks with many layers and few nodes per layer. Researchers in deep learning assert that such configurations enable easier learning, and result in better predictive powers, than networks with fewer layers but more nodes per layer. However, such observations probably hold true only for problems with a higher dimensional input vector (i.e., more predictors) as well as more data samples. Such feature-rich data sets are not common in finance, unless we have access to order book or unstructured (e.g., news) data.

Data Aggregation and Normalization

Machine learning algorithms benefit from lots of training data. If we are just trying to predict one instrument's returns (as we have been doing so far in this chapter), the model built tends to be overfitted. So instead of predicting SPY returns, can we try to predict the returns of every stock component of the SPX index? Surely, we will have 500 times more data in this case? In a sense, yes, but not if we just naively train a separate model on each stock, ending up with 500 models. We will only benefit from the increased data if we aggregate all these data into one vector and use that to train just one model. To do that, we will need to *normalize* the data first.

Data normalization is necessary when aggregating data from different stocks because their returns will have quite different volatility. For example, it won't be sensible to have a rule that says "Short the stock when the previous return is greater than 100 percent" because while WTW have gone up more than 100 percent on the day when Oprah decided to take a stake in it, WMT with its more than $188 billion market cap may never see such a day till the end of time. Clearly, we need to normalize the stocks' predictors by their volatilities before aggregating them and feeding them into any machine learning algorithm. (Of course, this applies only to those predictors that are not already normalized. A technical indicator such as the Relative Strength Index is already normalized and does not require further treatment.) Just as predictors need to be normalized, the response variable also needs to be normalized in a similar way. It won't be sensible to predict that a stock, any stock, is expected to have a next-day return of 10 percent, a return that would be much more onerous to achieve for WMT than for WTW.

In the example depicted in rTree_SPX.m, we use the same predictors featured in previous sections to predict the future one-day return of a stock in the SPX index, except that these predictors are all normalized by their past daily return volatilities:

```
ret1N=ret1./vol1;
ret2N=ret2./vol1;
ret5N=ret5./vol1;
ret20N=ret20./vol1;
```

We will do the same to the response variable

```
retFut1N=retFut1./vol1;
```

We could just as well have divided the returns by two-day return volatility, or three-day return volatility, and so on. The exact normalization factor is not important: what is important is to make sure all these normalized return variables have similar magnitude. These data, which range from January 3, 2007, to December 31, 2013, are obtained from CRSP and are survivorship-bias-free.[11] Furthermore, to avoid issues related to the consolidated closing prices (see discussion in Chapter 6), we use the midprice at the market close as our prices.

Unlike the variables in the previous sections, however, these variables are $T \times S$ matrices, where T is the number of historical days in the data, and S is the number of stocks (actually greater than 500, since we need to include stocks that were historically in the SPX index but are no longer there). To combine all the columns of data belonging to different stocks into one single $(T \times S) \times 1$ vector, we use the *reshape* function (see Example 2.2 for a similar procedure):


```
X=NaN(length(trainset)*length(syms), 4);
X(:, 1)=reshape(ret1N(trainset, :), [length(trainset)*length
  (syms) 1]);
X(:, 2)=reshape(ret2N(trainset, :), [length(trainset)*length
  (syms) 1]);
X(:, 3)=reshape(ret5N(trainset, :), [length(trainset)*length
  (syms) 1]);
X(:, 4)=reshape(ret20N(trainset, :), [length(trainset)*length
  (syms) 1]);

Y=reshape(retFut1N(trainset, :), [length(trainset)*length(syms) 1]);
  % dependent variable
```

Once the data are thus aggregated, the training and prediction can go on as before. We use the cross-validated regression tree as our learning algorithm. But once the best tree is selected, we need to unpack the vector containing

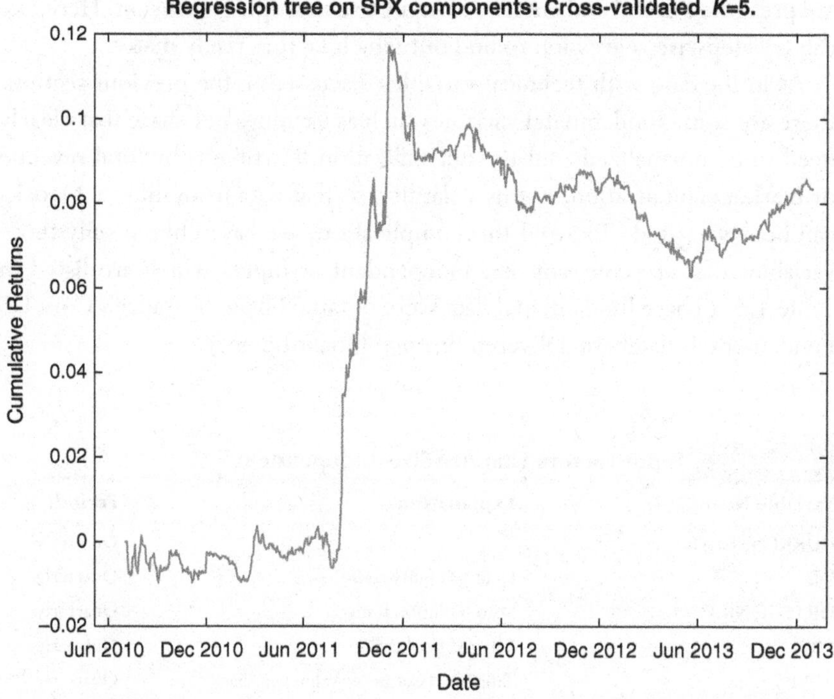

FIGURE 4.12 Cross-validated regression tree on SPX component stocks

the predicted returns back to a $T \times S$ matrix before we can compute our usual performance measures:

```
retPred1=reshape(predict(bestTree, X), [length(trainset)
   length(syms)]);
```

The out-of-sample CAGR of this strategy is 2.3 percent, with a Sharpe ratio of 0.9. As can be seen from the cumulative return curve in Figure 4.12, the strategy performed best during the financial turmoil in the aftermath of the US Treasury debt downgrade in August 2011.

In case you wonder what the performance is like if we did not normalize the variables, we would get a CAGR of −0.7 percent with a Sharpe ratio of −0.4.

Application to Stocks Selection

Throughout this chapter, we have stuck to using a few simple returns variables as predictors. But actually, one of the more interesting applications of machine learning to finance may be the discovery of predictive fundamental factors. Recall that when we discussed factor models in Chapter 2, all factors are presumed useful and entered as input to a multiple regression. Here, we can try stepwise regression to find out which factors really matter.

As in the case with technical variables discussed in the previous section, there are some fundamental variables such as earnings per share that clearly need to be normalized. But the normalization this time is by total revenue or market capitalization, not by volatility, so that data from different stocks can be aggregated. To avoid this complication, we have chosen only those variables that are company-size-independent as input, which are listed in Table 4.3. (These fundamental data were obtained from Sharadar's Core US Fundamentals database delivered through Quandl.com.)

TABLE 4.3 Input Factors That Are Size-Independent

Variable Name	Explanation	Period
CURRENTRATIO		Quarterly
DE	Debt to Equity Ratio	Quarterly
DILUTIONRATIO	Share Dilution Ratio	Quarterly
PB	Price to Book Value	Quarterly
TBVPS	Tangible Asset Book Value per Share	Quarterly
ASSETTURNOVER		Trailing 1 year
EBITDAMARGIN		Trailing 1 year
EPSGROWTH1YR		Trailing 1 year
EQUITYAVG	Average Equity	Trailing 1 year
EVEBIT	Enterprise Value over EBIT	Trailing 1 year
EVEBITDA	Enterprise Value over EBITDA	Trailing 1 year
GROSSMARGIN		Trailing 1 year
INTERESTBURDEN	Financial Leverage	Trailing 1 year
LEVERAGERATIO		Trailing 1 year
NCFOGROWTH1YR		Trailing 1 year
NETINCGROWTH1YR	Net Income Growth	Trailing 1 year
NETMARGIN	Profit Margin	Trailing 1 year
PAYOUTRATIO		Trailing 1 year
PE	Price Earnings Damodaran Method	Trailing 1 year
PE1		Trailing 1 year
PS		Trailing 1 year
PS1	Price Sales Damodaran Method	Trailing 1 year
REVENUEGROWTH1YR		Trailing 1 year
ROA		Trailing 1 year
ROE		Trailing 1 year
ROS		Trailing 1 year
TAXEFFICIENCY		Trailing 1 year

TABLE 4.4 Factors Selected by Stepwise Regression	
Variable name	**Period**
CURRENTRATIO	Quarterly
TBVPS	Quarterly
EBITDAMARGIN	Trailing 1 year
GROSSMARGIN	Trailing 1 year
NCFOGROWTH1YR	Trailing 1 year
PS	Trailing 1 year
ROA	Trailing 1 year

After aggregating these input variables in the same manner described in the previous section, and using the same function as we did in the "Stepwise Regression" section, we found that the algorithm[12] selected the variables displayed in Table 4.4 as significant predictors for the return in the next quarter (or more precisely, 63 trading days). These selections are based on data from January, 3, 2007, to December, 31, 2013. Note that most rows of X, the $T \times S$ predictors matrix, have NaN as values. This is because most stocks on most days have no quarterly earnings announcements that will determine these fundamental factors. But the delightful feature of the *stepwiselm* function, just as the *fitlm* or other functions in the Statistics Toolbox, is that it will automatically ignore rows in the predictors matrix with NaNs.

To turn this prediction into a trading strategy, we simply buy and hold for 63 days, whenever the predicted return is positive, and vice versa when it is negative. The code fragment for doing that is listed below:

```
longs=backshift(1, retPred1>0); %1 day later
shorts=backshift(1, retPred1<0);

longs(1, :)=false;
shorts(1, :)=false;

positions=zeros(size(retPred1));

for h=0:holdingDays-1
    long_lag=backshift(h, longs);
    long_lag(isnan(long_lag))=false;
    long_lag=logical(long_lag);
```

```
    short_lag=backshift(h, shorts);
    short_lag(isnan(short_lag))=false;
    short_lag=logical(short_lag);

    positions(long_lag)=positions(long_lag)+1;
    positions(short_lag)=positions(short_lag)-1;
end
```

Of course, this implies that we may end up buying one unit of capital every day for 63 days straight. Hence we need to divide the total P&L due to all these units of capital by 63 in order to compute a daily return that is not levered 63 times:

```
dailyRet=smartsum(backshift(1, positions).*ret1(testset, :), 2)./
  smartsum(abs(backshift(1, positions)), 2);
```

The out-of-sample CAGR is 4 percent with a Sharpe ratio of 1.1. The cumulative return curve is shown in Figure 4.13.

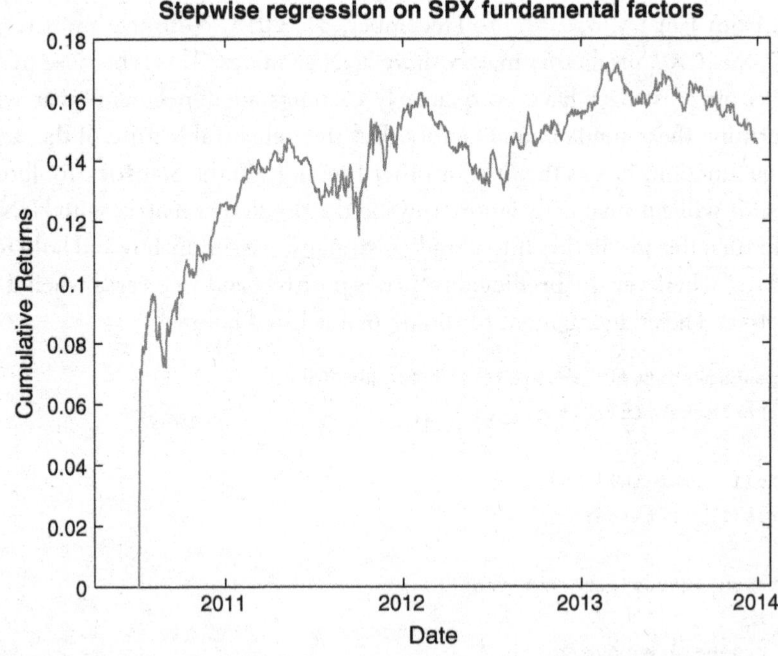

FIGURE 4.13 Stepwise regression on SPX component stocks using fundamental factors

■ Summary

One lesson that stands out from this plethora of AI techniques is that methods to improve on the weak learners and reduce overfitting are as important as which weak learner to start with. These methods include cross validation, bagging, random subspaces, random forests, and retraining and averaging. All these methods try to introduce artificial randomness in either the data or the predictor choices, and seek to train as many learners as possible based on this randomness. The hope is that the average over all these weak learners, or picking the best of these weak learners, will yield a model that generalizes better out-of-sample data, and we often succeed in doing that.

More training data (the number of rows in an input array) and more predictors (the number of columns) are always better for machine learning algorithms. It is therefore no surprise that many of these techniques have mediocre performance on our SPY training data set with just about 1,000 rows, and a paltry 4 columns. Even our SPX component stocks training data isn't much better: it has only about 10,000 rows,[13] and 27 columns. Typical machine learning problems often have millions of rows and hundreds of predictors. At the very least, for the SPY problem, we should try all the technical indicators that have ever been invented, and for the SPX component stocks problem, we should include factors that require normalization by market capitalization. Where else can we find data sets with orders of magnitude more data in the financial markets? One promising direction is to study high-frequency data (Rechenthin, 2014); in particular, level 2 quotes sampled at 1 millisecond frequency or higher. Another promising direction is to study unstructured data (Kazemian, 2014) such as news releases and social media and see if they portend financial market movements. Domingos (2012) wrote: "... efficacy of a machine learning algorithm relies heavily on the input features."

When faced with a new prediction problem, what techniques should you try? The answer is easy: Start with the simplest technique (such as stepwise regression) and proceed to the most complicated (such as neural network) if the simpler techniques do not yield good performance. In trading, complexity doesn't pay.

Exercises

4.1. When using stepwise regression to predict SPY's next-day return, retrain the model every day by adding the latest data to the training set. Does this increase the CAGR to above 10.6 percent and Sharpe ratio to above 0.7 over the period September 16, 2009, to June 2, 2014, for the trading model suggested in the section on Stepwise Regression?

4.2. Similar to Exercise 4.1, modify the trading strategy to generate buy or sell signals only if the return magnitude exceeds a certain threshold. What threshold works best in-sample? Does it also generate out-of-sample CAGR and Sharpe ratio that are higher than the original strategy?

4.3. Similar to Exercise 4.2, modify the trading strategy so that the dollar amount it buys or shorts is proportional to the magnitude of the predicted return. Adjust the proportionality constant so that the average absolute market value over the training set is $1. Then calculate the CAGR based on the levered return. Is the out-of-sample CAGR higher than the original strategy?

4.4. Use the fundamental data set presented in the section on "Application to Stocks Selection" and discretize the response variable to predict an up or down quarter. Apply the random subspace method and see if it improves out-of-sample predictive accuracy. Also, try the random forest method with classification trees to compare. What does "averaging the predicted response" mean when the response is a discrete (categorical) variable?

4.5. Improve on the performance of our basic SVM by trying out different Kernel functions and Kernel scale. What settings are best?

4.6. Look for software that implements online decoding of an HMM and use this to decode our SPY model's hidden states without using the for-loop.

4.7. Re-estimate the HMM model for SPY at every time step prior to prediction. Does this improve the out-of-sample CAGR of the trading strategy?

4.8. Use the HMM model for SPY and determine if today is a bull or bear market.

4.9. Pick your favorite AI technique from this chapter and compile data on as many technical indicators as you can find to be used as predictors for the SPY and the SPX stock components problems.
4.10. Apply random forest to the classification tree model for SPY returns prediction and see if it improves on the corresponding results for regression tree model.

Endnotes

1. This cannot be explained in simple language or rules that humans can understand.
2. The complete code is available for download as lr.m.
3. The complete code is available for download as stepwiseLR.m.
4. The complete code is available for download as rTreeBagger.m.
5. The complete code is available for download as cTree.m.
6. The complete code is available for download as svm.m.
7. While you may think that discovering what "regime" we are in must have more use than just answering questions on CNBC, ultimately we are only interested in expected returns. The regimes are just theoretical constructs, and so are regime shifts.
8. The complete code is available for download as nn_feedfwd.m.
9. The complete code is available for download as nn_feedfwd_retrain.m.
10. The complete code is available for download as nn_feedfwd_avg.m.
11. Specifically, the US Stock Databases. See Chapter 1 for more discussion of CRSP.
12. The complete code can be downloaded as stepwiseLR_SPX.m.
13. After aggregating all the stocks in SPX, we have about 654,583 rows in the training set. But since the fundamental factors only get updated quarterly, these really only represent about 10,000 rows of data that are not filled with NaNs.

CHAPTER 5

Options Strategies

It is hard to trade options algorithmically. This is not because the theories are mathematically advanced (although they are). We don't need to completely understand the derivation of the Black-Scholes equation or use stochastic calculus in order to backtest and execute options strategies profitably. You may be surprised to find that there are very few equations in this chapter, as there are many good books out there for those who want to learn about the theoretical derivations (Hull, 2014; Oksendal, 2013). There are also many well-known options trading strategies that have been explained in careful detail previously (McMillan, 2002; Augen, 2008; Augen, 2009; Sinclair, 2010; Sinclair 2013; James, 2015). But not many of these books actually describe backtests of intraday strategies or strategies that are applied to a large number of options on a portfolio of stocks, which is our main focus in this chapter. Since each stock (or any other type of underlying, such as stock index, future, bond, or currency) can have many options with different tenors (time-to-expiration) and different strikes, it can be quite a complicated task to backtest the selection of some of these options to form a portfolio.

The options strategies described here are mostly delta-neutral strategies. Delta is the rate of change of the option value with respect to the change in the underlying stock price. Delta-neutral means that the delta of our portfolio is zero, or nearly so. The reason we focus on such strategies is that, if you are interested in being exposed to delta, you might as well just buy (or short) stocks instead. You would incur far lower transaction costs trading stocks due to their much higher liquidity. Trading delta-neutral strategies means you are trading the other determinants of option prices: notably volatility and time-to-maturity. Many people think of trading options as trading volatilities. If we think volatility will be lower, we may collect the options premium by shorting them (covered in the section

"Trading Volatility without Options"). If we think volatility may spike up due to some events or because it is otherwise underpriced currently, we may buy them (see the section "Event-Driven Strategies"). But it is important to note that we seldom can make a pure bet on volatility: if you are net short options because you want to short volatility, you will be long theta (the change of option value due to the passage of time, other factors being unchanged), and vice versa.

Sometimes when we think that volatility is high, but instead of shorting options, we trade the underlying using a mean reversion strategy, which is effectively shorting volatility (Ang, 2014). At the same time, we want to protect against tail events. For this, the section on "Gamma Scalping" fits our needs. Sometimes we are not even betting on the direction of the volatility, but on the mean reversion of the implied volatilities between different instruments (discussed in "Cross-sectional Mean Reversion of Implied Volatility"). Other times, we may not even bet on volatilities at all, but on correlations (see the section on "Dispersion Trading"). In all these cases, we will not be buying a single option, since that won't have zero delta, but two or more of them, often in packages with names like straddles or strangles. We will give examples of the concrete implementation for each of the strategies in this chapter. Finally, we will explain why these backtest results are quite tenuous guides to whether the strategies will be profitable in live trading.

While no mathematical sophistication is required to understand these strategies, we assume the reader has some basic familiarity with options, so that concepts such as moneyness (e.g., OTM, ATM, ITM), tenor, implied volatility, and the Greeks (e.g., delta, gamma, theta, vega) won't be foreign concepts.

Trading Volatility without Options

A large and profitable industry has existed for centuries shorting volatility—the insurance industry. Similarly, hedge funds in aggregate make their money from shorting options (Ang, 2014, p. 219). The reason selling insurance (or equivalently, selling options) is profitable is that insurance has a decaying time value: as time goes on, if nothing bad happens, the value of the insurance contract continues to drop. Of course, the key condition is that "nothing bad happens." But that's the same risk we are taking by being long in equities. Assuming that we are comfortable with taking this risk, we only need to figure out how to extract the most return from it as consistently and efficiently as possible, and without bankrupting ourselves during financial crises.

The simplest strategy for an equity investor to profit from the equity risk premium is to buy-and-hold a stock index. This beats many sophisticated strategies in unlevered returns, though perhaps not in Sharpe ratio, over the long term. Similarly, the simplest strategy for an option investor is to short the futures or ETNs that track stock index volatility. For example, we can compare buy-and-hold SPY versus short-and-hold the front contract of the VX future. Of course, options and futures do expire, so it is not possible to really "hold" a constant short position in them. We need to continuously roll them to the next nearby contract. (We can short-and-hold the ETN VXX, but it has a relatively short history, which inconveniently misses the 2008 financial crisis for our comparison. In any case, holding VXX just means someone else is doing the rolling forward of the underlying VX futures on your behalf.) Also, the volatility of SPY is much smaller than the volatility of VX, so just comparing their returns is not very fair. One can manufacture a high positive return from practically any instrument or strategy as long as it has a positive return and we crank up the leverage. One fair way of comparison is to leverage each instrument by their Kelly-optimal leverage (see the section "Portfolio Optimization" in Chapter 1), and compare their compounded returns. This of course differs slightly from buying-and-holding, since maintaining a constant leverage requires daily rebalancing of our levered position in SPY or VX. Figure 5.1 shows a comparison of the optimally

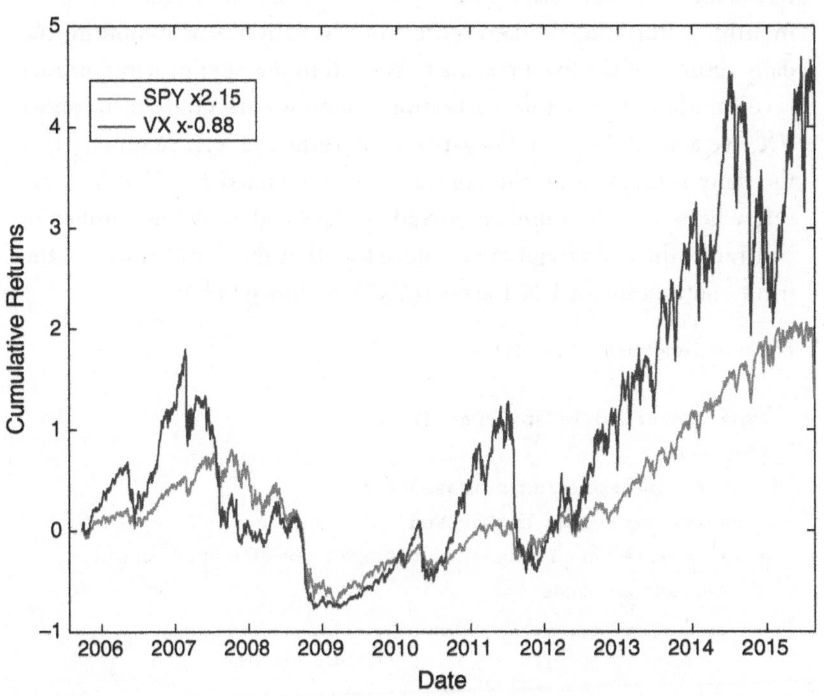

FIGURE 5.1 Long SPY vs. Short VX

levered compound returns of SPY versus that of VX from April 5, 2004, to August 19, 2015.

Table 5.1 includes some performance numbers for the two instruments:

TABLE 5.1 Performance Comparison between Long SPY vs. Short VX

	2.15 × SPY	−0.88 × VX
CAGR	7.2%	17.8%
Maximum drawdown	−86.3%	−91.8%
Calmar ratio (since inception)	0.084	0.19

Both "strategies" have dizzying drawdowns, but shorting volatility has much higher returns and Calmar ratio than buying the equity index. See Example 5.1 for the implementation details of this comparison.

Example 5.1: Comparing the levered, compounded returns of SPY and VX

Before we compute the levered, compounded returns of anything, we should first compute its unlevered, simple daily returns. This is quite trivial for SPY, but not so for the VX future. Since the VX future expires monthly, computing the daily returns of VX really means computing the daily returns of the front contract. We roll to the next nearby contract seven trading days before expiration. Since we are going to be short VX, we actually want the negative daily return of VX. Assuming that the daily returns of all the contracts are contained in a T × M array ret, where T is the number of trading days and M is the number of contracts, the code fragment to piece together the daily returns of the front contract into a T × 1 array ret_VX is shown below:[1]

```
for c=1:length(contracts)-1

  expireIdx=find(isExpireDate(:, c));
  if (c==1)
    startIdx=expireIdx-numDaysStart;
    endIdx=expireIdx-numDaysEnd;
  else % ensure next front month contract doesn't start until
      current one ends
```

```
      startIdx=max(endIdx+1, expireIdx-numDaysStart);
      endIdx=expireIdx-numDaysEnd;
    end

    if (~isempty(expireIdx))
      idx=startIdx:endIdx;

      ret_VX(idx)=-ret(idx, c); % assume short position

    end
end
```

To find the optimal Kelly leverage for SPY and VX, respectively, these codes will do:

```
kelly_vx=mean(ret_VX)/var(ret_VX)
kelly_spy=mean(ret_SPY)/var(ret_SPY)
```

Then finally, the levered, compounded cumulative returns are:

```
vx_kelly_cumret=cumprod(1+kelly_vx*ret_VX)-1; % 0.868334700884036
spy_kelly_cumret=cumprod(1+kelly_spy*ret_SPY)-1;
  % 2.152202064271893
```


Can we modify the VX strategy to reduce drawdown and improve the pitiable Calmar ratio? Since the ES future's returns anticorrelate very well with that of the VX future (Chan, 2013): We can buy VX *and* ES (with number of contracts in the ratio 0.3906:1) whenever VX is in backwardation with a roll return of −10 percent or less, and vice versa when it is in contango with a roll return of 10 percent or more. The Calmar ratio over the same period as Table 5.1 is 0.55—an improvement over the short-and-hold VX strategy, but not by much. See Figure 5.2 for the equity curve.

There is one detail worth noting in backtesting the VX-ES strategy: The daily settlement (closing) price of VX is obtained at 16:15 ET, while that of ES is obtained at 16:00 ET. Since we need the roll return of VX at its close to determine the trade signal, we cannot use the current day's roll return as a trading signal—we must use the lagged value. (See VX_ES_rollreturn_lagged.m from epchan.com/book3.)

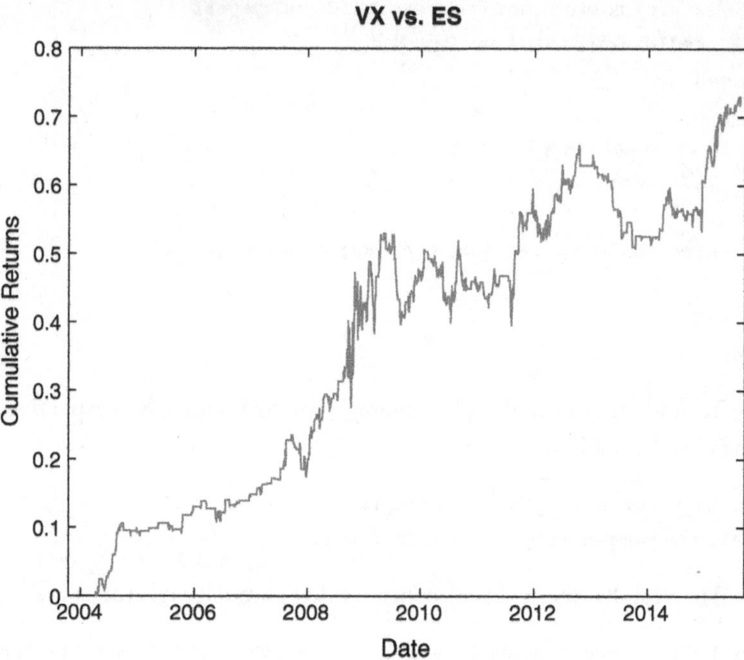

FIGURE 5.2 Cumulative returns of VX-ES roll returns strategy

(To complicate matters further, CME, the exchange where ES is traded, changed its settlement time for Globex equity index futures from 16:15 ET to 16:00 ET starting November 18, 2012. See Chicago Mercantile Exchange, 2012. I avoided any problem associated with this switchover in the VX-ES strategy above by using the previous day's VX price as signal. The actual entry times of VX and ES futures may differ by 15 minutes, but this poses no error or problem to our backtest. This fortunate situation, however, may not extend to other strategies or other backtests that involve arbitrage between the CME equity index futures and futures trading on other exchanges.)

Another issue with the strategy and its backtest methodology above is that the hedge ratio of 0.3906 between VX and ES is fixed (it was determined based on a linear regression of their values prior to June 2010). This single hedge ratio tends to overestimate the number of VX contracts per ES contract when the volatility is high and likely to increase further (typically when VX is in backwardation) and underestimate the number when the volatility is low and likely to decrease further (typically when VX is in contango). Hence, we can try the Kalman filter (see Chapter 3) as a dynamic update method for the hedge ratio to see if this will improve results. To simplify the program KF_beta_XIV_SPY.m, instead of trading VX vs. ES futures, we trade the XIV (the ETF that tracks the inverse of the VIX) and SPY, but otherwise the signals are the same as the VX vs. ES strategy. Of course, in this case, we will buy XIV and short SPY when the roll return of VX is negative, and vice versa. The hedge ratio is displayed on Figure 5.3.

Notice that since 2011 there is a general decline in volatility, which inversely increases the value of XIV. Hence, the number of XIV shares needed per SPY share is declining. We use the hedge ratio generated as the output of KF_beta_XIV_SPY.m as input into the program XIV_SPY_rollreturn_lagged.m that actually backtests the XIV vs. SPY trading strategy.

The Calmar ratio of 0.97 from November 30, 2010, to August 19, 2015, is an improvement from 0.41 using the fixed hedge ratio to trade VX vs. ES above over the same period. See Figure 5.4 for the equity curve.

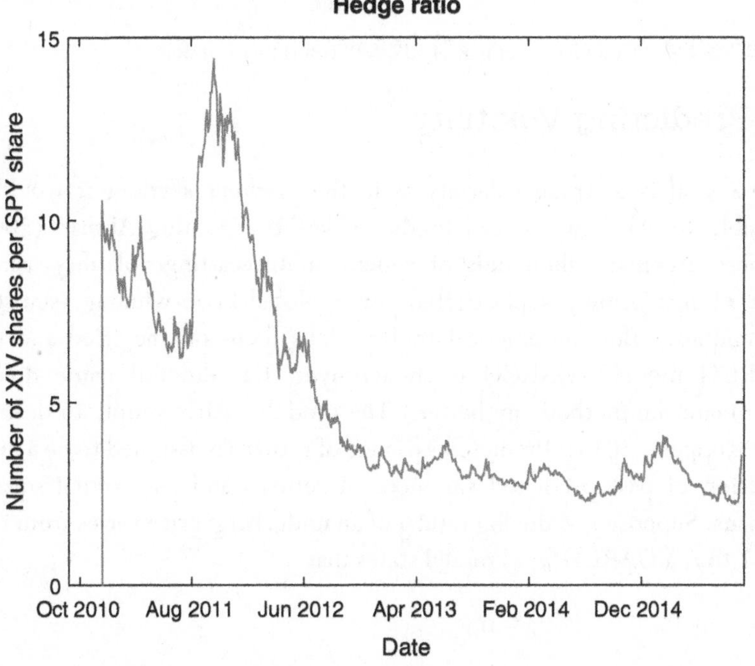

FIGURE 5.3 Hedge ratio between XIV and SPY determined by Kalman filter

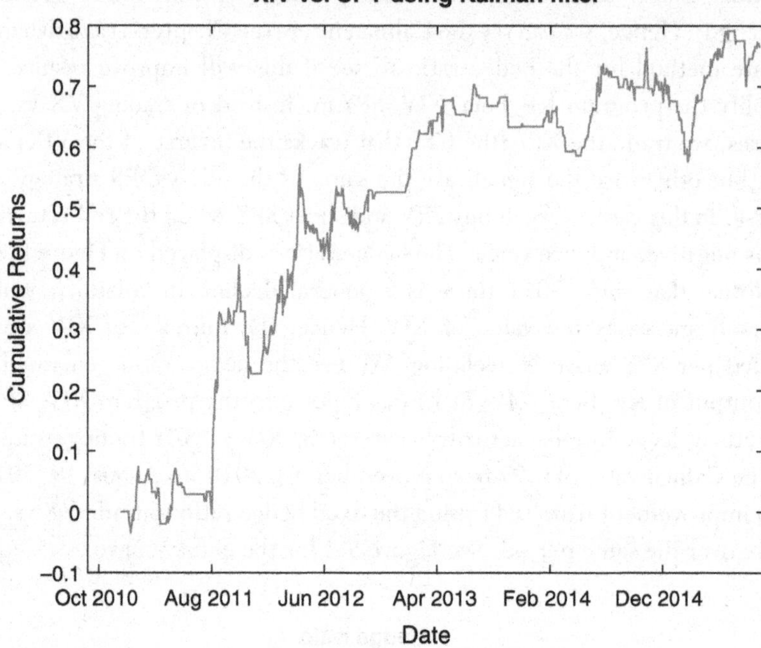

FIGURE 5.4 Cumulative returns of XIV-SPY roll returns strategy

Predicting Volatility

If our goal is to trade volatility as in the previous section, it would be sensible to ask how we can predict volatility. Quoting Ahmad (2005), "There are many thousands of papers on forecasting volatility using a host of increasingly sophisticated, even Nobel-Prize-winning, statistical techniques." But for practical traders, let's focus on the tried and true GARCH model. (GARCH is an acronym, but the full name doesn't illuminate the method any better.) The model is fairly simple to describe (see Ruppert, 2015): Predicted variance of returns is assumed to be a linear function of past predicted variances of returns and past actual squared returns. Suppose r_t is the log return of an underlying price series from time $t-1$ to t, a GARCH(p, q) model states that

$$r_t = \sigma_t \epsilon_t,$$

$$\sigma_t^2 = \omega + \sum_{i=1}^{p} \alpha_i \sigma_{t-i}^2 + \sum_{i=1}^{q} \beta_i r_{t-i}^2 \tag{5.1}$$

where ϵ is a random variable with zero mean, unit variance, and zero serial autocorrelation (i.e., it is white noise), and the parameters $p, q, \omega, \alpha_i, \beta_i$ will be optimized by maximum likelihood estimation on in-sample data. (Note that the definition of p and q in Ruppert, 2015, are opposite to equation 5.1. We adopt the convention that MATLAB uses.) Example 5.2 shows how we can apply this method quite painlessly to predicting the volatility of SPY. To be precise: We only want to predict whether the magnitude of the one-day return tomorrow will be higher or lower than today's. The resulting accuracy is quite high: We predicted the sign correctly better than 66 percent of the time, out-of-sample. We can, of course, apply the same technique to many other instruments. Here is a list, together with the out-of-sample accuracy, based on data from November 30, 2010, to March 11, 2016:

- SPY: 66%
- USO: 67%
- GLD: 59%
- AAPL: 60%
- EURUSD: 62%

Why it is so easy to predict the sign of the change in volatility, but typically so hard to predict the sign of the change in price? The answer is that it is easy to trade on price prediction, but hard to trade on volatility prediction. Hence, any accurate price prediction method will get arbitraged away pretty quickly. But why is it hard to trade on volatility prediction? Didn't we just suggest a VX future or VXX/XIV strategy in the previous section? If we predict that volatility will increase, why not just buy VXX, and vice versa? Actually, if we do that, we will lose money, as Example 5.2 shows. In fact, it is shown there that the opposite trading strategy works. The sign of change in VXX has negative correlation with the sign of change in realized volatility!

Predicting the sign of change in realized volatility isn't the same as predicting the sign of change in VXX because a change in VXX does not represent purely a change in implied volatility. The price of VXX reflects the value of a portfolio of options, and option price is a function of a number of variables, not just implied volatility. One of the most important variables is time-to-expiration, which cannot be constant. Even if implied volatility and all other variables are unchanged, the value of VXX or VX is still going to decline due to negative theta. In fact, a negative theta is what's behind the often negative roll returns of the VX future.

(As a side note, the VIX index itself does not have theta, because the index represents the value of a portfolio of options whose composition changes frequently, sometimes minute to minute. As CBOE explains,[2] VIX is the weighted average price of a portfolio of OTM SPX options with tenor of

23 to 37 days. There is no time decay in the collective option premium if you can always replace an aging option with a younger one!)

Example 5.2: Predicting volatility of SPY

Since there are many numerical packages that we can use for parameter optimization and prediction based on GARCH, we need not trouble ourselves with the technical details. What we do need to understand is the intuitive meaning of this equation. It allows us to predict the magnitude of the next-period return, and it can be shown that σ_t^2 is the conditional variance of r_t ("conditional" because we know the previous values of σ_t^2 and r_t^2). Thus, σ_t is none other than the predicted volatility that we want.

To see whether this volatility prediction method is any good, let us use the GARCH function in MATLAB's Econometrics toolbox[3] to train a model and then use it to predict the magnitude of next day's SPY return.[4] Notice that we first estimate $p \times q = 10 \times 9$ different GARCH models on the trainset from December 21, 2005, to December 5, 2011, each with a fixed value of (p, q) and a log-likelihood as an output.


```
for p=1:size(PQ, 1)
    for q=1:size(PQ, 2)

        model=garch(p, q);
        try
            [~,~,logL] = estimate(model, ret(trainset),'print',
               false);
            LOGL(p, q) = logL;
            PQ(p, q) = p+q;
        catch
        end
    end
end
```

We then use the BIC criterion to pick the best model (i.e., the best p and q values), which is the best compromise between maximizing likelihood and preferring models with fewer parameters.

```
[~, bic]=aicbic(LOGL_vector, PQ_vector+1, length(ret(trainset)));
```

It turns out that the best model is GARCH(1, 2). Hence, we use this model to forecast the next day's variance, or equivalently, the magnitude of the next day's return. We cannot, of course, expect this forecast to be exactly the same as the next day's return magnitude. But from a practical viewpoint, what is important is whether the *sign* of the change in magnitude of the return from one day to the next agrees with the forecast. Hence, we compute the percent agreement on the trainset and the test set from December 6, 2011, to November, 25, 2015. These turn out to be 72 percent and 69 percent, respectively, which are very respectable numbers. Unfortunately, a straightforward application of this to buy (sell) VXX and hold for one day when we expect positive (negative) change in variance fails miserably. How can our volatility prediction achieve good accuracy yet generate such poor returns when applied to VXX?

The reason is, of course, that we succeeded only in predicting realized volatility (as measured by the magnitude of one-day return), but we used that to trade VXX, which is a proxy for implied volatility. Change in realized volatility does not coincide with the change in implied volatility, not even in the direction of the change. To see this, let's compute the percentage of the days where the magnitude of the one-day returns move in the same direction as VXX, on the complete data set from December 21, 2005, to November 25, 2015 (using compareVolWithVXX.m). This turns out to be only 35 percent—far less likely than random! Now, you may think this is because many of these one-day returns may be positive, and we know that a big upward move in the equity index is correlated with a big downward move in implied volatility, and you would be partially right. But even if we restrict ourselves to those days with negative equity index returns, VXX and the return magnitude only move in the same direction 43 percent of the time. So all in all, we can conclude that realized volatility actually moves in the opposite direction to VXX on a daily basis!

Based on the above observation, we should be able to exploit this fact in a trading strategy that is opposite to the one suggested before. Whenever GARCH predicts an increase in realized volatility, we should short VXX at the close, and vice versa. Hold only one day. On the test set used in the GARCH model above, this strategy has a CAGR of 81 percent, with a Calmar ratio of 1.9. The equity curve is shown in Figure 5.5. I call it the $RV(t + 1) - RV(t)$ strategy because the change in realized volatility (RV) is the trading signal. The backtest code is included as part of SPY_garch.m.

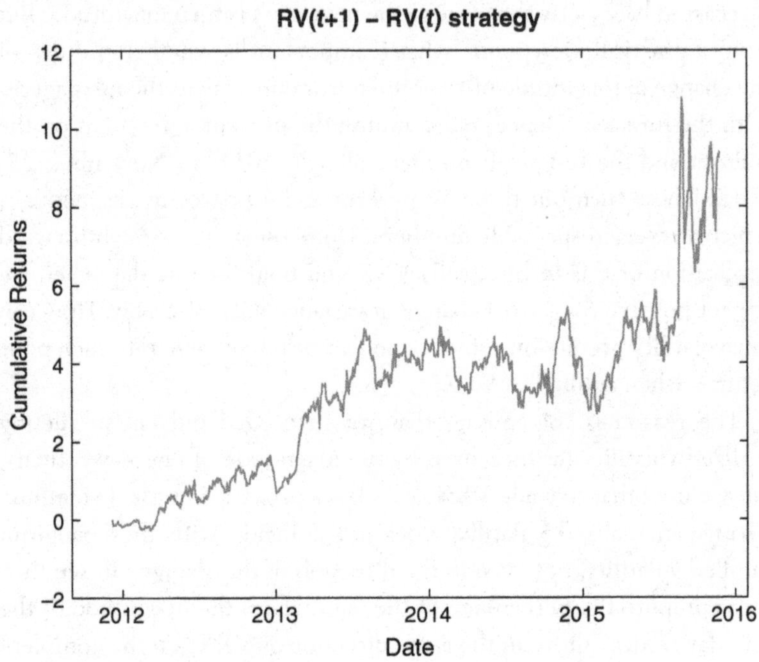

FIGURE 5.5 Cumulative returns of $RV(t+1) - RV(t)$ Strategy

If we are able to predict volatility using GARCH reasonably well, there is an alternative trading strategy we can try. This strategy is inspired by Ahmad (2005), who suggested that if the predicted volatility is higher than the current implied volatility, we should buy an option and delta-hedge until expiration. So analogously, we will buy the front month VX future when the predicted volatility is higher than the current VIX value, and short when the opposite occurs (even though Ahmad, 2005, did not recommend the short trade). We call this the $RV(t+1) - VIX(t)$ strategy. We have shown on Figure 5.6 the value of $RV(t+1)$ and $VIX(t)$ over time. We can see that GARCH predicts a much lower volatility than VIX does during the two financial crises in this period.

The trading strategy has a CAGR of 41.7 percent from November 30, 2010, to March 11, 2016, but with a Calmar ratio of only 0.5. The performance has deteriorated sharply since March 2014. The equity curve is displayed in Figure 5.7. (The backtest code can be downloaded as VX_GARCH_VIX.m.)

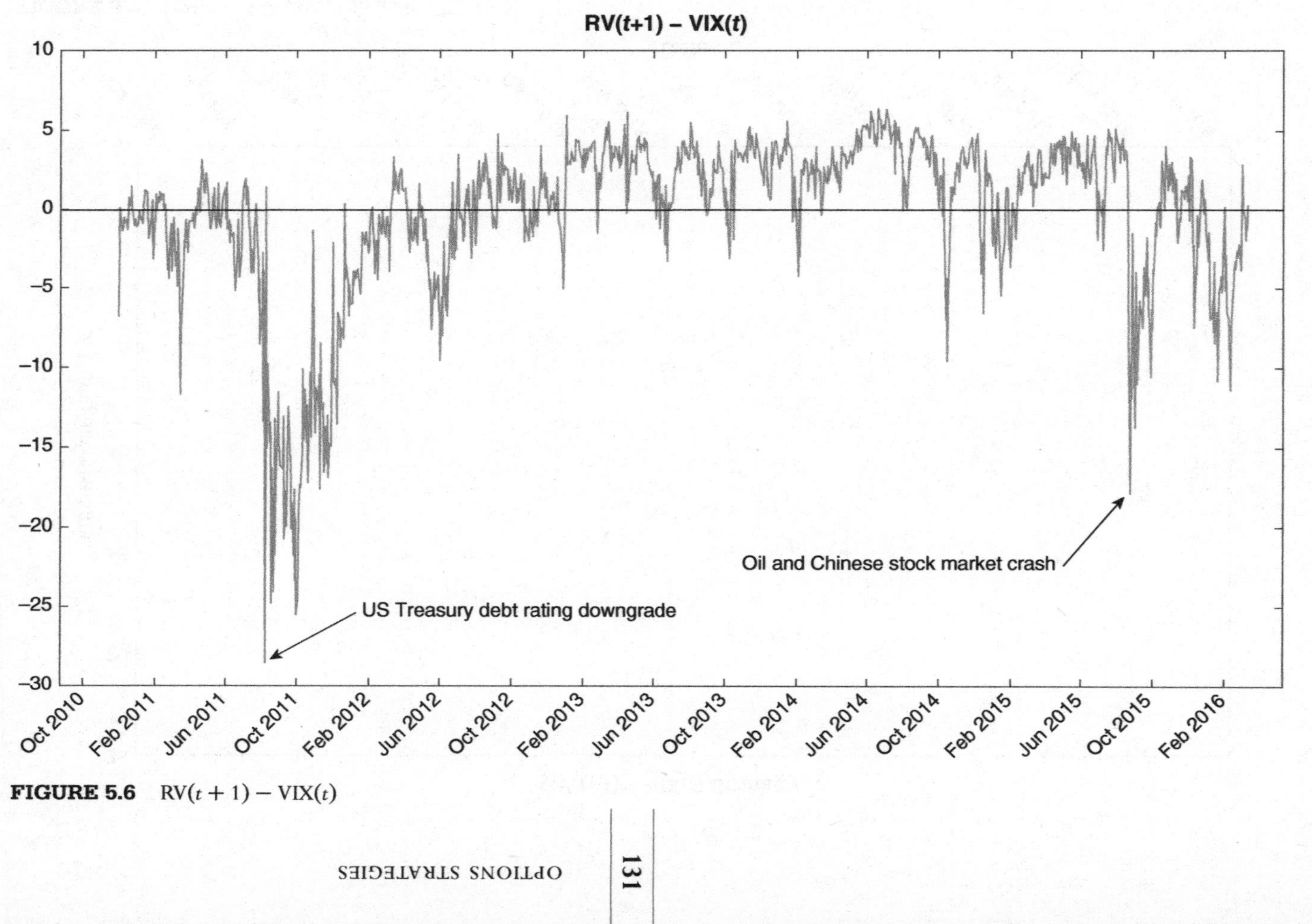

FIGURE 5.6 $RV(t+1) - VIX(t)$

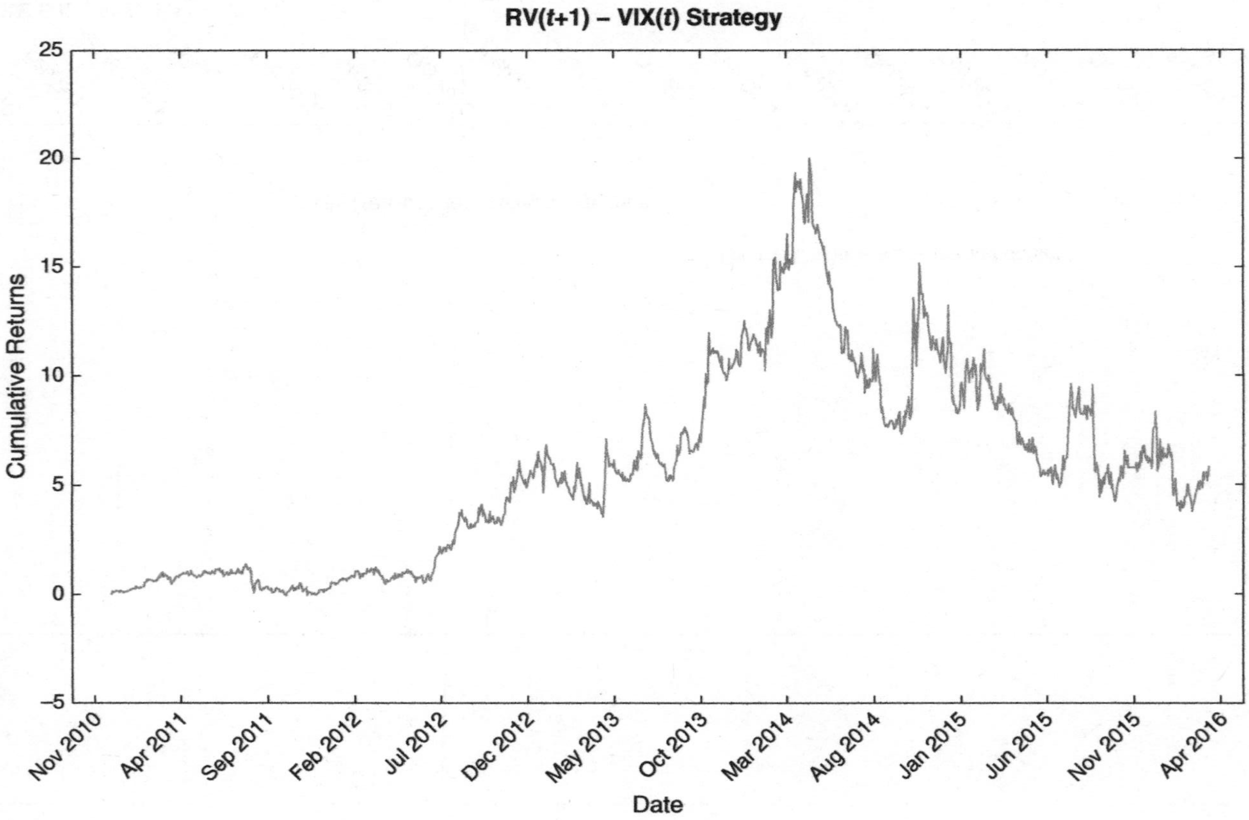

RV(t+1) – VIX(t) Strategy

Cumulative Returns

25
20
15
10
5
0
−5

Nov 2010 Apr 2011 Sep 2011 Feb 2012 Jul 2012 Dec 2012 May 2013 Oct 2013 Mar 2014 Aug 2014 Jan 2015 Jun 2015 Nov 2015 Apr 2016

Date

FIGURE 5.7 RV($t+1$) − VIX(t) Strategy

Event-Driven Strategies

Regularly scheduled market events are good candidates for volatility trading strategies. After all, it is not easy to predict whether the Fed will increase or decrease interest rates, or whether the unemployment numbers will be good or bad, but it is a safe bet that there will be a larger-than-average movement in prices after the announcement. The only question is: Has the option market already priced in the expectation of volatility increase, or is there still profit to be made? (As we learned from Example 5.2, an increase in implied volatility does not usually accompany an increase in realized volatility.) We will look at the evidence from one market event and see if we can build a successful strategy around it: the "Weekly Petroleum Status Report" released by the US Energy Information Administration.

The "Weekly Petroleum Status Report" contains supply-side statistics on crude oil in the United States, and it often has major impact on crude oil futures prices. This report is typically released on Wednesday mornings at 10:30 a.m. ET (for weeks that include holidays the release date is delayed by one day and the time changed to 11:00 a.m.) The exact schedule can be found on www.eia.gov. If one believes that the release will increase volatility in crude oil futures, we can try buying a straddle (a call and a put at the same strike price with the same expiration date) on them in the morning of the release at 9:00 a.m., and sell the straddle one minute after the schedule is released. Shockingly, this long volatility strategy loses about $27,110 per straddle per year! Perhaps the spike of volatility is too well-anticipated by traders, which inflates the entry price, or perhaps implied volatility once again goes in the opposite direction from realized volatility. Since buying implied volatility before the event isn't successful, we may try the opposite. But that loses even more: $36,060 per straddle per year. The reason that both the long and short trade lost money is due to the wide bid-ask spread. We have assumed we enter into the position using a limit order at midprice (the average of bid and ask prices), but exit the position using a market order. Options bid-ask spreads are notoriously wide (even for crude oil futures ATM options with a two-week tenor, it can be as high as 1.2 percent). Hence, the method of execution has an enormous effect on profitability. If we always assume executions with market orders, most options strategies won't be profitable. But options traders do not always use market orders for position entry. (There is no difficulty ensuring that both legs of the straddle are filled at the same time using limit orders at entry, since CME allows traders to submit a limit order on a straddle as a single unit. In fact, we can submit any order type to trade the straddle as a single unit.)

We can also try selling volatility during uneventful periods: We can short a straddle at 9:00 a.m. on the day *after* the release and buy cover it at 10:29 a.m. on the *following* Wednesday (just before the next release). Hopefully, this would capture the period in the week that has the least volatility and risk. The backtest detailed in Example 5.3 shows that this strategy does have promise: It generates a profit of $13,270 per straddle per year, excluding commissions, with a maximum drawdown of about $4,050. Granted, we only backtested this on one year of data, so this is very flimsy evidence.

We can also short a strangle instead of a straddle, where the strangle can consist of a call and a put that has a strike price, say, 5 percent out-of-the-money (but with the same expiration date). Assuming midprice entry and market exit, we obtain a profit of $10,640, which is comparable to the straddle trade, but the maximum drawdown is $3,410, which is smaller than that of the straddle.

Besides the "Weekly Petroleum Status Report," there is a report published by the American Petroleum Institute (API) that often moves the crude oil market. This is the "API Weekly Statistical Bulletin" published on Tuesdays at 4:30 p.m. ET (or Wednesdays at 4:30 p.m. if the preceding Monday is a holiday). We can adapt the short strangle strategy to exit just one minute before this release, and the profit is $9,750, similar to the other variations above, but the maximum drawdown is further reduced to $2,950.

There are other regularly scheduled events in the futures markets that may be exploited. One is the National Oilseed Processors Association (NOPA) monthly crush report for soybeans that takes place at 12:00 noon ET on the 15th of each month (or the next business day, if that is a holiday). We can potentially trade the option OZS on the future ZS around that event. Another is the US employment report issued by the Bureau of Labor Statistics (BLS) every Thursday at 8:30 a.m. ET (or the previous business day, if that is a holiday). We can trade the ES option on the ES future for that. For stock options, earnings announcements are good (and popular) candidates for event-driven strategies.

Our trading rule is a very simplistic seasonal strategy. Interested readers may explore refinement of this. For example, would the Calmar ratio be higher if we short the straddle/strangle when the ratio of implied volatility over historical volatility is higher than some threshold? Should we short it when theta is lower than some threshold so that the straddle loses value quicker? Should we impose a stop loss or profit cap? These are variations we are leaving as exercises.

Example 5.3: Shorting Crude Oil Futures Options Straddles

The short crude oil futures options straddle strategy seems simple: Just short a straddle on the day after the release date of a "US Weekly Petroleum Status Report," and buy a cover just before the next release. But as with any options strategy, especially strategies that trade intraday, the implementation details can be staggering. This will be a good example of some of the issues we face.

Crude oil futures (symbol CL) on CME Globex expire around the 22th of every month ahead of the delivery month. For example, the February 2015 contract (denoted as CLG15 in our data and our program) will cease trading on or around January 22, 2015. However, its options (symbol LO) expire three (3) business days ahead. Table 5.2 offers a summary of the first and last dates that each contract will be a candidate for trading by our strategy. Note that we trade only options on the front (nearest to expiration) futures contract, but at the same time we require the option to have a tenor (time-to-maturity) of about two weeks. The option expiration date is approximate only, and the first trading date of J12 and the last trading date of J13 are irregular due to the limitation of our data. Furthermore, there is no guarantee that this choice of tenor produces the optimal returns: It should be treated as a parameter to be optimized. (Similarly, the exact entry and exit dates and times are free parameters to be optimized, too.) The data are from Nanex.net, which are time-stamped to the nearest 25 milliseconds.

The information in Table 5.2 corresponds to the values used in the contracts, firstDateTimes, and lastDateTimes arrays in the program. (The dateRanges array refers to the range of dates in the data files we happen to have acquired, and have no direct correspondence to the range of dates for each contract to be traded.)

As a straddle consists of one pair of an ATM put and call, we need to find out what strike price is ATM at the moment of the trade entry. Hence, we need to first retrieve the quotes data for the underlying CL futures contracts and determine the midprice at 9:00 a.m. Eastern

TABLE 5.2 Contracts Trading Dates

Contract	Options Expires (approx.)	First Trading Date	Last Trading Date
J12	20120319	20120301	20120305
K12	20120419	20120306	20120405
M12	20120519	20120406	20120505
N12	20120619	20120506	20120605
Q12	20120719	20120606	20120705
U12	20120819	20120706	20120805
V12	20120919	20120806	20120905
X12	20121019	20120906	20121005
Z12	20121119	20121006	20121105
F13	20121219	20121106	20121205
G13	20130119	20121206	20130105
H13	20130219	20130106	20130205
J13	20130319	20130206	20130227

Source: Nanex.net

Time on Thursdays. Notice that this is already a simplification: We have treated those holiday weeks when the releases were on Thursdays at 11:00 a.m. in the same way as the regular weeks. But if anything, this will only deflate our backtest performance, which gives us a more conservative estimate of the strategy profitability. In case either a Thursday and the following Wednesday is not a trading day, our code will take care not to enter into a position. After finding the underlying future's midprice and thus the desired options strike price, we go on to retrieve the BBO (best bid offer) quotes data for the call and put with this strike price. This is quite a slow and tedious step, as every entry date requires us to download two options data files.

Retrieving historical data from a data file with regularly spaced time bars is easy, but what we have is a tick data file with quotes that may arrive within the same 25 milliseconds, which is the time resolution of our data. We will assume that quotes with the same time stamp are arranged in chronological order in the file; thus, we take only the last quote. Also, we cannot expect there is a new quote update at exactly the entry or exit time—we will take the quotes with the most recent time stamp just before entry or exit time as our execution prices.

We have a choice of whether to enter into the short straddle position at the bid (using market orders), at the ask (using a limit order), or at midprice (also using a limit order). We can backtest all three alternatives. As for the buy cover exit, we use a market order to buy at the ask prices. While the P&L in points is computed here just by taking the differences between entry and exit prices (and multiplying that by −1 since this is a short position), we should remember that P&L in dollars is one thousand (1,000) times the points difference.

The code can be found in shortStraddle_LO.m. However, data files are not available for download due to their sizes and licensing restrictions.

Gamma Scalping

In the previous section, we weren't able to profit from a long option position even when there is predictably a big price move. There are at least two reasons why it is hard to be profitable with a long option position:

1. Options can become very valuable during extreme market events (*black swans*), but these events rarely happen. So most of the time we are paying insurance premiums for nothing (as we do for, say, life insurance).
2. Option premiums decay with time. The rate of change of the value of an option with respect to time is called theta, and theta is usually negative.

However, a short option position carries the risk that when a black swan event does occur, we will suffer a catastrophic loss. Is there a way to benefit from being short volatility and yet be protected against extreme loss? This motivates a *gamma scalping* strategy.

In a gamma scalping strategy, we will run a mean-reversion strategy on an underlying, taking a long position in the underlying when its price moves lower or a short position when it moves higher. At the same time, we will long a straddle or strangle as a hedge. As is explained in Ang (2014), Chapter 4, a mean reversion strategy (or equivalently, a portfolio rebalancing strategy) is short volatility, while the long straddle is, of course, long volatility. The profit of this strategy is usually from the short-volatility, mean-reverting strategy, while the long straddle merely provides a hedge against extreme movements and is typically a drag on profits. (Though the mean reversion part of the strategy is short volatility, at any moment the static portfolio has positive vega and negative theta.)

At first glance, a long straddle combined with a long (or short) position in the underlying would seem to result in a portfolio that would have a delta of one (or minus one), thus fully exposed to the underlying's movement. (The straddle would be delta neutral, while the underlying of course has a delta of one or minus one.) But actually, we will put on the underlying's position only when there is a significant movement from the strike price of the options in the straddle. For example, if the underlying's price suddenly increases significantly, the put's delta will be almost zero (very much OTM), while the call's delta will be almost one (very much ITM), and entering into a short position in the underlying will render the portfolio almost delta-neutral again. The change of the delta of the straddle per unit change in the underlying's price is its gamma; hence, this strategy is called gamma scalping, as we try to profit from the changing delta by entering and exiting the underlying's position as its price moves up and down. (*Scalping* is traders' parlance for market making or mean reversion trading.) The more positive the gamma of the straddle, the faster the delta changes, and the more scalping profit opportunities. Note that unlike the strategies already described, the profit of a gamma scalping strategy is *path-dependent*. It depends not only on the initial and ending values of the underlying or the options, but on the exact path that the underlying took from the inception time to the liquidation time of the portfolio. The more often the underlying price oscillates around some mean value, the more profit we will generate. At the same time, unlike a typical mean reversion strategy as described in Chan (2013), the gamma scalping strategy does not have unlimited risk. For example, if we enter into a long position in the underlying, then if the price goes down further, the loss of the underlying will be offset by the gain in the put position almost exactly. Of course, if the price suddenly reverses and goes up, the gain of underlying will more than offset the loss due to the straddle as its delta returns to zero. This, of course, does not guarantee that a gamma scalping strategy will be profitable: If the underlying's price changes little, the mean reversion strategy will have nearly zero profit, while the time-decay of the straddle's premium, together with the probable decrease in realized volatility (and positive vega), will generate negative P&L.

In Example 5.4, we describe the codes for the backtest of a gamma scalping strategy on crude oil futures. This strategy establishes a long straddle position at 9:00 a.m. ET on Thursday, and liquidates everything at 2:30 p.m. ET on Friday. The reason we pick the weekly trading period to be Thursday morning to Friday afternoon is that the main profit driver of this strategy is due to the mean reversion of the underlying future contract, not the long straddle or strangle. Hence, we want to pick a period that is most favorable to mean-reversion—that is, it is devoid of expected announcements that might affect crude oil price. Also, we do not wish to hold positions over the weekend, which will incur negative theta without the compensating profits from mean reversion trading. The CL price at the inception of the straddle is used both as the strike price of the options, as well as the mean price level for the mean reversion strategy on the CL future. As CL goes up every 1 percent beyond this mean price, we will short one contract, up to a maximum of N contracts at a maximum deviation of N% from the mean. We will buy contracts in the same way if CL goes down every 1 percent instead of up, down to a maximum of $-N$ contracts at $-N$% from the mean. When we enter into a new position in CL, we assume we are using a limit order to enter at the midprice, but if we exit an existing position, we will use a market order to exit at the market price (as we did in the short straddle strategy before). N is a parameter to be optimized, as is the width of 1 percent between the levels. To hedge a maximum of N futures contracts, we will buy N straddles at inception time.

With an arbitrarily chosen $N = 1$, the total annual P&L of this strategy is negative: The straddle lost a lot more than the mean reversion strategy was able to make. If we gamma-scalp an LO *strangle* instead at 5 percent OTM, the annual P&L is $6,370, while the maximum drawdown is at $9,400. An improvement, though still not a great Calmar ratio. The 5 percent OTM strangle is chosen so that any loss in the underlying for a price deviation beyond 5 percent will be neutralized by one of the option positions. In other words, the maximum loss of the CL position is limited to 4 percent, or about $4,000 (assuming crude oil is worth $100 per barrel). The loss of the strangle will, of course, be limited to the initial premium. So we are assured that there cannot be extreme losses under any circumstances.

A less arbitrary way to fix the separation between the limit price levels is to set it equal to the historical volatility of CL, as in the usual Bollinger band approach. Alternatively, these price levels can be spaced based on the delta of OTM options. For example, each leg of the strangle can be chosen to have a delta of ±0.25. Then each price level can be set equal to the strike price of an option with delta at ±0.45, ±0.40, ±0.35, ±0.30, and ±0.25.

We can also try to impose a rule that the ratio of implied volatility to historical realized volatility must be below some threshold before we would enter into a position. This is naturally opposite to the rule proposed for improving the short LO straddle strategy discussed in the section "Event-Driven Strategies."

You may wonder if this strategy will work on stocks as well, especially after an earnings announcement when the price has settled down to a new level. But there is an advantage of running a gamma scalping strategy on futures instead of stocks: Futures and their options are traded throughout the evening (in ET) during the trading week, whereas we cannot do any scalping on stocks or their options during those times.

Example 5.4: Gamma scalping crude oil futures with a straddle

The code for gamma scalping CL and LO is very similar to that of shorting an LO straddle. Instead of entering into a short straddle position, we enter into a long straddle position just before 9:00 a.m. ET on Thursdays, assuming midprice execution, and we exit that using market orders just before 2:30 p.m. ET on Fridays. The major difference with shortStraddle_LO.m[5] is the section that deals with the mean reversion strategy on CL. My code deals with each level (1 percent, 2 percent, … , up to 5 percent away from the initial value of CL) separately.


```
for entryThreshold=levelWidth:levelWidth:numLevels*levelWidth
     exitThreshold=entryThreshold-levelWidth;
  ...
end
```

For each level, we determine when we enter a long or short position, and when we exit those positions, based on whether the price exceeds the entry threshold for that level and when it reverts toward the initial value of CL by 1 percent. For example, for level 3, we will buy a CL contract if the return of CL is lower than −3 percent from the initial value, and we will hold this long position until the return of CL increases to higher than −2 percent. At the exit time on Fridays, we will liquidate all futures and options with market orders.

```
pos_Fut=NaN(length(idx), 1);
pos_Fut(1)=0;
pos_Fut_L=pos_Fut;
pos_Fut_S=pos_Fut;
```

```
pos_Fut_S(retFut_bid > entryThreshold)=-1;
pos_Fut_S(retFut_ask <= exitThreshold)=0;
pos_Fut_S=fillMissingData(pos_Fut_S);

pos_Fut_L(retFut_ask < -entryThreshold)=1;
pos_Fut_L(retFut_bid >= -exitThreshold)=0;
pos_Fut_L=fillMissingData(pos_Fut_L);

pos_Fut=pos_Fut_L+pos_Fut_S;
pos_Fut(end)=0;
```

After the desired future position pos_Fut(t) at time *t* is determined, we still need to figure out the entryPrice (at mid-quote), and the exitPrice (at market).

```
for i=2:length(idx)
      myidx=idx(i);
      if (pos_Fut(i-1)==0 && pos_Fut(i) > pos_Fut(i-1))
        % Buy entry
          entryPrice=(bidFut(myidx)+askFut(myidx))/2;
        % Enter at mid-quote
      elseif (pos_Fut(i-1)==0 && pos_Fut(i) < pos_Fut(i-1))
        % Short entry
          entryPrice=(bidFut(myidx)+askFut(myidx))/2;
      elseif (pos_Fut(i-1) > 0 && pos_Fut(i) < pos_Fut(i-1))
        % Sell long
          exitPrice=bidFut(myidx); % Exit at MKT
          PL_Fut=PL_Fut+(exitPrice-entryPrice);
          if (pos_Fut(i) < 0) % Short entry
              entryPrice=(bidFut(myidx)+askFut(myidx))/2;
          end
      elseif (pos_Fut(i-1) < 0 && pos_Fut(i) > pos_Fut(i-1))
        % Buy cover
          exitPrice=askFut(myidx);
          PL_Fut=PL_Fut-(exitPrice-entryPrice);
          if (pos_Fut(i) > 0) % Buy entry
              entryPrice=(bidFut(myidx)+askFut(myidx))/2;
          end
      end
end
```

Dispersion Trading

Dispersion trading is an arbitrage between options on stocks that are components of an index, and the option on the index itself. It can be understood in analogy with index arbitrage. In index arbitrage (Chan, 2013), we buy the stocks that are components of an index such as the S&P 500, and we simultaneously short the index future, or vice versa. We hope to benefit from temporary discrepancies between market value of the stocks and the index future. Similarly, in dispersion trading, we buy the stock options and simultaneously short the index option—but there is no vice versa. We usually want to short index options and seldom want to buy them because index options are typically overpriced due to the need of portfolio managers to protect their long index portfolios. The sale of structured products linked to indices also increases demand for them (Bennett, 2014).

Dispersion trading is also called *correlation trading,* since by buying the stock component options and shorting the index option we are in effect shorting the implied correlation of the stocks, hoping that it will converge to the lower value of the realized correlation. (The mathematical demonstration of this can be found in the Bennett article as well.) When there is a financial crisis, stocks of all stripes tend to suffer big drops at the same time. Conversely, sometimes major macroeconomic announcements may prompt a huge rise in market sentiment and all stocks surge. In both extremes, stock returns experience *tail-dependence* (Ruppert, 2015), as normally uncorrelated stocks suddenly move in the same direction. These are times where implied correlation will spike up. Naturally, if one was short implied correlation (i.e., long stock options and short index options), one will suffer a big loss when tail dependence hits. However, if one shorts implied correlation after extreme events occur, one may well profit from a decrease in correlation in the aftermath. Hence, the return-risk profile of a dispersion or correlation trade is quite similar to that of a short VXX position that was discussed in the section "Trading Volatility without Options."

A dispersion trade can be implemented by buying stock option straddles or strangles, and shorting index option straddles or strangles. This way, the portfolio starts off being delta-neutral. We can impose additional constraints on the portfolio to minimize exposure to other risks. For example, if we want to have a pure exposure to correlation decrease, and not to volatility changes, we can make the portfolio vega-neutral by weighing the short index option position so that its vega is equal to that of the long stock option positions. Alternatively, if we want to minimize the change of the portfolio value due to the passage of time alone, we can make it theta-neutral also by adjusting the weight of the short index option position. Our example strategy in Example 5.5 adopts the vega-neutral weighting scheme.

Just as for index arbitrage, we often find it more profitable not to include all the component stocks or stock options in the portfolio. Instead, we can select a particularly favorable subset of the index components. In our example strategy, we decide to pick the 50 stocks whose straddles have the highest (i.e., least negative) theta in order to minimize time decay of their premiums. Assuming that we are able to trade options at midprice, and ignoring commissions, we find that our example strategy has a CAGR of 19 percent (the percentage is based on the daily P&L divided by the total gross market value of the options), a Calmar ratio of 0.4, and a maximum drawdown of 51 percent from 2007 to the end of 2013. Another way to measure the profit versus risk is to note the average annualized profit is about 86 percent of the maximum drawdown in NAV (which is different from Calmar ratio based on gross market value of the portfolio). Surprisingly, neither the financial crisis of 2008 nor the market turmoil in August 2011 caused much of a drawdown, despite the inevitable increase in realized correlations. (See the equity curve in Figure 5.8.)

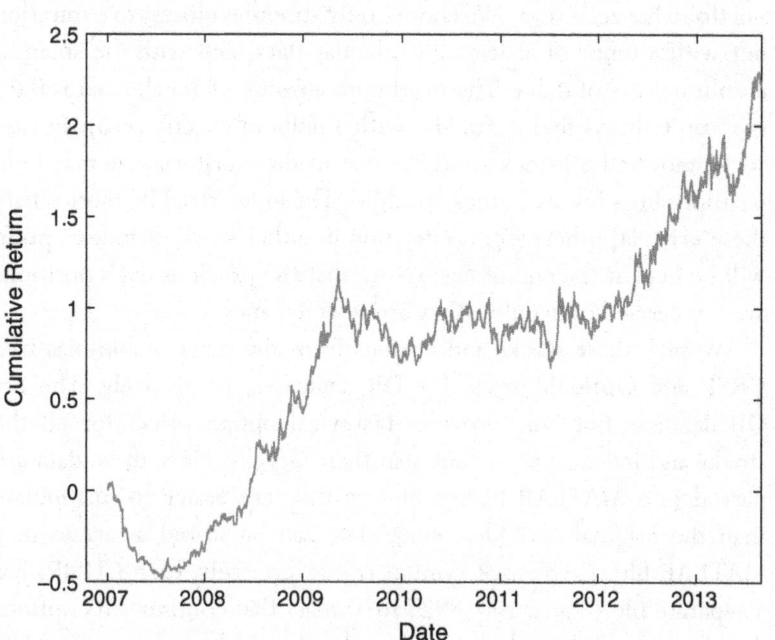

FIGURE 5.8 Dispersion trading of SPX

Our dispersion strategy rebalances the options positions at the market close every day to ensure that the portfolio remains delta-neutral, vega-neutral, and has maximal theta. The main challenge of generating profits from this strategy is to avoid incurring exorbitant transaction costs in trading options during this daily rebalance. A more cost-effective implementation would be to delta-hedge using stocks and SPY, in the same manner as in the gamma scalping strategy, instead of liquidating options that are no longer ATM. Since this needs to be done for every stock in the portfolio, it would, of course, make our already complicated backtest code more complicated. Even with that, we won't be able to avoid updating option positions regularly in order to look for the maximal theta set, or adjusting the weight of the index option to achieve vega-neutrality.

Example 5.5: Dispersion trading of SPX component straddles vs. index straddle

Our example strategy for dispersion is to select 50 stocks within SPX with straddles that have the highest theta at the end of each day and buy these straddles, while shorting an SPX index straddle such that the portfolio has zero vega. We choose only straddles closest to expiration but with a tenor of at least 28 calendar days, and with the smallest absolute value of delta. The maximum absolute delta allowed is 0.25 (we can't always find a straddle with a delta of exactly zero). In case we cannot find 50 stock straddles that fit these criteria, we may hold positions in as few as 1 stock straddle. The index straddle must satisfy these criteria; otherwise, no position in either stock or index option will be held at the end of day. (Note that the previous day's positions are not carried over unless they are selected anew.)

We pick these stocks and options from the survivorship-bias-free CRSP and OptionMetrics' Ivy DB databases, respectively. The Ivy DB database not only provides historical option prices for all the stocks and index options, but also their Greeks. Here these data are parsed into MATLAB binary files as they are easier to manipulate than the original text files, since data can be stored as arrays in a MATLAB file. Each stock symbol (more precisely, each CUSIP) has a separate file (e.g., cusip_89235610.mat) that continues its options data for the entire period. On the other hand, the index option data has a separate file for each trading day (e.g., 20040102.mat) due to the more voluminous data. A few of these files are available for download as illustrations.[6] (For other options historical data sources, see Chapter 1.)

Backtesting a stock options portfolio is much more complicated than backtesting a stock portfolio due to the extra dimensions (strike prices, expiration dates, and whether an option is a call or put) involved. There is not sufficient memory in MATLAB to store an array containing all the options prices of all the stocks with each dimension corresponding to one attribute of an option. Hence, we have to read in the data for one stock at a time and selectively store only those data we need for the strategy. So we store only the option prices and Greeks for various strikes for a given tenor in a $T \times M$ array, where T is the total number of days and M is the total number of strike prices. In contrast, the prices and Greeks of the index options data are stored in $1 \times M$ arrays since we read in their data one day at a time.

After loading these $T \times M$ arrays with option prices and Greeks into memory, the dispersion program goes through each day in a loop and finds all strike prices of the calls and puts of a symbol (either stock or index) which satisfy the tenor and net delta constraints, and determines their indices in the price array. This way, we can collapse the expiration date and strike price dimensions and achieve our needed data compression. The index that points to the location of the option data in the $T \times M$ arrays with the chosen expiration and strike price is then stored in the array ATMidx(t, c, [1, 2]), where t is time index, c is the symbol index, and [1, 2] points to a call or put, respectively. At this point, we have determined and stored what the eligible straddle is for one symbol. For example, ATMidx(10, 2, 1) has a value of 101. This means that on the 10th date (20080117) and the second stock (CUSIP = 438516106), the bid (ask) for the call is located in row 10 and column 101 of the $T \times M$ array "bid" ("ask"). The Greeks of these straddles are simultaneously stored in arrays such as totTheta or totVega. ATMidx, totTheta, and totVega all have dimension $T \times N$ where N is the number of stocks in the index (in contrast to the $T \times M$ array for each stock). What we have done so far is to compress N data files, each with several $T \times M$ arrays, into four $T \times N$ arrays, which can easily fit into memory. The following is the code fragment that does that:

```
optExpireDate_uniq=unique(opt.optExpireDate(t, :));
optExpireDate_uniq(~isfinite(optExpireDate_uniq))=[];
```

```
if (~isempty(optExpireDate_uniq))
    time2Expire=datenum(cellstr(num2str(optExpireDate_uniq')),
        'yyyymmdd')-datenum(cellstr(num2str(stk.tday(tt))),
          'yyyymmdd'); % in calendar days

    optExpireDate1month=optExpireDate_uniq(time2Expire >=
        minTime2Expire); % Choose contract with at least 1 month
          to expiration

    if (~isempty(optExpireDate1month))
        optExpireDate1month=optExpireDate1month(1); % Choose the
            nearest expiration

        minAbsDelta=Inf;
        minAbsDeltaIdx=NaN;
        strikes_uniq=unique(opt.strikes(t, :));
        strikes_uniq(~isfinite(strikes_uniq))=[];

        for s=1:length(strikes_uniq) % Go through each strike

            if (c<=length(cusip8))
                idxC=find(opt.strikes(t, :)==strikes_uniq(s) &
                    opt.optExpireDate(t, :)==optExpireDate1month
                        & isfinite(opt.delta(t, :)) & ...
                    opt.bid(t, :)>0 & opt.ask(t, :)>0 & strcmp
                        ('C', opt.cpflag(t, :)) & opt.bid(t+1, :)>
                            0 & opt.ask(t+1, :)>0);  % Ensure
                                we can exit position day after
                                    entry!
            else
                idxC=find(opt.strikes(t, :)==strikes_uniq(s) &
                    opt.optExpireDate(t, :)==optExpireDate1month
                        & isfinite(opt.delta(t, :)) & ...
                    opt.bid(t, :)>0 & opt.ask(t, :)>0 &
                        strcmp('C', opt.cpflag(t, :)));
            end

            if (length(idxC) > 1)
                if (t > 1) % if duplicate, use old option data
                    assert(c~=length(cusip8)+1, 'We cannot deal
                        with SPX for duplicates yet!');
```

```
            idx2=find(~isfinite(opt.strikes(t-1, idxC)));
            idxC(idx2)=[];
            if (length(idxC) > 1)
                idxC=[];
            end
        else
            idxC=[];
        end
    end

    if (c<=length(cusip8)) % stock options
        idxP=find(opt.strikes(t, :)==strikes_uniq(s) &
          opt.optExpireDate(t, :)==optExpireDate1month &
               isfinite(opt.delta(t, :)) & ...
            opt.bid(t, :)>0 & opt.ask(t, :)>0 & strcmp
              ('P', opt.cpflag(t, :)) & opt.bid(t+1, :)>0
                & opt.ask(t+1, :)>0);  % Ensure we can
                    exit position day after entry!
    else % index options
        idxP=find(opt.strikes(t, :)==strikes_uniq(s) &
            opt.optExpireDate(t, :)==optExpireDate1month
              & isfinite(opt.delta(t, :)) & ...
            opt.bid(t, :)>0 & opt.ask(t, :)>0 & strcmp
                ('P', opt.cpflag(t, :)));
    end

    if (length(idxP) > 1)
        if (t > 1) % if duplicate, use old option data
            assert(c~=length(cusip8)+1, 'We cannot deal
                with SPX for duplicates yet!');
            idx2=find(~isfinite(opt.strikes(t-1, idxP)));
            idxP(idx2)=[];
            if (length(idxP) > 1)
                idxP=[];
            end
        else
            idxP=[];
        end
    end

    if (~isempty(idxC) && ~isempty(idxP))
        assert(length(idxC)==1 && length(idxP)==1);
```

```
                totAbsDelta=abs(opt.delta(t, idxC)+opt.delta
                   (t, idxP));
                if (totAbsDelta < minAbsDelta)
                    minAbsDelta=totAbsDelta;
                    minAbsDeltaIdx=[idxC idxP];
                end
            end
        end
        % finding the straddle with the smallest absolute delta
        if (minAbsDelta <= maxNetDelta)
            totTheta(tt, c)=sum(opt.theta(t, minAbsDeltaIdx));
            totVega(tt, c) =sum(opt.vega(t, minAbsDeltaIdx));
            ATMidx(tt, c, :)=minAbsDeltaIdx; % Pick the strike
              prices for call and put to use

        end
    end
end
```

After locating a straddle for each stock, we then go through each day again to find the 50 of them that have the highest theta, using the array totTheta. Next, we weigh these options by the number of shares of underlying stocks required to contribute a market value of \$1. (To put it another way: The market value of the stocks each option position has the right to buy or sell has a market value of \$1.) We then compute the total vega of these stock options, using the array totVega (which, despite its name, gives the total vega for just one stock straddle, not the total vega of all the stock straddles). The number of options required for each stock is stored in a position array *pos* which also has dimension $T \times N$. All the stock options have positive positions. But the index option will have a negative position with a vega equal to the negative of the total vega of the stock positions. Here is the code fragment for that:

```
for t=1:lastDayIdx-1
      candidatesIdx=find(isfinite(totTheta(t, 1:end-1)) &
        isfinite(stk.cl_unadj(t, :)) & isfinite(totVega(t, 1:
          end-1))); % consider all stock straddles

      if (length(candidatesIdx) >= 2 && all(isfinite(ATMidx
        (t, end, :))) && all(isfinite(ATMidx(t+1, end, :))) &&
```

```
isfinite(totVega(t, end))) % Can have positions
        only if enough stock candidates AND SPX index
            options are available both on t and t+1.
    [foo, maxIdx]=sort(totTheta(t, candidatesIdx),
        'descend');

    assert(all(isfinite(stk.cl_unadj(t, candidatesIdx
        (maxIdx(1:topN))))), 'Some candidates have no
            stock price!');
    pos(t, candidatesIdx(maxIdx(1:topN)))=1./stk.cl_unadj
        (t, candidatesIdx(maxIdx(1:topN)))/100; % Number of
            straddles set equal to $1 of underlying. Recall
                each option has rights to 100 shares.

    assert(all(isfinite(totVega(t, candidatesIdx(maxIdx
        (1:topN))))), 'Some candidates have no vega!');
    totVega_stk=sum( pos(t, candidatesIdx(maxIdx
        (1:topN))).*totVega(t, candidatesIdx(maxIdx
            (1:topN))));

    %                assert(isfinite(totVega(t, end)),
         'Index option has no vega!');
    totVega_spx=totVega(t, end);
    pos(t, end)=-totVega_stk/totVega_spx; % Set number of
         index straddles such that their total vega is
             negative that of total stock straddles' vega

  end

end
```

(An alternative capital allocation among the stock options is to weigh them by the number of shares of underlying stocks required to contribute to their index weight. For example, if AAPL contributes 3.8 percent to the SPX, and we assume the stock portfolio is worth $500, we need to compute the number of shares of AAPL that have the market value $3.80, and divide this by 100 as the number of AAPL straddles to buy.)

After computing the number of straddles we need on each side, we can proceed to compute the P&L of holding these positions.

Finally, we can also compute the gross market value of these positions by multiplying the number of straddles by their call and put prices and summing across all stocks and index straddles. This way, we can compute the daily returns of the portfolio.[7]

```
pnl=zeros(size(pos, 1), 1);
mktVal=zeros(size(pos, 1), 1); % gross market value of all stock
   and index options
for c=1:size(pos, 2)-1
    load(['C:/Projects/Ivy/SPX_200701_201308/cusip_', cusip8{c}],
        'bid', 'ask');

    mid=(bid+ask)/2;

    for t=2:lastDayIdx-1

        if (pos(t-1, c) ~= 0)
            assert(all(isfinite(mid(t-1, ATMidx(t-1, c, :)))));
            pnl(t)=pnl(t)+100*sum(pos(t-1,c)*(mid(t,ATMidx
                (t-1,c,:))-mid(t-1,ATMidx(t-1,c,:)));
            mktVal(t-1)=mktVal(t-1)+100*sum(abs(pos(t-1, c)*mid
                (t-1, ATMidx(t-1, c, :))));
        end

    end
end

% SPX index
for t=2:lastDayIdx-1

    if (pos(t-1, end) ~= 0)
        opt1=load(['C:/Projects/Ivy/SPX_index_200701_201308/',
            num2str(stk.tday(t-1))], 'strikes', 'optExpireDate',
               'bid', 'ask', 'cpflag');
        opt2=load(['C:/Projects/Ivy/SPX_index_200701_201308/',
            num2str(stk.tday(t))],   'strikes', 'optExpireDate',
                'bid', 'ask', 'cpflag');

        % prices at t-1
        bid1=opt1.bid(1, ATMidx(t-1, end, :)); % 1x2 array,
            [idxC idxP]
        ask1=opt1.ask(1, ATMidx(t-1, end, :));
```

```
            % We need price at t corresponding to strikes and
            % optExpireDate at t-1

            idxC=find(opt2.strikes==opt1.strikes(ATMidx(t-1, end, 1))
                & opt2.optExpireDate==opt1.optExpireDate(ATMidx(t-1,
                  end, 1)) & strcmp('C', opt2.cpflag) );
            idxP=find(opt2.strikes==opt1.strikes(ATMidx(t-1, end, 2))
                & opt2.optExpireDate==opt1.optExpireDate(ATMidx(t-1,
                  end, 2)) & strcmp('P', opt2.cpflag) );

            assert(length(idxC)==1 && length(idxP)==1);


            bid2=opt2.bid(1, [idxC idxP]); % 1x2 array, [idxC idxP]
            ask2=opt2.ask(1, [idxC idxP]); % 1x2 array, [idxC idxP]

            mid1=(bid1+ask1)/2;
            mid2=(bid2+ask2)/2;

            % We need price at t+1 corresponding to strikes and
            % optExpireDate at t-1

            pnl(t)=pnl(t)+100*pos(t-1, end)*smartsum(mid2-mid1)
            mktVal(t-1)=mktVal(t-1)+100*sum(abs(pos(t-1, end)*mid1));

        end


    end

    pnl(lastDayIdx+1:end)=[];
    mktVal(lastDayIdx+1:end)=[];

    cumPL=smartcumsum(pnl);


    dailyret=pnl./backshift(1, mktVal);
    dailyret(~isfinite(dailyret))=0;
    cumret=cumprod(1+dailyret)-1;
```

Some readers may be concerned about whether we have adjusted for dividends and splits for the options when computing P&L. Even though a call option price will drop on the dividend ex-date, unlike stock, there will be no compensating dividend payout so this is a real loss, and thus no historical adjustment is needed. Owners of a call would typically sell it before ex-date. We, however, do not take into account the need to sell a call before dividend ex-date in this strategy. (The same argument applies to puts.) On the ex-date for a split, option price do not change, but each option will be the right to buy or sell a different number of shares based on the split factor. For example, if it is a two-for-one split, a call option that was issued prior to the ex-date would allow you to buy 200 shares instead of 100 on or after the ex-date. Since the option price doesn't change, there is no need for historical adjustment, either.

Cross-Sectional Mean Reversion of Implied Volatility

One of the advantages of being an algorithmic options trader is the ability to choose among a large portfolio of stock options to find the ones that have the "best" prices. But what does the best price mean for options? Clearly, it doesn't just mean that an option is cheap: OTM options are always cheaper than ATM or ITM options, and options with shorter tenors are always cheaper than those with longer tenors, but that doesn't mean they have better value. Instead, we may measure the "cheapness" of an option by its implied volatility. If it has the lowest implied volatility of all the options for the same underlying, we may consider it the "cheapest." But even if an option is cheap, it doesn't necessarily mean that we should buy it: We would only do so if we think its price is going to mean-revert.

Notice I didn't say that we should only buy an option if its price is going to "increase." There are two types of mean reversion: time-series and cross-sectional. Time-series mean reversion in this context means that we expect a cheap option will indeed increase in price later on. This has to be an unusual occurrence, though: As we know, option prices tend to decrease due to the decay of time value. A cheap option will increase in price only in the unusual situation that expectation of future realized volatility increases significantly. Another way to look at this is that a low implied volatility may indeed increase later on, but this doesn't mean that the option's price will increase. However, in cross-sectional mean reversion, we do not require that an option will increase in price in the *absolute* sense. We only require that it will increase in price in a *relative* sense: that it will become more expensive relative to other options of the same underlying and perhaps the same tenor. In other words, we expect that the price difference between an option with the lowest implied volatility and its peers with higher implied volatility will narrow over time, and might even change sign.

Of course, the earlier discussion concerning the cheapest option applies in an opposite way to an "expensive" option, too. In cross-sectional mean reversion of option prices, we would expect a relatively expensive option to become relatively cheaper.

Do cross-sectional mean reversions actually occur regularly? We can easily find out by constructing a trading strategy that should be profitable (at least in a backtest) if this is true. We start with the S&P 500 universe. Every day and for every stock in the universe, just as in the dispersion strategy, we select a slice of options that have the nearest expiration date but that have a tenor of at least 28 calendar days. We select the call option with the lowest implied volatility among them and add it to a candidate list of call options. Similarly, we select the put option with the highest implied volatility and add it to a candidate list of put options. After going through all the stocks in the universe, we form a long portfolio of 50 call options by choosing the ones with the lowest implied volatilities from the call option candidate list. Similarly, we form a short portfolio of 50 put options by choosing the ones with the highest implied volatilities from the put option candidate list. We will hold all these options positions for just one day, and rebalance the portfolio as necessary on the following day's market close.

Naturally, due to put-call parity, we can just as well implement this strategy by shorting calls and buying puts instead. (Put-call parity is only exactly true for European options. But with the risk-free rate so low, it is almost true for American options, too, especially for the short-tenor ones we choose.)

The implementation of this backtest is structurally similar to that of the dispersion strategy, and the program is available for download as impVolCrossSectionalMeanReversion.m. The backtest of this strategy achieved an astounding *daily* return of 1.1 percent from 2007 to the end of 2013, without subtracting commissions, and assuming midprice executions. There are several reasons why the return is so high, and may be unrealistic. Unlike the dispersion trading strategy before, we don't insist on using ATM options in this strategy. OTM options tend to have higher embedded leverage, and since the return we quote is the P&L of an option position divided by its market value, it is essentially a levered return that will go up with leverage.

(Leverage is calculated as delta times the price of the underlying divided by the price of its option. Figure 5.9 shows the leverages of puts and

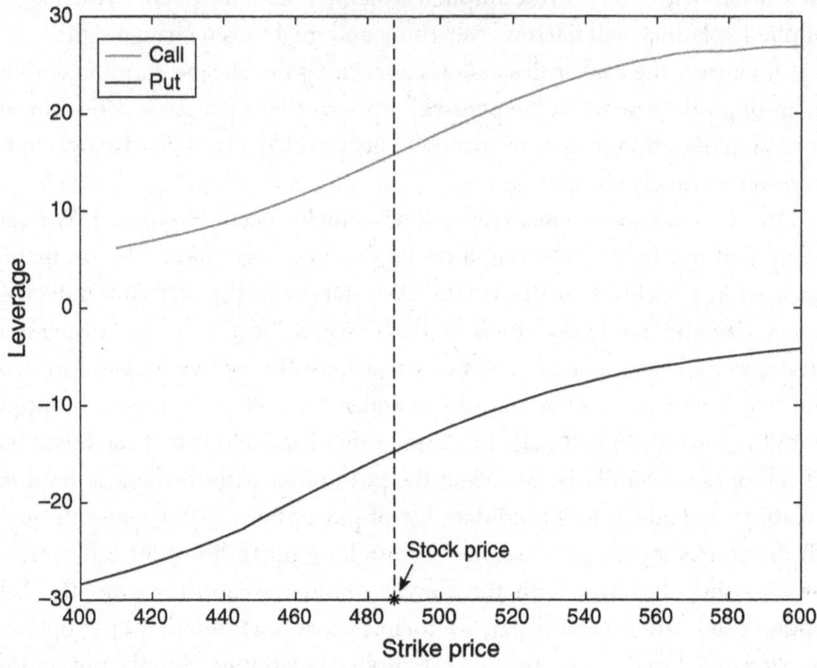

FIGURE 5.9 Leverage of AAPL options

calls of AAPL as a function of strike price. Either leverage is evidently a monotonically increasing function of strike price, but the absolute values of the leverages are increasing as a function of the options' out-of-moneyness. Since delta for puts is negative, their leverage is also negative. The code to generate this curve can be downloaded from computeLeverage.m.)

OTM options also tend to be less liquid and have wider bid-ask spread. Our backtest assumes midprice executions, which may be unrealistic when the bid-ask spread is wide. Strategies often have high returns on paper when those returns cannot actually be captured in live trading due to high transaction costs, which may be the case here. Nevertheless, the highly positive theoretical return illustrates that cross-sectional mean reversion of implied volatility does occur regularly.

What about the risk of this mean reversion strategy? Since we are long calls and short puts, we are certainly not market or delta neutral. This can easily be remedied by delta hedging the portfolio with a short SPY position. We will leave that as an exercise to see if it reduces the maximum drawdown. But even after delta-hedging this portfolio, it is still short vega, since we are short options with high implied volatility and long options with low implied volatility. Might this strategy work with just the long side, thus eliminating vega risk? Or can we weigh the long and short options positions to enforce vega-neutrality, just as in dispersion trading? We will leave all that to you to explore.

Summary

It isn't easy to profit from buying options unless one is Nassim Nicholas Taleb (Chung, 2015). Even when we think realized volatility will go up due to expected events ("Event-Driven Strategies" section), we end up extracting returns only in the aftermath by shorting volatility. Even though we bought straddles in the "Gamma Scalping" section, we were only able to profit from the mean reversion trading of the underlying, which is short volatility. At best, we were able to be vega-neutral in the "Dispersion Trading" section. But by shorting correlation there, we were exposed to the same tail risks as shorting volatility. In the section on "Cross-Sectional Mean Reversion of Implied Volatility," we actively sought options with high implied volatilities and short them, though we hedged by buying those options with low implied volatilities. We were still net short implied volatility as a result. We were acting like an insurance company in these trades. Even though Taleb is celebrated for his ability to earn 20 percent in one day during market crashes, one should note that his year-to-date return was also 20 percent, since the long volatility makes practically nothing until that day. A short volatility strategy (like the FX mean reversion strategy we run in our fund) is able to earn more than 20 percent in a year, though one will have to suffer steep drawdown during risk-off periods. It is therefore not surprising to hear expert options traders saying that they spend most of their time shorting options (Chan, 2015).

If we are to sell volatility, we might as well find the most efficient and least risky way to do it. That is why various different short volatility strategies are explored. With the aid of a computer, even independent traders are not limited to just trading a few familiar options. They can choose among a portfolio of hundreds of different options, with different underlyings, tenors, and strike prices and select the most advantageous ones to hold positions. Of course, it is quite complicated to backtest such high-dimensional strategies. The main problem is that storing high dimensional arrays in memory is not feasible in most common programming languages. We demonstrated how to get around this problem using special programming structures in the "Dispersion Trading" and "Cross-Sectional Mean Reversion of Implied Volatility" sections.

But these backtests are only suggestive—they can't really tell us whether the strategies will be profitable in live trading. The reason for such tentativeness is the especially large bid-ask spreads of options compared to their underlyings. (We saw that even an option on a very liquid future like CL can have a bid-ask spread that is over 1.2 percent wide.) The strategies were mostly backtested by assuming that we can enter a position at midprice. In a few cases, we even assume that we can exit a position with midprice. This is not an impossible pipe dream, as options traders do manually and expertly adjust their limit prices so that they get filled without paying the full-spread, taking into account the instantaneous condition of the order book and order flow. But this is often an art rather than science. The science of balancing the opportunity cost (for not getting filled) and bid-ask cost can be explored only if one has an options trading simulator, or of course in live trading. Hence, a sophisticated automated market-making program is necessary to execute many of these strategies.

I did describe in the sections on "Trading Volatility without Options" and "Predicting Volatility" some pseudo-options strategies that can both long and short the ETF VXX or the future VX at different times. They are far easier to backtest and execute than the strategies that really trade stock or even index options themselves.

You are no doubt aware that there are many more options strategies out there than the ones covered in this chapter, involving structures such as butterflies, condors, ladders, and so on. Hopefully, the techniques introduced here will allow you to automatically search for the best structure among the hundreds or thousands of choices every day, or every millisecond.

Exercises

5.1. What is the sign of the vega for SPX options? How do you reconcile this sign with the fact described in Exercise 5.2 that implied volatility seems to anticorrelate with realized volatility on a daily basis?

5.2. Backtest various refinements of the trading rules suggested at the end of "Event-Driven Strategies."

5.3. Assuming a CL contract is initially quoted at 100, demonstrate that the maximum loss of the mean reversion strategy on CL described in "Gamma Scalping" is $4,000 for holding one contract. (The maximum loss here does not include the options premium.)

5.4. Add a delta hedging strategy to the strategy described in the section on "Cross-Sectional Mean Reversion of Implied Volatility" by trading SPY, and show how it affects the daily returns and maximum drawdown.
5.5. Backtest trading only the long side of the strategy described in the section on "Cross-Sectional Mean Reversion of Implied Volatility."
5.6. Backtest weighing the options positions so that the portfolio is vega-neutral on the same strategy in Exercise 5.5.
5.7. In Example 5.2, we found that the one-day change in daily SPY returns volatility is usually opposite in sign to that of the one-day change in VXX. Check if this is true also for hourly bars. (If you program in Python, you can try this on Quantopian.com, which provides free one-minute-bar data for US stocks and ETFs.)
5.8. Instead of trading the VX future, can we implement the $RV(t+1) - VIX(t)$ strategy in Example 5.2 by trading the ETF VXX instead? (*Hint*: Study in detail the VX-ES Roll Returns Strategy in the same section.)
5.9. If an ATM call option has gamma $= \Gamma$, by how much would the delta of this option decrease if the underlying price changes by δS?

Endnotes

1. The complete code can be downloaded as VX_SPY_returns.m, with complete definitions of parameters such as numDaysStart, and arrays such as isExpireDate.
2. See www.cboe.com/micro/vix/vixwhite.pdf.
3. R users can use the ugarchfit function in the rugarch package for estimating the GARCH model.
4. The complete code can be downloaded as SPY_garch.m.
5. The codes are available for download as gammaScalp_straddle_LO.m. The corresponding code for buying a strangle instead of straddle can be downloaded as gammaScalp_strangle_LO.m.
6. The programs for converting the text files into .mat files are also available for download as parseIvyOptions.m and parseIvyOptions_index.m.
7. The complete program can be downloaded as dispersion.m. However, data are not available for download due to licensing restrictions.

CHAPTER 6

Intraday Trading and Market Microstructure

Suppose you are given a choice of two investment strategies. Both have the same unlevered average annualized returns net of all costs, but one has an average holding period of one hour and the other has a holding period of one month. Which strategy would you prefer?

Most investors would prefer the first, intraday strategy. The reason is obvious: intraday strategies typically have higher Sharpe ratio than longer-term ones, given the same average returns. This is because intraday strategies can make more independent bets in one day. By the law of large numbers, the difference between an intraday strategy's realized mean return and expected return will be smaller than that of a strategy that makes only monthly bets. Because of the higher Sharpe ratio, we can also apply a higher leverage to the strategy as per Kelly's formula. So even if the unlevered average returns of the two strategies are the same, the levered compound return of the intraday strategy will be higher.[1] Quite apart from earning higher returns, it is also obvious that the longer one holds a position, the more vulnerable we are to black swan risks.

So why don't we all become day traders, or taking this to the extreme, high frequency traders? First, there is the issue of capacity. If you are a billionaire (or manager of a billion-dollar fund), it is almost impossible to find a day trading strategy that can generate significant returns on your asset. For example, even AAPL has an average daily trading volume of only about \$4 billion. Worse, the average top-of-book quote size for AAPL at Nasdaq is only 189 shares (Cartea, Jaimungal, and Penalva, 2015, Table 4.7). A day trading strategy cannot have orders that are much bigger than the quote size "at-the-touch"[2] without having major market impact that destroys any theoretical profit (though using dark pools can alleviate part of this problem, as we shall see.) Of course, you might consider trading stock index futures instead, which is even more liquid than AAPL. But even the ES future for the S&P 500 stock index has an at-the-touch quote size of about \$30 million only. If we submit a market order that approaches \$1 billion, we will instantly "walk the book" (take out multiple layers of the order book).

But even if one does not have a billion dollars to deploy, intraday traders still need to worry a lot about transaction costs that may comprise of bid-offer spread, slippage, market impact, adverse selection, opportunity cost, and so on. To understand transaction costs and how best to minimize them, we need to understand better what is generally called *market microstructure* in the academic literature. Part of this chapter is intended to be a primer on this topic, which includes the study of latency reduction, smart routing, market fragmentation, optimal order types, and dark pools. But beyond such execution issues, just backtesting intraday strategies involves some subtle issues that can significantly affect their accuracy. We will discuss various problems with supposedly high frequency data for such backtests. Fortunately, not everything is toil and trouble in intraday trading. We will discuss some research that uses order flow and order book information for high frequency trading.

Most of the discussion in this chapter focuses on the US stock market, since microstructure issues are most complex there. However, we will comment on relevant issues in the US futures and spot currency markets as well.

Latency Reduction

There are three types of latencies we have to contend with in trading:

1. Order submission: The time between our submitting an order, and the order's arrival at the market venue.
2. Order status: The time between the execution (full or partial) or cancellation/rejection/modification of our order and our receipt of the order status notification.

3. Market data: The time between the occurrence of a tick on a market venue and our reception of that tick. (A tick can be an execution or a change of a quote on that market.)

Whatever latency is, common sense tells us that it can't be good for trading. For example, if having your order execute just a few milliseconds later will be beneficial, we could have just submitted it a few milliseconds later. Reducing latency is an important part of reducing execution costs. We will discuss how to minimize each type of latency in this section.

In this era of low-cost colocation, even retail traders can easily reduce the order submission latency to below 5 milliseconds (ms) in some circumstances. For example, you can rent a virtual private server at Equinix's NY4 data center in Secaucus, New Jersey, through Fluid Hosting for hundreds of dollars a month, and cross-connect (for some extra hundreds of dollars) to Interactive Brokers' (IB) Point of Presence (POP) there. Alternatively, you can rent a virtual private server at DuPont Fabros's NJ1 data center in Piscataway, New Jersey, through Speedy Trading Servers (www.speedytradingservers.com) for a much lower price, which has an extranet connection with IB's Stamford, Connecticut, trading servers. Either option will get your order to IB below 5 ms. Of course, IB will then reroute your order to various exchanges such as the NYSE, Nasdaq, or Globex, unless you are trading currencies in which case your order is immediately routed to IB's FX liquidity partners that include various global banks. The rerouting time from IB to an exchange is, however, quite fast. You can beat IB's time-to-market only if you pay huge sums of money to invest in microwave or laser transmissions, and if you meet the necessary capital requirement for your brokerage account (which can be as low as several hundred thousand dollars for currency trading) to opt for direct "sponsored" access to the various market centers. In this scenario, you will be collocated at the market center itself, and your order goes directly from your program to the market without going through your broker's server. You will need a prime broker to provide you with credit for such sponsored access.

If you have minimized the latency of submitting an order, then you have also minimized the latency of receiving an order status confirmation, whether your order has been filled, cancelled, or otherwise modified. Just as in the case of order submission, we are also at the mercy of the broker, unless we have direct sponsored access to the market venue. The time it takes for your order to be transmitted to the market is usually similar to the time it takes for the order status to be transmitted back to you.

Market data latency, however, is a whole different matter. Most brokers (except FX brokers, since they often run their own FX market) do not bother to provide you with low-latency market data. This is not their core competency. For example, IB provides snapshots of stock prices at 250 ms intervals only. (The IB latency for futures, and option-on-futures, data is the same as for stocks. But for stock options it is 10 ms, and for FX, just 5 ms). In fact, there are very few market data providers that can offer stocks and futures data with lower than 10 ms latency—among them, S&P Capital IQ (previously QuantHouse), SR Labs, and Thomson Reuters are some examples. However, one should prepare to pay dearly (i.e., a few thousand dollars per month) for such data feeds. Of course, one can also subscribe to the market venues' data feed directly. Nasdaq, for example, offers the ITCH feed which has a lot more information beyond price and size (more on this later) besides being low latency. Such an enriched, direct data feed from the market venues is generally much more expensive than the consolidated data feeds distributed by SIP,[3] unless one is subscribing to a "Managed" version that a broker may provide to its clients.[4]

All the latencies we have described so far concerned the time of travel of data. But of course, there is also the issue of computational latency—the time it takes your trading program to turn market data into trading decisions. As we saw in Chapter 1, many programming languages can turn a trading strategy into an automated execution platform that can receive market data and submit an order through a broker or an exchange API, but they differ greatly in speed. In a nutshell, complied languages such as C++, C#, or Java generally run at least 10 times faster than scripting languages such as MATLAB, R, or Python (Aruoba, Borağan, and Fernández-Villaverde, 2014), and so we should use only compiled languages for intraday trading. However, there are ways to replace computationally intensive functions in a scripting language with compiled codes. If we use Mex files written in C++ for such functions in MATLAB, or if we use Numba or Cython compilers for Python, then their speed comes within a factor of 2 of that of C++. The speed of R, however, cannot yet be increased to match these.

If one doesn't want to write automated execution platforms using universal languages such as C++ or MATLAB, one can use the special-purpose trading platforms such as Deltix, Progress Apama, and S&P Capital IQ's Quanthouse. Though their speed may not be as fast as custom-built C++ codes, their performance won't be too different from compiled scripting languages.

Latency affects transaction costs in two distinct ways, depending on whether one is running a mean-reversion or a momentum strategy.

We usually execute a mean-reversion strategy by placing limit orders on the order book. If our placement is a few milliseconds later than our competitors' (other mean reversion traders or market makers), the opportunity for our order to get filled may be lost. That is because most order books use time priority[5] to decide which order will get filled first, for orders at the same prices. In other words, we may suffer *opportunity cost* due to latency. For high-frequency traders who provide liquidity in order to earn rebates provided by some exchanges, this opportunity cost can be measured quite precisely. In addition to opportunity cost, latency also induces *adverse selection*. That is to say, one's limit orders only get filled when the market goes against us immediately after execution. For example, if we place a buy limit order, we may only get filled when the price drops after the execution. This is often because the counterparties who sent market-sell orders to execute against our limit-buy orders are more informed traders, who only send out these market orders when they can accurately predict that prices will soon drop. If we have lower latency than other traders (including both market makers and informed traders), and if we are also good at predicting the short-term price movement, we may be able to cancel or modify our limit orders before they get adversely executed against. Even if we do not possess this predictive ability but enjoy the lowest latency, we can at least hope that the profits we earn from frequently providing liquidity due to our head-of-queue status will offset the losses when there are adverse executions.

If we are momentum traders, we are the informed party in such transactions. In order to immediately benefit from our information, we have to use market orders. Latency in our market orders getting executed will result in slippage—other informed traders may have already taken the quotes with better prices a few milliseconds before us. Note that here we use "information" in the broadest possible sense. Naturally, we include information such as news and fundamental analysis. But we also include predictions that come from quantitative or technical analysis.

Order Type and Routing Optimization

Now that we have configured our trading infrastructure with the lowest physical latency, we need to consider what sort of order types best achieve our goals within the shortest time and the lowest cost. Once again, we have to distinguish between mean-reversion (liquidity-providing, market-making) strategies, and momentum (liquidity/market-taking) strategies. Note that this section pertains only to US stocks trading, and the special order types discussed are mainly of interest to traders with institutional prime broker accounts (though retail traders may be able to access these through a membership in a proprietary trading firm).

Adding Liquidity

The prototypical order type for a mean-reverting strategy is the limit order. But the problem with a plain-vanilla limit order is that it is difficult to compete in priority with the limit orders with special modifiers that many high-frequency traders use for US stocks. These special modifiers can push a limit order to the head of the queue in execution priority, so they have the best chance of getting filled ahead of everybody else and enjoy the exchange's rebate of about 1 to 3 mils[6] per share (as well as possibly earning the bid-ask spread as all market-making strategies are supposed to). One of these modifiers is generically called *hide-and-light*. Examples of the hide-and-light order are Hide Not Slide Order on BATS, and Post No Preference Blind Order on NYSE ARCA (see Mackintosh, 2014; Nasdaq, 2014; and DirectEdge, 2015). To understand how a hide-and-light limit order works, one has to understand a bit about the US stock market structure.

There isn't one US stock market—there are more than 50 of them. Eleven or so of these market centers are exchanges, and the rest are dark pools. As a result, the US stock market is very fragmented, and when you submit a limit order to your broker, it is quite difficult to figure out to which market center it will be routed (unless your broker allows you to directly route to a specific market center: the so-called Direct Market Access, or DMA). Each market center maintains its own order book. But these order books are not totally independent—they are governed by a rule established by the SEC around 2007, called the Order Protection Rule (Rule 611) of the Regulation National Market System (Reg NMS). The gist of this rule is that any arriving market order (or marketable limit order) must be routed to the exchange with the best *displayed* quote where the order can be filled. (Only exchanges but not dark pools will have displayed quote.) The best displayed quotes across all the exchanges are called the NBBO (National Best Bid Offer), and the best displayed quotes (BBO) on each of these exchanges are "protected" by the Order Protection Rule, in the sense that their prices must be checked by all the exchanges to determine where an order should be routed.

Suppose a stock has best bid offer of $10-10.02 at exchange L (some "local" exchange) and best bid offer of $10-**10.01** at exchange N (the exchange that has the National best offer). Assume the quote sizes are all for 100 shares (see Table 6.1). Now if a trader sends a limit buy order for 100 shares at $10.01 to exchange L, it will not stay there. It has to be routed

TABLE 6.1 Order Book for Exchanges L and N

Offers are in gray boxes; bids are in white boxes. Quote sizes are indicated in each column under L and N, and NBBOs have boldface quote sizes.

Prior to Hide-and-Light Order Placement

Bids/Offers	L	N
$10.02	100	
$10.01		**100**
$10.00	100	

After Hide-and-Light Order Placement

Bids/Offers	L	N
$10.02	100	
$10.01		**100**
$10.00	200	

After N Raised the Offer to $10.02

Bids/Offers	L	N
$10.02	**100**	**100**
$10.01	**100**	
$10.00	100	

to N and will be immediately executed there as a market order against the National Best Offer (NBO), which is noted in **boldface**. If the intention of the trader is to earn a rebate from the exchange L, this execution as market order is bad because the trader will instead be charged a liquidity taking fee by N. However, if we specify this limit buy order as a hide-and-light order, then the exchange will automatically lower its display limit price to $10 so that it can stay on its order book, while remembering that it has a hidden working price of $10.01. If and when the national best offer is raised to $10.02, then the display price of this order will also be automatically lifted to $10.01, which is now the national best bid. This change of limit price is managed by the exchange itself, requiring no further instruction from the trader—hence, it has practically zero latency. More importantly, it was time-stamped at the original time that the order was received by the exchange, not at the time that the order was repriced at $10.01, and hence it has higher priority over all other orders (except an ISO order, which we will discuss later). Therefore it is very likely that this order will be executed and the trader will earn the liquidity rebate.

Now you may wonder how one can be so sure that the national best offer would be lifted from $10.01 to $10.02 shortly after the trader placed the hide-and-light order. There is one way to be sure: See into the future. What I mean is that the trader can use the fast direct data feed from the exchanges mentioned in the section on "Latency Reduction" to see whether the offer has been raised to $10.02 before placing the hide-and-light order. Note that the NBBO is based on the slower SIP data feed, which is about 0.5 ms slower than the direct feed. (Ding, 2014. See also Hunsader, 2016(1) and (2).) So even if the offer has actually been raised at exchange N to $10.02, anyone placing a limit buy order at $10.01 will still be routed to exchange N, only to find that it will be sitting at the top of the order book at N some time (0.5 ms?) *after* the hide-and-light order has already been placed at the top of book at exchange L at the same price. Therefore, placing a hide-and-light order is one way to increase the chance that the order will be at the head of the queue.

The exchange L benefits from providing such exotic order types to high-frequency traders because they will get to keep the limit orders local (instead of routing them to N) and earn exchange fees when market orders get routed to its NBBO for executions. Higher volume at an exchange will also attract more orders, begetting higher volume, and so on. Finally, more volume at an exchange means that more traders will pay them high market data fees for their direct feeds. To an exchange, this is one big profitable virtuous circle.

Unfortunately, retail brokerages do not make available the hide-and-light order to their customers, since retail brokerages do not allow their customers to have direct sponsored access to the market centers. The hide-and-light order is only useful if you can submit it to the exchange faster than the latency of the SIP feed as explained above, which is just 0.5 ms or so. Even if by some good luck, your limit order did end up getting filled, some retail brokerages still would not pass on the exchange rebates to you. Instead, they simply pocket them. Only select retail brokers such as Interactive Brokers, and institutional brokers such as Lime Brokerage, will pass on the rebates. So the hide-and-light order type is really useful only if you are trading for an account large enough that can be served by a prime broker or if you are trading your membership account of a proprietary trading firm.

If getting head-of-queue priority for our limit order is the goal, and we have information from our fast direct market data feed that tells us where the NBO will be in the next millisecond, then there is another order type that is useful—the intermarket sweep order (ISO). Thankfully, this order type is sometimes available[7] to retail investors.

The ISO is also a type of limit order. But unlike an ordinary limit order, a buy ISO need not be routed to the market center that has the National Best Offer (we called it market N), even if its limit price is equal to the NBO. The sender of this order is supposed to separately send another buy ISO to execute against the NBO and remove that quote. This is easy enough to accomplish, because, as we mentioned in this chapter's introduction, the NBBO quote size is often quite small. The original ISO will be allowed to sit at the top of the order book of the local market center L as the best bid (see an illustration of this in Table 6.2). As in the case of the hide-and-light order, we may choose to do this only when we know via the fast direct data feed that the actual best offer at N is higher than the NBO. So when the SIP feed finally broadcasts the new, higher NBO to everybody, our bid at L will be the National Best Bid (NBB) and is at head-of-queue. In fact, because no repricing of the order is needed here, our bid has even higher priority than the hide-and-light order in the queue.

There are reasons other than earning rebates that make it advantageous to use the hide-and-light or the ISO orders. As already mentioned, getting our limit orders filled more frequently reduces adverse selection. (Otherwise, we may only get filled in a trending market.) Also, in this era of high-frequency trading, prices change very quickly but order routing takes time. So by the time an order is routed to the exchange with the NBBO, it might no longer be the best price. (Some exchanges actually charge a fee to liquidity providers, and pay a rebate to liquidity takers. See Box 6.1 for an example.)

TABLE 6.2 Order Book for Exchanges L and N

Offers are in gray boxes; bids are in white boxes. Quote sizes are indicated in each column under L and N and NBBOs have boldface quote sizes.

Prior to ISO Placement		
Bids/Offers	**L**	**N**
$10.02	100	
$10.01		**100**
$10.00	**100**	**100**
After Sending Buy 100 @ $10.01 ISO to Both L and N		
Bids/Offers	**L**	**N**
$10.02	**100**	
$10.01	**100**	
$10.00	100	100

Box 6.1: Why does BATS' BZX exchange *charge* fees for adding liquidity?

The concept that a trader will earn a rebate for adding (making) liquidity, and will be charged a fee for taking liquidity (the "maker/taker" model), is familiar. For example, BATS' BYX exchange pays a rebate of 0.18 cents per share (also called 1.8 *mils*) for adding liquidity (placing a limit order on its order book that is not immediately executable and is executed later against an incoming marketable order), and charges 0.15 cents per share for taking liquidity (sending an order to it that is immediately executed against a resting order). However, BATS' BZX exchange does the opposite: It charges a fee of 0.20 cents for adding liquidity, and pays a rebate of 0.30 cents for taking liquidity (see www.batstrading.com/support/fee_schedule). This seems bizarre at first sight, but the reason for sending a limit order to BZX is to gain head-of-queue priority for execution, though obviously not for rebate-earning purpose. It is for those mean-reversion traders that are able to earn liquidity-providing profits through other means (such as the many mean-reversion trading models I described in this and my previous books). By charging a fee, this exchange essentially discourages those HFT rebate-seekers from getting in front of us old-fashioned statistical arbitrageurs. It relieves us from engaging in such high-tech weaponry as using hide-not-slide orders or ISO, which are typically not available to traders without prime broker sponsored direct access to trade on exchanges. For another explanation, see Hasbrouck (2014).

Taking Liquidity

When we are the informed traders, we want our orders to execute quickly, lest other informed traders executed ahead of us and drive prices away. A good old-fashioned market order would seem to fit our need here. However, the market order has one problem—it will have to be routed to the exchange with the NBBO. As we saw above, an uncertain fate meets our order once it arrives there: The NBBO might not actually be the best price available in the market. If we have a direct market data feed, we may know better where to send our order. But we still need to ensure that the exchange to which we send our order will not be obligated (as a result of the Order

Protection Rule) to reroute it to the exchange with the official, though not actual, NBBO. The best way to do this is to use the Intermarket Sweep Order we just discussed. There is one difference from our previous usage of the ISO—our limit price for a buy ISO order will be set higher than the best offer at the local exchange L, so that execution is immediate. ISOs are executed faster than non-ISOs even without routing, because the exchange to which the ISO is sent does not need to spend time checking the protected quotes of other exchanges before executing it.

Another circumstance where an ISO is warranted is when our order size is bigger than the NBBO size. If we didn't apply the ISO modifier, part of the order not filled by the top-of-book quote may be rerouted to another exchange that has the best price after the original NBBO quote is filled by our order. But again, any rerouting causes latency, and when the market is moving fast due to breaking news, prices may have changed adversely after our partial order arrives at the new exchange. Adding the ISO modifier will allow the order sent to the local exchange L to "walk" the book—that is, fill the entire order against quotes on L by sweeping several layers of the order book, without routing any part to the exchange with the official NBBO. In fact, if we have a large market order, and if we know the order books of several exchanges, we might send multiple ISOs to the individual exchanges simultaneously to take advantage of their instantaneous liquidity. In other words, ISO allows *parallel processing* instead of *sequential processing* of our large order, reducing the chance that HFT can sniff out our order trail and front-run us (see Example 6.1).

Example 6.1: How ISOs walk a book

Suppose we have only three exchanges, with their order books for a stock shown below (only bids are relevant for this example):

Order book for exchanges L, N1, and N2

Bids	L	N1	N2
$10.03		**100**	
$10.02	**100**		
$10.01		300	
$10.00	200		**100**

The "protected" quote sizes are in **boldface**. Note that N1 has the NBB. A trader sends "sell 300 limit $10.00 ISO" to L. In order to satisfy the Order Protection Rule, the trader needs to send separately to N1 a "sell 100 limit $10.00 ISO" to N1. The first ISO sent to L will then walk the book and sell 100 shares at $10.02 and 200 shares at $10.00. But this last trade could have been done at a better price of $10.01 on N1.

Does the Order Protection Rule require the exchange L to route a sell order of 200 shares to N1 after it executes the first 100 shares at $10.02? The answer is no: The 300 shares at $10.01 on N1 is not a protected quote, since it is not at the top of book on N1.

Does the Order Protection Rule require the trader to send an ISO to N2? The answer is also no: The protected quote at N2 does not have a *superior* price to the limit price of the first ISO, so no routing would be needed. As SEC Rule 300(30)(ii) says, "Simultaneously with the routing of the limit order identified as an intermarket sweep order, one or more additional limit orders, as necessary, are routed to execute against the full displayed size of any protected bid, in the case of a limit order to sell, ... , for the NMS stock with a price that is *superior* [emphasis added] to the limit price of the limit order identified as an intermarket sweep order. These additional routed orders also must be marked as intermarket sweep orders." (See Hasbrouck, 2014, p. 24.)

Suppose that after the ISO was sent, but before it was executed, N2's NBB was increased to $10.03. The trader still would not need to send an order to N2 immediately to satisfy the Order Protection Rule. As Wood, Upson, and McInish (2013), explained, "Execution of ISOs are based on the state of the market at order submission and are [sic] not impacted by changes in the market state during processing."

To ensure that our limit ISO will behave like a market order, and not end up as a resting limit order on the book if there is not enough liquidity on the book to execute against it, we can add the immediate-or-cancel (IOC) modifier to it. This way, the unexecuted part of the limit IOC will simply be canceled. As we will discuss in the section on "Adverse Selection," adding the an IOC modifier is generally a good way to prevent adverse selection against a limit order.

(An IOC modifier can be applied to a market order, too. In this case, the market order will similarly not be routed to the exchange with a protected quote that has a better price than the quotes at the local exchange. But it also won't be allowed to execute against quotes that are not NBBO at L. Instead, it will be cancelled after executing the portion that matches with an NBBO quote. See Exercise 6.2.)

Simply put, latency is bad for informed traders, rerouting causes latency, and using ISO can avoid rerouting. And apparently, because only professional traders use ISO, order flow (a concept to be discussed later in a separate section) generated by an ISO has more information content than order flow from ordinary market order (Chakravarty, Jain, Wood, and Upson, 2009).

While ISO sounds like a very useful way to get our order to the head-of-queue as described in the subsection "Adding Liquidity," or to quickly capture liquidity as described in this subsection, it may have some unpleasant side effects. It has been blamed as a cause of "flash crashes" or "mini flash crashes" (Golub, Keane, and Poon, 2012). The most famous flash crash occurred on May 6, 2010, but there have been many mini flash crashes in individual stocks both before and after that. One definition of a flash crash (assuming a downward crash in prices) is that the stock ticks down at least 10 times, and this ticking down happens within 1.5 seconds, and the price change exceeds −0.8 percent. (A symmetrical definition applies to an up crash.) One can see that an ISO can cause such crashes, since it is allowed to walk the book at an exchange despite the possible existence of better quotes elsewhere. Those better quotes are not "protected" by the Order Protection Rule, since they are not the BBO at that exchange, and there is no need for any order to be routed to them. But a large but ordinary market order can also walk the book, except that a small portion of it will be routed by the local exchange to the exchange with the NBBO. So it is not clear *a priori* whether ISOs or market orders are the cause of flash crashes. Only after a careful examination by Golub, Keane, and Poon (2012), have they determined that fully 71.49 percent of them are caused by ISO.

Routing to Dark Pools

Dark pools are market centers that do not display any of their quotes—traders can submit *hidden* orders to them. But just like any market center, they do have to report their trades after execution.[8] There are over 40 dark pools for stocks in the United States. Examples of dark pools are Goldman Sachs's Sigma X, ITG's POSIT, and formerly IEX.[9] Not all hidden orders reside on dark pools—they can reside on any of the 11 or so exchanges discussed above. But an order sent to a dark pool is unique in that it will usually be executed at the midprice within the NBBO, and thus only the side (buy or sell) and size but not limit price are attached to such an order. On some dark pools, traders can agree to pay a premium above/below midprice for priority executions (see Nimalendran and Ray, 2011), and on others, traders can specify "price protection." Price protection specifies the worst price at which an order can get executed. When an order arrives at a dark pool, and there is no unexecuted (resting) order on the opposite side, the order will rest in the pool, undisplayed. (Similarly, if the aggregate resting order is smaller in size than the incoming order, the unexecuted part of the incoming order will rest in the pool.) Whenever an opposite order arrives, part or all of the unexecuted resting orders will get filled at the NBBO midprice. A typical dark pool will allocate these fills on a pro rata basis, not on a time priority basis (Hasbrouck, 2015). For example, if trader A has a buy order for 1,000 shares resting on the dark pool, and trader B has a buy order for 2,000 shares resting, and there is an incoming sell order of 1,500 shares, then 500 shares of A's order and 1,000 shares of B's order will be filled.

If we are an informed trader (in the special sense that we have been using), there is a big advantage in sending an order to a dark pool instead of sending a market order, or a limit IOC order, to a lit market. The first reason is obvious: The execution at a dark pool will save us half the NBBO spread compared to a market order. The second reason is also easy to understand. If we send a large market order to an exchange, it is likely to walk the book and the average execution price won't be the NBBO. But if we send it to the dark pool, we may just need to wait for a short time before our order is completely filled, and there is a chance that the NBBO midprice won't move adversely against us over that short period. The third and most important reason for sending our order to the dark pool is that, as we shall see below, market orders carry information, and this information is captured by the "order flow" measure that we will discuss in the section on "Order Flow." If we plan to send more orders on the same side, this order flow information will cause other traders to front-run our subsequent orders. If our order is executed in a dark pool, no order flow is generated because there is no "aggressor" side to the trade.

However, there are reasons to avoid dark pools, too. The most problematic is that the NBBO midprice can be front-run or manipulated so that executions in the dark pool are disadvantaged.

Front-running the NBBO midprice is a form of latency arbitrage. Recall that NBBO is determined by the slow SIP market feed. Hence, a trader subscribing to fast direct feeds from the exchanges knows where the NBBO midprice will be in the next millisecond or two. If that midprice will go higher, the trader just needs to send a buy order to the dark pool now and then send a sell order later once the new official NBBO is established. It is true that many dark pools no longer use the official NBBO midprice as their matching price. Instead, they also subscribe to the direct feeds of various exchanges to determine the actual NBBO. However, they are apparently still some *micro*seconds behind some high-frequency traders. This is the reason why the former dark pool IEX was established to much fanfare (Lewis, 2014). It has introduced a 350-microsecond delay between order submission and execution, so that it has the time to update to the latest actual NBBO before allowing an order to match at that midprice (Aisen, 2015).

Manipulating the midprice is an altogether more nefarious activity. A trader S sends a small buy limit order to an exchange to increase the NBB, and thus, the midprice. S then sends a large sell order to the dark pool for execution at this raised midprice. S next cancels the buy limit order at the exchange, and sends a small sell limit order to that exchange to decrease the NBO. S sends a buy order to the dark pool to cover its short position. Finally, S cancels its sell limit order at the exchange. Note that even if the small limit orders that S placed on the exchanges were filled before S got the chance to cancel them, no big harm was done, since they were small, and in that case S does not need to follow up with the large order to the dark pool. We call this trader "S" because this is considered *spoofing*, an illegal activity. But just because it is illegal doesn't mean it is not happening, and that other dark pool users won't be disadvantaged by it.

The two ways to game the dark pool midprice described are all done by third-party traders, through little or no fault of the dark pool itself. But some dark pools are actually complicit in taking advantage of the slower traders. They would, for example, reveal information on resting orders to their affiliated proprietary trading group (e.g., Pipeline, ITG; see Hasbrouck, 2015), or they would let high-frequency trading partners get access to such information (e.g., Barclays, Hasbrouck, 2015.) Such dark pools are only dark to the general public—they are brightly lit for insiders and partners! Some dark pools also allow their partners to submit a special order type which price-improves the NBBO midprice by less than a penny (e.g., UBS, Hasbrouck, 2015.) These partners who submit subpenny orders are likely to get filled first when they detect that the order flow is not informed (and where the order flow information comes from inside information on the dark pool order book). Naturally, all these gaming and information leaks introduce a high degree of market impact and adverse selection to large orders sent to these dark pools.

So in conclusion, is it recommended to route market orders to dark pools? The short answer is: You can always route them to dark pools that do not have such problems, which formerly would include IEX. Beyond IEX, you can quantitatively measure the degree of adverse selection (as will be discussed in the next section) for the dark pools that you are considering routing to, and route orders to dark pools with lowest adverse selection first (Saraiya and Mittal, 2009).[10] You can also add the IOC modifier to your order, so that it won't be subject to adverse selection. This means that if there is not enough liquidity resting on the opposite side of the order book on the dark pool, the unexecuted part of your order will be cancelled. Finally, if your order isn't that large, my personal experience is that routing to any dark pool often beats sending a market order and letting your broker route it to the NBBO.

Adverse Selection Reduction

Sometimes we have a buy limit order on the book, but we never manage to get it filled because no one hits our bid. A little later, the best bid goes above ours, making our purchase further out of reach. We incur opportunity cost. Other times, our buy limit order does get filled quickly, but right after our purchase, the BBO goes lower, generating (unrealized) loss for us. If these two situations happen often, then we are suffering from adverse selection in that market.

Adverse selection happens when prices on average go down after we buy something, and go up when we sell something. This happens because the traders on the other side of our trade (the "aggressors") are *informed* ones—they possess information or models that are good at short-term prediction of prices.

Who, then, would be the *uninformed* traders? There is a saying: "If you can't spot the sucker at the poker table, it's probably you." If we are running a rebate-earning or market-making strategy, we would be the uninformed traders, since our only model is to buy when prices are cheap, no matter why they are cheap. If we are running a large mutual fund, and suffer some redemption requests from our retail customers, we may need to sell some holdings to raise cash. In that case, we would also be the uninformed traders—we are selling because of our immediate liquidity need, not because we know where the prices will go. (See the section on "Mutual Funds Asset Fire Sale and Forced Purchases" in Chan, 2013, and also Harris, 2003, for a general discussion of informed versus liquidity traders.) Adverse selection can be measured quite accurately by computing the difference between the P&L of unfilled orders and the P&L of filled orders over a short time frame from 1 second to 30 minutes (Saraiya and Mittal, 2009). As we will discuss in the section on "Order Flow," market orders generate order flow, and market orders from highly informed traders generate "toxic" order flow (Easley, Lopez de Prado, and O'Hara, 2012). It is toxic to market makers and mean-reversion traders because of adverse selection.

Adverse selection only affects orders that are resting on the order book—in other words, it only affects the passive orders that provide liquidity. Such passive orders include limit orders and market orders sent to dark pools that are not immediately executable. If we are the informed traders, we would be sending market orders to the lit exchanges so that our information does not get stale, and of course such market orders always get filled immediately. Whether the trade turns out to be profitable or not, it is not the fault of the counterparty—it is the fault of our own price prediction model. The counterparty is not selectively filling our unprofitable market orders. Sending limit IOC orders to the lit exchanges, or market IOC orders to the dark pools will also protect us from adverse selection. Either way, the order will not rest on the order book and cannot be adversely selected against. Limit and market IOC orders take, not make, liquidity.

As we mentioned in the section on "Latency Reduction" and that on "Adding Liquidity," if our strategy does involve providing liquidity, then we should at least make sure that our orders are at the head of the queue in execution priority. This way, we will hopefully benefit from exchange rebates or other forms of market-making profits more often in order to offset the losses inflicted by toxic flow. Lower-order submission and confirmation latency, and using special order types such as hide-and-light and ISO, also help.

Most of what we have discussed applies generally to US stock and futures markets. (Some of them may apply to the US stock options markets, too.) It also applies to currency markets, with one notable exception.

Currency markets are even more fragmented than the US stock market. There is no consolidated order book, no routing, and no Reg NMS to encourage best executions. Anybody (at least anybody outside of CFTC and other national regulators' jurisdiction) can start an FX brokerage and run their own currency market. Liquidity (i.e., orders that sit on the book) is often provided not by other buy-side traders, but by large banks or hedge funds, and all manner of mark-ups can be applied as the brokerage see fit. In other words, the spot currency market is an over-the-counter market, not an exchange-based market. Despite all this opaqueness, the spot currency market is still the most liquid market, and often has narrower bid-ask spreads in percentage terms than even currency futures which are traded on exchanges.

There is one feature in the spot currency market, however, that is particularly troublesome to traders. This is the "last look" feature. *Last look* means that some of the quotes we see on the order book are not firm: Market makers (often called "LP" for liquidity provider, or liquidity partner, in the industry) can simply not honor the quotes after they have received our marketable orders. They have many milliseconds to check whether the quotes they pose on different market centers are all being hit in the same direction simultaneously, and decide what, if any, fraction of these quotes to honor. This may sound reasonable: Because the currency market is not consolidated, not even virtually as for the US stock market, the LP has no choice but to post quotes on many different market centers. But if all these quotes were filled, the LP will end up with a large unbalanced position, and such positions pose significant risks.

In addition to avoiding getting hit on multiple markets simultaneously, LPs can also use the last look period to check if the BBO changes significantly across all these markets. If so, this would indicate a large informed trader is on the other side of the trade, and they would decline to fill this order to avoid adverse selection. Unfortunately, this act of avoiding adverse selection on the part of the LP *induces* adverse selection for the buy-side traders. If market makers can pick and choose when to fill our market orders or marketable limit IOC orders, then there is no doubt that our orders will suffer from adverse selection.

I was a victim of last look on one occasion. Our team backtested a fairly high-frequency strategy based on order flow (similar to the one discussed in the section on "Order Flow"). It was very profitable not only in backtest, but also in live walk-forward test using HotspotFX's UAT (user acceptance testing) account. This account uses real-time quotes from the real HotspotFX order book for simulation. However, when we started trading in a production account, our strategy was devastated. Why? Our market orders that got filled were unprofitable, and the ones that got rejected due to last look were the ones that turned out to be profitable—a classic symptom of adverse selection. It is true that we can request last look to be turned off for the quotes presented to us. But once we did that, the BBO spread widened considerably, and the strategy was still unprofitable despite the absence of last look.

It is important to note that last look induces adverse selection on market or limit IOC orders, but has no effect on limit orders that we place on the order book. This is quite in contrast to adverse selection in the stock or futures markets, which affects limit orders on the book but not market or limit IOC orders. Hence, last look only adversely affects FX momentum strategies, but not mean-reverting or market-making strategies.

As my experience above shows, the presence of last look also presents a problem for backtesting or even walk-forward-testing FX momentum strategies: One can never be sure which one of our orders will actually get filled. So accuracy of such backtests or forward tests is questionable.

Fortunately, not every FX market center has the last look feature (e.g., LMAX does not have last look), and even for those market centers that do have this feature (e.g., HotspotFX and FXall), there is an effort underway to tighten constraints on its use (Albanese, 2015). They may shorten the period where last look can take place, and they can set minimum acceptance rates for liquidity partners (i.e., they cannot reject too many orders based on last look).

Backtesting Intraday Strategies

To properly backtest intraday strategies that use market orders, we have to at least use NBBO (or BBO, in the case of instruments such as futures that trade on a single market center) data sampled at whatever frequency is appropriate to our strategies. This is because liquidity can vary greatly intraday,[11] and so can execution cost. It is quite inaccurate to backtest an intraday strategy by assuming half an average bid-ask spread as execution cost.

When backtesting US stocks strategies, even such top-of-book data are not sufficient for reasons that we have touched on before: thin NBBO liquidity means that our order size can easily be bigger than the NBBO size, so it will have to walk the book at the local exchange, or parts of it will have to be rerouted to another exchange. This means a true backtest requires at least level 2 quotes. But even level 2 quotes won't be able to accurately reflect the actual route that our order, or pieces of it, will take across the 60+ market centers, and what prices it will execute against during its excellent adventure.

(Why does even a stock like AAPL have a typical NBBO size of 189 shares, as mentioned in the introduction? Those may be "sniffer" orders placed by high-frequency traders to gauge market demand, or to gauge the quantity of hidden orders inside the NBBO, or to earn liquidity rebates by always standing at the head-of-queue using hide-and-light orders or ISOs. In any case, due to the fear of adverse selection by large informed traders, nobody wants to post a large order at the NBBO. In fact, these small orders may be a way to detect the toxic flow that induces adverse selection, so that the high-frequency traders can trade in the same direction!)

Even more difficult is to backtest a mean-reverting or market-making strategy that uses limit orders. A static snapshot of the order book(s) will not tell us whether our limit order will be filled, because we don't know what priority we have in the queue. One has to use the stream of historical order book messages such as the aforementioned Nasdaq ITCH data[12] that allows us to reconstruct the history of the order book. HotspotFX also provides an ITCH feed for its currency market. These messages include events such as a limit order addition (only for displayed orders), execution[13] (in full or in part, for displayed or hidden orders), cancellation, and the associated ticker, price, size, side, the unique market participant ID, the unique order ID (only for displayed orders), and, of course, the time stamp in millisecond or higher frequencies.[14] Incoming market orders are not recorded by these messages, but their interactions with the order book can be inferred from the executions of the limit orders. These ITCH messages are available to subscribers during live trading. But missing from them are the modifiers, so we still won't know if an order will get ahead of us in queue priority because it is a hide-and-light order, or an ISO. Naturally, backtesting a strategy using these messages is not a simple task, but there are platforms such as Lime Brokerage's Strategy Studio that incorporate a fill simulator for limit orders, and many high-frequency trading firms as well as brokers have built advanced simulators for their internal or customers' use.[15] (Sometimes an exchange or a data vendor will only provide us with historical ITCH messages but not the BBO quotes for our backtest. In this case, we will have to construct the BBO ourselves using these messages. Example 6.2 shows you how.)

Example 6.2: Constructing the BBO using ITCH messages

This coding example shows how one can find out the BBO of an order book at every instant by processing a time series of messages similar to the ITCH messages from Nasdaq or HotspotFX. However, I do not have samples of Nasdaq or HotspotFX ITCH messages—I only have samples of bitcoin (see Chapter 7) messages from the Coinsetter exchange. But the algorithm for constructing the order book is, of course, the same no matter what the actual traded instrument is.

The Coinsetter messages have five important fields that describe an event: ExchangeTime (in nanoseconds based on UTC time), Side (BUY or SELL), Level (i.e., order price), EventAmount (i.e., order size), InformationType (one of "WORKING_CONFIRMED," which means order addition, "CANCELED_CONFIRMED," "FILL_CONFIRMED," "PARTIAL_FILL_CONFIRMED"). One way to simulate an order book is to use the binary search tree data structure, implemented in MATLAB as part of a free Data Structures package by Brian Moore (www.mathworks.com/matlabcentral/fileexchange/45123-data-structures). One binary search tree will keep us updated as to which bid (active, not filled, or cancelled) has the highest price (best bid), and another tree will similarly handle the offers, amidst all the additions, cancellations, fills, and partial fills events. So actually, the order book is split into two independent halves: the *buyOrderBook* and the *sellOrderBook*.

To initialize the binary search trees, a.k.a. order book, we add the first orders:

```
assert(strcmp(action(1), 'WORKING_CONFIRMED'));
if (strcmp(side(1), 'BUY'))
    bid(1)=price(1);
    bidSize(1)=orderSize(1);
    buyOrderBook.Insert(price(1), bidSize(1));
elseif (strcmp(side(1), 'SELL'))
    ask(1)=price(1);
    askSize(1)=orderSize(1);
    sellOrderBook.Insert(price(1), askSize(1));
end
```

The bid(1) (ask(1)) represents the best bid (offer) at the time of the first event. Note that the arrays bid and ask are indexed by events, not by regular time intervals. These are truly "tick" data.

Then we need to process the subsequent events sequentially in a for-loop, assuming they appear in chronological order. For example, if we add a buy order, we need to find out if its price is better than the current best bid. If so, we reset the best bid, and its size, and insert that bid into the buyOrderBook. If its price is the same as the current best bid, we merely increase the best bid size, and update the bid size in the buyOrderBook (a delete followed by an insert). If its price is inferior to the current best bid, then we will just insert it into the buyOrderBook, and copy forward the current best bid. The following code fragment illustrates this:

```
if (strcmp(action(t), 'WORKING_CONFIRMED'))
    if (strcmp(side(t), 'BUY'))
        if (price(t) > bid(t-1) || isnan(bid(t-1)))
            bid(t)=price(t);
            bidSize(t)=orderSize(t);
            buyOrderBook.Insert(price(t), bidSize(t));
        elseif (price(t) == bid(t-1))
            bid(t)=bid(t-1);
            bidSize(t)=bidSize(t-1)+orderSize(t);
            buyOrderBook.Delete(buyOrderBook.Search(price(t)));
            buyOrderBook.Insert(price(t), bidSize(t));
        else
            bid(t)=bid(t-1);
            bidSize(t)=bidSize(t-1);
            buyOrderBook.Insert(price(t), orderSize(t));
        end
        ask(t)=ask(t-1);
        askSize(t)=askSize(t-1);
    end
end
```


If there is a buy order cancellation or a fill (full or partial), we need to see if that order is the best bid. If so, we need to find out what the next best bid is from the buyOrderBook and update the best bid. Otherwise, we just copy forward the current best bid, and delete that order from the order book or update its size.

```
if (strcmp(action(t), 'CANCEL_CONFIRMED') || strcmp(action(t),
  'FILL_CONFIRMED') || strcmp(action(t), 'PARTIAL_FILL_
    CONFIRMED') )
    if (strcmp(side(t), 'BUY'))
        if (price(t) == bid(t-1))
            if (orderSize(t) < bidSize(t-1))
                bid(t)=bid(t-1);
                bidSize(t)=bidSize(t-1)-orderSize(t);
                buyOrderBook.Delete(buyOrderBook.Search
                  (price(t)));
                buyOrderBook.Insert(price(t), bidSize(t));
```

```
            else
                assert(orderSize(t)==bidSize(t-1));
                buyOrderBook.Delete(buyOrderBook.Search
                   (price(t)));
                if (~buyOrderBook.IsEmpty)
                    T=buyOrderBook.Maximum();
                    bid(t)=T.key;
                    bidSize(t)=T.value;
                end
            end
        elseif (price(t) < bid(t-1))
            bid(t)=bid(t-1);
            bidSize(t)=bidSize(t-1);

            T=buyOrderBook.Search(price(t));
            if (~isnan(T)) % Some trades are wrong
                if (orderSize(t) == T.value)
                    buyOrderBook.Delete(T);
                else
                    %                               assert(orderSize(t)
                       < T.value);
                    if (orderSize(t) > T.value)
                        fprintf(1, 'Trade size %i > bid size
                            %i!\n', orderSize(t), T.value);
                    end
                    buyOrderBook.Delete(T);
                    buyOrderBook.Insert(price(t), T.value -
                        orderSize(t));
                end
            end
        end
    end
end
```

Naturally, a symmetrical process occurs for sell orders events. The complete code can be downloaded as buildOrderBook.m.

For those of us who may not have the time to build such sophisticated backtesting platforms for ourselves or the resources to rent them, we can at least backtest strategies that can be executed with market orders and still remain profitable. (See Chapter 1 for commercially available backtesting platforms.) We will demonstrate in Example 6.3 how we can backtest an intraday futures strategy using MATLAB with BBO data sampled at 25 ms. But the essential difference between backtesting using BBO bar data (whether it is daily, minute, 25 ms, or 1 ms bars) and *tick* data is that bar data have prices for every bar while tick data, even if they are sampled at regular intervals, may show prices at irregular intervals in the historical file. If the instruments' quote price changes more frequently than the frequency of the time stamps, we may also find multiple ticks to have the same time stamp. One can, of course, create bars from tick data, but if quotes change infrequently, we would be utilizing both CPU and memory very inefficiently when backtesting. Hence, backtesting algorithms (such as that in Example 6.3) that are designed specifically to handle prices with irregular time stamps are needed.

Where can we find intraday data that are suitable for backtesting intraday strategies? We already mentioned the ITCH data, but that captures only stock tick data from Nasdaq and is quite expensive to obtain unless you are an academic researcher. NYSE will also sell you the consolidated trades and quotes (TAQ) data[16] reported to the SIP. There are also many third-party vendors that will sell you high frequency data for stocks, futures, and options. However, not all high frequency data are of equal quality. For example, CQG Data Factory's TAQ data are time-stamped only at one minute, and we have no idea whether the ticks in a block of quotes with the same time stamp are in chronological order. Furthermore, I have verified that they miss a number of trade ticks in their ES futures data files. Similarly, Algoseek's 1-millisecond TAQ data available for *rent* through QuantGo.com misses many end-of-day auction prices even for AAPL. (They are also missing data on some days for some important futures contracts such as CL, even for front months.) Importantly, one may need such high-frequency data even if one wants to backtest interday strategies accurately, and such missing ticks cause inaccuracies for such interday backtests as well (see Box 6.2).

Box 6.2: Beware of Low Frequency Data

(Part of this section is taken from a talk I gave at QuantCon 2015 and published on my blog as epchan.blogspot.com/2015/04/beware-of-low-frequency-data.html.)

One may think that the TAQ tick data I mentioned in this chapter is important only for backtesting intraday strategies. But even when we are backtesting stock strategies that only trade at the market open or close, the usual consolidated daily historical data that most data vendors (e.g., csidata.com, Quandl.com) provide will induce substantial noise, and may dangerously inflate backtest performance, especially for mean-reverting strategies.

Consolidated daily data come from the trades recorded on the SIP feed. Since the SIP feed captures trades from more than 60 stock market centers in the United States, the "opening" or the "closing" trade can come from any of these places quite by chance. (For example, the open price may come from whichever market center happens to have the first trade at or just after 9:30 a.m. ET, and the close price may come from whichever market center that has the last trade at or just before 4:00 p.m. ET.) These trades may be the result of an execution of a mere hundred shares, and their prices can be quite different from the prices based on the open or close auctions at the primary exchange for these stocks. A primary exchange of a stock is the exchange where the stock is listed. For example, AAPL is listed on the Nasdaq, and IBM is listed on the NYSE. What's special about the primary exchange of a stock is that whenever we send a Market-on-Open (MOO), Limit-on-Open (LOO), Market-on-Close (MOC), or Limit-on-Close (LOC) order to our broker, it will be routed to the primary exchange to participate in the auction there. Every exchange runs an auction on every stock, but only the auction at the primary exchange of a stock has significant volume due to all these routings. So the price we will get for our MOO/LOO/MOC/LOC orders is the primary exchange auction price, not the consolidated open or close price that we see from the typical data vendor. The consolidated open or close prices are not the most accurate for backtesting purposes.

How big are their differences? On April 27, 2010, for example, AAPL's primary exchange auction closing price is $262.26, while the consolidated closing price is $262.04, an 8 bps difference. This may seem small, but remember that this difference is essentially uncorrelated white noise—its sign fluctuates from day to day randomly. Hence, if we invent a mean-reverting strategy that buys whenever the consolidated close is lower than the primary exchange close, and short when it is the opposite, then we will be picking up these 8 bps differences regularly, generating a significant but fictitious excess return in backtest. This excess return is fictitious because we can't really guarantee execution at the consolidated price.

Where can we find the historical primary exchange open/close prices? Bloomberg provides that, but is expensive. Here is where the TAQ data come in handy. We can rent such tick data quite cheaply (certainly cheaper than a Bloomberg subscription) from Algoseek through QuantGo.com. These TAQ data time-stamped at 1 ms come with a special flag ("Cross") that indicates a trade participated in the opening/closing auction, and if we select only those Cross trades that took place on the primary exchange, we will theoretically know the primary exchange open/close prices for our backtest. However, as mentioned in the main text, Algoseek sometimes misses many ticks in their data. For example, on October 28, 2014, they are missing all the AAPL trades that occurred on Nasdaq at the close, and thus we can't figure out what the primary exchange close price was!

Another data provider, Nanex, provides only the top 10 layers of the order book (which isn't too much of a problem), and with only 25 ms time stamps, which isn't a problem here because the ticks are in chronological order as they are stored in a tape format. But the main problem is that because their data are stored in a tape format, it takes quite a bit of programming to extract them. Tickdata.com (now part of onemarketdata.com) sells only BBO quotes (and trades), so we can't really backtest orders larger than the BBO quote size (though they do have 1 ms time stamps). Kibot.com also sell tick data at a reasonable price, but they do not report quote sizes, nor do they provide the aggressor tags for futures trades. As we shall see in the section on "Order Flow," such tags are very handy for determining order flow. (When backtesting futures strategies you may find that some quotes are marked "implied". These are legitimate quotes that can be traded on. See Box 6.3 for a detailed explanation.)

Box 6.3: Calendar spread quotes data

When backtesting futures strategies using BBO data, one often see quotes that are marked "implied." These are quotes are that are "implied-out" by limit orders on calendar spreads, and they can be executed against any market orders. To understand how a calendar spread limit order can imply a quote on the outright contract, we use an example taken from Aikin (2012).

Let's say we have the following state (Table 6.3) of the BBO for the outright market for the Eurodollar futures ED, for the contract months March 2002 (H2) and June 2002 (M2). The numbers in parentheses are the quote sizes (number of contracts).

TABLE 6.3	BBO for Outright Market for ED		
	H2	M2	H2M2
Offer	98.79 (100)	98.56 (100)	0.24 (100)
Bid	98.78 (100)	98.55 (100)	0.22 (100)

Note that we have included the "implied-in" prices of the calendar spread H2M2 (meaning long 1 H2 contract and short 1 M2 contract, or H2-M2) in the last column. These are the limit prices for the calendar spread implied by the outright limit prices. Hence, the best offer for H2M2 is 98.79 − 98.55 = 0.24, and the best bid is 98.78 − 98.56 = 0.22. The sizes of the implied-in quotes are 100 by 100. Now, suppose a trader places a limit order to buy 50 contracts of H2M2 at 0.23, which is the midprice between the H2M2 BBO shown in Table 6.3. This will update the outright BBO, as shown in Table 6.4.

TABLE 6.4	BBO for Outright Market after Adding New Calendar Spread Limit Order		
	H2	M2	H2M2
Offer	98.79 (100)	98.56 (**150**)	0.24 (100)
Bid	98.78 (**150**)	98.55 (100)	0.23 (50)

Note that the implied-out BBO prices have not changed, but the sizes (in **bold**) have (Aikin, 2015). If there is an incoming market order to sell 50 contracts of H2, the buy calendar spread order will be filled—it has higher priority in the queue than outrights. This outright market order will let the original calendar spread order buy 50 H2 contracts at 98.78, and it will trigger an execution of the outright buy limit order for M2 at 98.55 so that the calendar spread order can sell 50 contracts. Similarly, if there is an incoming market order to buy 50 contracts of M2, the buy calendar spread order will also be filled. This implied-in and implied-out pricing is highly advantageous for both market taker and maker, since it improves the quote size for the market taker, and it allows the market maker's calendar spread order to get filled with a market order on just one leg. So if you are backtesting futures strategies, make sure the data vendor has included implied-out quotes. For further information, see Aikin (2012) or www.cmegroup.com/confluence/display/EPICSANDBOX/Implied+Orders.

Order Flow

Order flow is *signed* transaction volume: If a transaction of size s is the result of a buy market order,[17] the order flow is $+s$; if it is the result of a sell market order, the order flow is $-s$. Order flow is typically aggregated over a period of time and over many transactions in that period to create a more robust measure. Researchers have long known that order flow is positively correlated with future price change (see Lyons, 2001, or Cartea, Jaimungal, and Penalva, 2015). This makes intuitive sense: On average, traders using market orders are more likely to possess superior information since they are apparently so sure of the future price change that they are willing to pay the bid-ask spread to get into position quickly. In contrast, market makers do not usually know which way the market will move, and they are content to place a limit order passively on the order book, hoping to profit from the bid-ask spread. If we can determine the order flow at the moment, we can join the bandwagon of the aggressive, informed traders and enter trades in the same direction as well.

The only hitch in this beautiful strategy is that most data feeds don't tell you whether a trade is due to a buy or sell market order. Only data feeds such as the Nasdaq or HotspotFX's ITCH feeds contain all the limit order messages (as discussed in the previous section) necessary to compute order flow. (In the case of HotspotFX, order flow lags by a second or so.) These low-latency direct feeds enable us to determine whether the disappearance of a buy (sell) limit order was due to cancellation or execution. If it was an execution, we can infer that it was hit with a sell (buy) market order, which contributed to the negative (positive) order flow. Another example of a direct data feed from an exchange that contains such detailed information is CME's MDP Market Data, which contains a tag for each trade that is called the "aggressor" tag. For example, Tag 5797-AggressorSide indicates a buy when its value is 1, and a sell when its value is 2 (CME, 2015). As we shall see in Chapter 7, some bitcoin exchanges also provide either the ITCH messages or aggressor flags.

For those of us who do not have subscriptions to such potentially pricey direct feeds, researchers have developed methods to estimate order flow using only price and volume. There is the *tick rule,* where a trade that transacts at a price higher than the previous trade generates a "buy" (positive order flow), and vice versa for a "sell" (if the trade price is the same as the previous one, the order flow is assigned the same sign as that of the previous trade). There is the *quote rule,* where a trade that transacts at a price higher than the midprice is considered a buy, and vice versa for a sell (it generates zero order flow if the trade occurs at the midprice). There is also the Lee-Ready algorithm that uses the quote rule for trades away from midprice, and the tick rule for trades at the midprice. More recently, there is a technique called *bulk volume classification* (Easley, Lopez de Prado, and O'Hara, 2015) that demonstrates how one can use price change and volume per bar instead of per trade to determine order flow. (See Box 6.4 for an explanation.) Using bulk volume classification (BVC) obviates the need for a tick data feed, and is therefore much less data intensive to either backtest or live-trade a strategy that uses order flow.

All these methods involve a certain amount of guess work and statistics, and are therefore not as accurate as having direct data feeds. Applying the tick rule or Lee-Ready algorithm to the US stock markets is especially inaccurate because of the presence of nondisplayed orders both on exchanges and dark pools, which together account for more than one-third of all executions. As you may recall, most dark pool executions happen at midprices and generate no order flow. For executions on lit exchanges against hidden orders, we would not know whether the hidden orders were buy or sell orders, so order flow cannot be computed, either. The CME is a bit more transparent in this regard: An order must display at least part of its total quantity (the so-called *iceberg* order). Despite such inaccuracies, we will demonstrate a trading strategy in Example 6.3 based on estimated order flow on the E-mini S&P 500 index futures on CME Globex. We will compare the performance of the strategy using order flow computed exactly from the exchange-provided aggressor tags and order flow estimated using BVC with volume bars.

Box 6.4: Determining order flow using bulk volume classification (BVC)

Bulk volume classification is a method of estimating order flow using only bar data with volume and trade prices, instead of tick data for every trade. This makes order flow computation much less computationally intensive, with the added advantage that executions due to hidden orders will be included in the calculation.

The bar data used in BVC can be the usual fixed-time bars, or fixed-volume bars. Volume bars have variable time durations, but each has the same volume (number of shares or contracts executed). Log returns on volume bars are found to have a more Gaussian distribution, and as the BVC formula assumes Gaussian distribution of log returns, volume bars instead of time bars are the preferred input.

It is quite easy to turn trade tick data (or time bars) into volume bars, so we will assume that our input is volume bars.

If the fixed volume of a bar is V, ΔP is the price change from one bar to the next, and $\sigma_{\Delta P}$ is the standard deviation of ΔP, then the "buy" order flow is just

$$V \cdot Z\left(\frac{\Delta P}{\sigma_{\Delta P}}\right), \tag{6.1}$$

where Z is the cumulative distribution function (CDF) of the Gaussian distribution with zero mean and unit variance. (See Figure 6.1 for a plot of Z.) As you can tell from Figure 6.1, the buy order flow will be equal to V if price change is very large and positive (compared to its standard deviation), and it will be equal to 0 if it is very negative. The "sell" order flow is just $-V \cdot \left[1 - Z\left(\frac{\Delta P}{\sigma_{\Delta P}}\right)\right]$, and the net order flow is thus $V \cdot \left[2Z\left(\frac{\Delta P}{\sigma_{\Delta P}}\right) - 1\right]$. The net order flow will be equal to V if price change is very large and positive, and it will be equal to $-V$ if it is very negative.

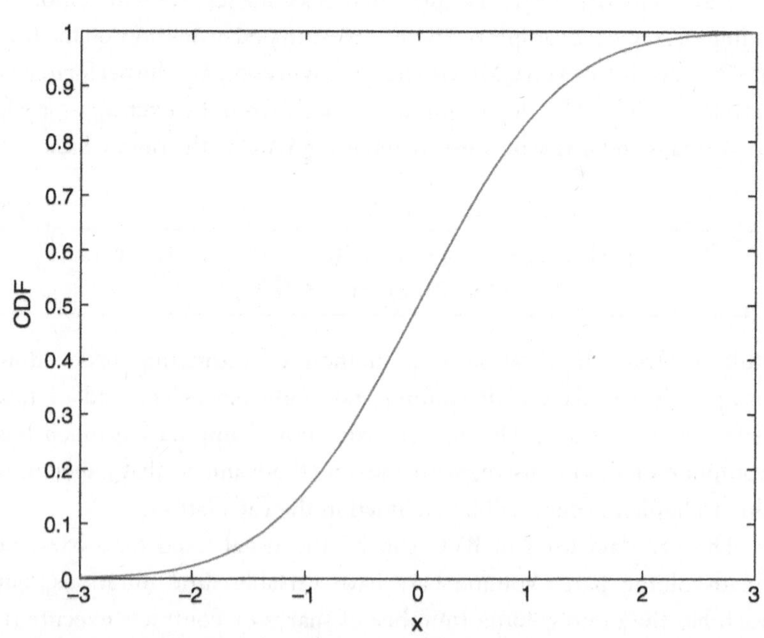

FIGURE 6.1 Z (CDF of a Gaussian with zero mean and unit variance)

The trading strategy is in principle very simple. If we are using aggressor tags for order flow, then we can compute exactly the order flow due to every trade tick within the past minute. If we are using the BVC method, then we will use a fixed number of past volume bars to compute the order flow in that period. This means we will only trade when a volume bar completes, unlike the aggressor tag method, where we may trade whenever a new trade tick arrives. Either way, if this order flow is greater (smaller) than some threshold, we send out a buy (sell) market order. We will exit the resulting position, again using market orders, whenever the order flow is zero or has the opposite sign from the one triggering the entry. Naturally, both the entry threshold and the implicit exit threshold of zero, as well as the lookback period of one minute, should be optimized in-sample and tested out-of-sample.

Example 6.3: Order flow strategy

We use two different methods, aggressor tag and BVC, to compute order flow, and compare how well a trading strategy based on each fares.

The instrument we trade is the front contract of the E-mini S&P 500 futures (symbol: ES) on the CME Globex. Each point move in this contract is worth $50, with the minimum tick equal to 0.25 points ($12.50). It is traded from Sunday to Friday around the clock from 6 p.m. to 4:15 p.m. ET on the next day, and from 4:30 p.m. to 5 p.m. ET. In this example, we will just pick one day (October 1, 2012) of data for the contract ES.Z12 to illustrate the method.

For the aggressor tag method, data are from Algoseek, provided through QuantGo.com's platform,[18] and it is time-stamped at 1 ms. It consists of BBO quotes, as well as trades. The quote sizes are typically in the hundreds during the "regular" trading hours of 9:30 a.m. to 4:15 p.m. ET. The trade sizes, however, are typically far smaller—in the double or even single digits. Some days, the average trade size is under three contracts (Hunsader, 2015). There can, however, be many quote updates and trades within 1 ms. (One-third of ES's volume is due to high-frequency trading. See Clark-Joseph, 2013.) With the aggressor tag method, it is important to determine the BBO whenever a trade occurs. We have preprocessed the data and align the BBO and trades to appear in MATLAB arrays with the same number of rows. Schematically, they can be represented in tabular form, as shown in Table 6.5.

TABLE 6.5 Data Structure for Aggressor Tag Method

Datenum	Best Bid	Best Offer	Trade	Trade Size
735143.0000072338	1428.5	1428.75	1428.75	1
735143.0001270254	1428.5	1428.75	1428.75	25
735143.0002248264	1428.5	1428.75	1429	17
735143.0002251157	1428.5	1428.75	1429	11
735143.0002256945	1428.75	1429	1429	28
735143.0002271412	1428.75	1429	1429	3

The first column is the MATLAB serial date number of a tick, where the integer part represents the number of days since some arbitrary reference time.

Now that the data are properly aligned, we can use the aggressor tag to determine the order flow for each trade tick:

```
ordflow=zeros(size(price));
ordflow(strcmp(event, 'T') & strcmp(aggressor, 'B'))= quantity
  (strcmp(event, 'T') & strcmp(aggressor, 'B'));
ordflow(strcmp(event, 'T') & strcmp(aggressor, 'S'))=-quantity
  (strcmp(event, 'T') & strcmp(aggressor, 'S'));
```


As in all backtests using tick data, we need a for-loop that advances one trade at a time in this program in order to find out exactly which ticks are within one minute of the current trade tick. To do this, it is easiest to compute the cumulative sum of the order flow since the first tick, and then take the difference between the value one minute ago and now:

```
lookback=60; % 1 min
cumOrdflow=cumsum(ordflow);
for t=1:length(cumOrdflow)
   idx=find( dn <= dn(t)-lookback/60/60/24);

   if (~isempty(idx))
       ordflow_lookback=cumOrdflow(t)-cumOrdflow(idx(end));
   end
end
```

Now we are ready to apply the trading rule: buy if aggregate order flow is greater than a threshold, exit a long position if it is not positive, and vice versa for shorts. We also need to update the existing position (denoted *pos*), update the latest entry price (*entryP*) for P&L computation, and the daily P&L (*dailyPL*) itself. If the aggregate order flow is not positive enough to trigger a buy, and not negative enough to trigger a sell, we just need to update the daily P&L based on the midprice.

```
if (ordflow_lookback > entryThreshold)
    if ( pos <= 0)
        if (pos < 0)
            dailyPL=dailyPL+(entryP-ask(t)); % Aggressive
            entryP=ask(t); % Aggressive
        else
            entryP=ask(t); % Aggressive
        end
        pos=1;

    end
elseif (ordflow_lookback < -entryThreshold)
    if (pos >= 0)
        if (pos > 0)
           dailyPL=dailyPL+(bid(t)-entryP);
           entryP=bid(t);
        else
            entryP=bid(t);
        end
        pos=-1;

    end
else
    if (ordflow_lookback <= exitThreshold && pos > 0)
        dailyPL=dailyPL+(bid(t)-entryP);
        pos=0;
    elseif (ordflow_lookback >= -exitThreshold && pos < 0)
        dailyPL=dailyPL+(entryP-ask(t));
        pos=0;
    end
end
```

If we choose the *entryThreshold* to be 66 (which is roughly the 95th percentile of order flow for that day), we find that the daily P&L is $300 ($4 per trade). This assumes we are using market orders that cross the bid-ask spread. If we assume midprice executions instead, the daily P&L is $762.50 ($10.17 per trade). But this is an unrealistic assumption. We have not included the minimum exchange and clearing fee of $0.095 per contract. (If you are not a high frequency trader generating tremendous volume, this total fee is more typically $0.16 per contract. Interactive Brokers charges $2.47 per contract.) The complete code can be downloaded as aggressorTag_algoseek.m.

Note one defect in our aggressor tag trading algorithm: We make a trading decision only when we encounter a trade tick. What if the aggregate order flow in the past minute needs an update because some old trades fall out this lookback, but there is no new trade? In a proper backtest (just as in live trading), we need to update the order flow at the same frequency as our data, which is 1 ms.

For our volume bar tests, we use data from Nanex.net that are time-stamped at 25 ms. To generate the volume bars suitable for the BVC method, we first aggregate those trade ticks in Table 6.5 so that we have 500 contracts per bar. This number means that each volume bar will typically span a few 25 ms bars. (It is OK to have fewer than 500 contracts so that each 25 ms bar will span a few volume bars, but we then must be careful in aligning with the BBO quotes, which will all have the same time stamps but may, in fact, be ahead or behind the end of a volume bar. To ensure proper alignment, we would need to assume that the trades and quotes are sorted chronologically in the ticker stream.) After aligning with the BBO quotes, a few sample volume bars are shown in Table 6.6.

TABLE 6.6 Data Structure for Volume Bars

Datenum	Best Bid	Best Offer	Last Price
735143.0080653935	1428.25	1428.50	1428.50
735143.0162265626	1428	1428.25	1428
735143.0215283565	1428	1428.25	1428.25
735143.0384505208	1427.75	1428	1427.75
735143.0452291666	1428	1428.25	1428.25
735143.0512219329	1427.75	1429	1428.75

To determine the order flow, we need to compute the change in price ΔP in equation 6.1, denoted deltaPrice in the code below:

```
prevTradePrice=backshift(1, fillMissingData(lastPrice));
deltaPrice=lastPrice-prevTradePrice;
```

Then we use a 100 volume-bar lookback to determine the Gaussian CDF function Z. This lookback is a parameter that can be optimized in-sample. (Instead of normalizing ΔP by $\sigma_{\Delta P}$ as in equation 6.1, we can enter standard deviation as an additional parameter in the MATLAB cdf function.)

```
lookback=100; % Num bars used for stddev of volume-weighted
   price changes
buyVol=NaN(size(lastPrice)); % Buy volume as fraction of
   total volume
for t=lookback+1:length(buyVol)
    myDeltaPrice=deltaPrice(t-lookback:t-1);
    myDeltaPrice(~isfinite(myDeltaPrice))=[];
    buyVol(t)=cdf('Normal', deltaPrice(t), 0, std(myDeltaPrice));
end
```

We have computed *buyVol(t)* as the fraction of order flow due to buy orders. The fraction for sell orders is just 1 − *buyVol(t)*. Our trading rule is to buy whenever the fraction for buys is greater than 0.95, and we will exit a long position if the fraction falls below 0.5. The exact opposite holds for sells. Otherwise, the code is very similar to the one for the aggressor tag method:


```
entryThreshold=0.95;
exitThreshold =0.5;
for t=lookback+1:length(buyVol)

    if (buyVol(t) > entryThreshold)
        if ( pos <= 0)
            if (pos < 0)
                    dailyPL=dailyPL+(entryP-ask(t));
                      % Aggressive
                    entryP=ask(t);
            else
                    entryP=ask(t);
            end
            pos=1;

        end

    elseif (1-buyVol(t) > entryThreshold)
        if (pos >= 0)
```

```
                if (pos > 0)
                        dailyPL=dailyPL+(bid(t)-entryP);
                        entryP=bid(t);
                else
                        entryP=bid(t);
                end
                pos=-1;
            end
        else
            if ( buyVol(t) <= exitThreshold && pos > 0)
                dailyPL=dailyPL+(bid(t)-entryP);
                pos=0;
            elseif ( 1-buyVol(t) <= exitThreshold && pos < 0)
                dailyPL=dailyPL+(entryP-ask(t));
                pos=0;
            end

        end
    end
```

The daily P&L using BVC is −$3,975 (−$5.8 per trade), which is much worse than the aggressor tag strategy on a per trade basis. If we assume the unrealistic midprice executions, the daily P&L is $400 ($0.58 per trade), again worse than the aggressor tag strategy. The complete code can be downloaded as volumeBar.m.

Note a defect in our BVC trading algorithm (similar to the one for using the aggressor tag): We make a trading decision only when a volume bar ends. We should actually compute the past volume bars every 25 ms, and use those to make trading decisions.

The problem with the aggressor tag-based strategy is that even when there is no trade tick, we are still supposed to update our aggregated order flow calculation, because some older trades would have rolled out of our one-minute lookback window. Unfortunately, this update would make the code quite a bit more complicated as we have to record the "expiration time" of each trade and insert into our chronological trade sequence these expiration events. We omit this detail in Example 6.3. There is a similar problem with the BVC version of the strategy: we can only trade at the end of a volume bar, which creates unnecessary delays. In theory, if our tick data has 1 ms time stamps, we need to check for the one-minute order flow every 1 ms, even if this means creating a whole new series of volume bars. This of course is very computationally demanding.

Our example applied this strategy to only one day of ES data for illustration purpose. But even with this limited amount of data, some pertinent issues emerge. The strategy is not very profitable if we assume our orders have to cross the bid-ask spread to be filled, and highly profitable if we assume they can be filled at midprice. Since the strategy is trend-following (with the trend set by the sign of the order flow), there is an urgency in getting our orders filled, and therefore we must use market orders. So the not very profitable scenario is probably more realistic. However, hypothetically profitable executions at midprice tell us that changes in midprices do go in the same direction as past order flow, so the premise of the strategy is sound.

Comparing the returns of the strategy using aggressor tag vs. using BVC volume bars, we see that the BVC method generates much worse results. This is consistent with some research indicating that order flow based on this method may not be very accurate (Andersen, 2013).

Are there ways to improve on the profitability of this order flow strategy? Naturally, we should eliminate delays for trades due to the absence of triggering ticks for the aggressor tag method or due to predefined finite volume bars for the BVC method. But more interestingly, we may notice that the sensitivity (regression coefficient) of the price change in response to past order flow may not be constant. We can choose to send a market order only when we believe that the price change as a function of both order flow and sensitivity is large. This sensitivity may depend on the state of the order book (less liquidity probably means higher sensitivity), and some high frequency traders may actually be probing this sensitivity continuously using small orders (Clark-Joseph, 2013). Alternatively, we can use linear regression over some moving lookback period or the Kalman filter to continuously compute the sensitivity of midprice change relative to order flow.

Given the evidence that order flow can predict returns, it is no surprise that institutional traders prefer to trade in dark pools (where trades generate no order flow) and with hidden orders (where order flow can only be estimated quite roughly using the BVC method). This is perhaps also why currency exchanges do not typically publish trades information in a timely manner—why do that when one's proprietary trading desk can make better use of the information!

Order Book Imbalance

We see from above that order flow, which is a function of signed trades and not quotes, is predictive of midprice movement. In this section, we will discuss research that uses quotes, or more specifically, order book imbalance to predict midprice movement.

Order book imbalance is simply defined as the total bid size minus the total offer size, normalized by their totals:

$$\rho = \frac{V_B - V_S}{V_B + V_S}, \tag{6.2}$$

where V_B is the total bid size on the order book, and V_S is the total offer size on the book. Some researchers have found that it is often sufficient to capture the BBO size in equation 6.2, ignoring the rest of the book. Cartea, Jaimungal, and Penalva (2015) found that there is a significant correlation between order book imbalance of a stock (ORCL) and future price change that persists up to 200 seconds. Over a period of one second, the correlation can be as high as 0.5. Naturally, the correlation may vary over time, and over various stocks in question. Hence, a continuous adaption of a linear predictive model just as we described at the end of the last section may be applied here, too.

Also noted by Cartea, Jaimungal, and Penalva (2015) is another curious phenomenon associated with order book balance: a buy imbalance attracts buy market orders, and vice versa. If one is a market maker posting sell limit orders, this is yet another reason to adjust the quote price upward when ρ is large and positive.

Summary

Intraday trading is an attractive trading style, due to its typically shorter drawdown and therefore a shorter time frame for validating or rejecting a strategy. However, transaction cost has a larger impact on intraday strategies' profitability than on longer-term trades, since the profit on each trade is lower. In an extreme case, if one is running a liquidity-rebate-earning strategy, the profit of each trade will be measured in mils, not cents, per share. We discussed many techniques in this chapter to reduce transaction cost. They include reducing physical latency of signal generation and order submission/confirmation and market data. They involve reducing the time needed for order routing and gaining priority in the order queue on an exchange's order book by using special order types. They involve trading in dark pools to avoid the bid-offer spread and hiding information. (Remember, order flow and order book imbalance is predictive of midprice change!) And they involve avoiding adverse selection by choosing order types and dark pools carefully. But even before we get to execute these strategies, just backtesting them involves data and techniques that are much more onerous than required for interday strategies. To make things worse, while interday strategies may rely on "factors" that can last for years if not decades (see Chapter 2, "Factor Models"), intraday strategies often depend sensitively on market microstructure that may change rapidly in response to regulatory changes, the rise of high-frequency trading, and the introduction of new technologies, exchanges, and algorithms. Alpha, after all, is ethereal.

Exercises

6.1. Refer to the (bid-side only) order book displayed in Example 6.1. A trader sends a market order to sell 600 shares to L.

a) What orders do L have to reroute, and to which exchanges?

b) Suppose that after the order was sent, but before it was executed, N2's NBB was increased to $10.03. Does L need to reroute part of the order to N2?

6.2. Suppose we have only two exchanges, with their order books for a stock shown below (only bids are relevant for this exercise):

Order Book for Exchanges L and N

Bids	L	N
$10.03	**100**	
$10.02		**100**
$10.01		300
$10.00	200	

The "protected" quote sizes are in **bold**. Note that L has the NBB. A trader sends "sell 300 MKT IOC" to L. How many shares of this order will be executed in total?

6.3. Referring to Box 6.3, suppose the bid price for EDH2 is 98.77 instead of 98.78.

a) Would the trader's limit order to buy 50 contracts of H2M2 at 0.23 still result in a best bid size of 150 for H2, and a best offer size of 150 for M2?
b) If a buy market order for 100 contracts of M2 arrives, would the calendar spread limit order in (a) be filled?
c) If the trader sends a limit order to buy 50 contracts of H2M2 at 0.24, how would this affect the outright order book?
d) If the trader sends a limit order to buy 50 contracts of H2M2 at 0.21, would that add an implied-out quote to the outright order book?

6.4. Modify code in Example 6.3 so that a trade tick that falls out of the one-minute lookback window will update the aggregate order flow value immediately, instead of waiting for the next trade tick for the update. Similarly, update the past volume bars every 25 ms for trading decisions. How do these modifications change the returns?

6.5. Find out the meanings of the following terms and write them down here for your own future reference. (Their explanations are throughout this chapter.)

Adverse selection
Aggressor
At the touch
BBO
DMA
Hide-and-light
Hidden orders
Implied-in quotes
Implied-out quotes
Informed traders
IOC
ISO
ITCH
LOC
LOO
Midprice
Mil
MOC
MOO
NBB
NBBO

NBO
Order Protection Rule
Primary exchange
Pro-rata priority
Protected quotes
Reg NMS
SIP
TAQ
Toxic flow
Walk the book

Endnotes

1. In Chapter 1, we noted that the levered compound return of a strategy that adopts the optimal Kelly leverage is $S^2/2$, where S is the Sharpe ratio, assuming that the risk-free rate is zero.
2. *At-the-touch* means the top-of-book best bid/offer quote.
3. SIP stands for securities information processor.
4. For example, Lime Brokerage provides such a "managed" data feed to its clients who are collocated in its data center, allowing them to significantly reduce the cost of subscribing to the "raw" direct feed from the exchange. Managed data feed means that the broker has user authentication and audit capabilities to prevent unauthorized usage of the data.
5. The exceptions to time-prioritized queuing are the many dark pools for US stocks, and the CME order book for the Eurodollar futures. They prioritize order fills on a pro-rata basis. See the later subsection on "Routing to Dark Pools" for details.
6. One mil is 0.1 cent.
7. At Interactive Brokers, the Sweep-to-Fill Order is a form of ISO. In fact, by default, IB sends all orders as ISO. See www.interactivebrokers.com/Universal/servlet/Registration_v2.formSampleView?ad=order_routing_disclosure.html.
8. Trades from dark pools are reported through FINRA's ADF (alternative display facility).
9. On June 17, 2016, SEC approved IEX to become an exchange. So they now have displayed quotes.
10. Ironically, this white paper on avoiding adverse selection was published by ITG, a few years before SEC fined them $20 million for gaming their dark pool customers.

11. For example, Cartea, Jaimungal, and Penalva (2015) found that the spread of AAPL can change by a factor of 6 over the course of a trading day.
12. Historical Nasdaq ITCH data are available to academic researchers for a low fee through lobsterdata.com.
13. Execution messages in HotspotFX's ITCH may be delayed by one second when offered as a live feed.
14. Time stamps of one nanosecond are available nowadays (Cartea, Jaimungal, and Penalva, 2015).
15. For example, Quantitative Brokers (Almgren, 2014) offers a market simulator for fixed income and futures.
16. NYSE TAQ microsecond data can be purchased from www.nyxdata.com/Data-Products/Daily-TAQ. It is also available at lower cost to academic researchers through Wharton Research Data Services at wrds-web.wharton.upenn.edu.
17. A buy market order also includes a limit order with price higher than the best ask price, and a sell market order also includes a limit order with price lower than the best bid price.
18. As mentioned in Chapter 1, QuantGo.com's data cannot be downloaded. Readers interested in trying this algorithm out can rent their data at a low monthly cost.

CHAPTER 7

Bitcoins

Currencies and bitcoins are the ideal playground for the quantitative analyst. Unlike stocks, bonds, or their derivatives, they are quite immune to fundamental factors (Lyons, 2001), at least on the shorter time scales that we will be concerned with in this chapter. This is not to say that, for example, a Fed interest rate decision would not affect exchange rates (of course it would!), but that such fundamental events cannot be used as *predictive* factors. They are contemporaneous factors that can only be used to explain exchange rates or bitcoins movement after the fact. Since as traders we are mostly interested in predictions only, we might as well look for the best technical analysis techniques instead.

When I mention *technical analysis*, you may immediately think of the Bollinger band, RSI, or stochastic indicators, and the like. But I use this term in a very broad sense. I just mean predictive techniques that only require prices and volumes as input. These include many of the tools we discussed in Chapters 3 and 4. Hence, this chapter provides another proving ground for those techniques, and would be of interest to those of you who want a fresh look at them without the baggage of too many methodological details. Other techniques include order flow analysis and cross-exchange arbitrage. Both of these techniques have wide applicability outside of bitcoins, and bitcoins serve to highlight their power in a particularly simple context.

■ Bitcoin Facts

Since bitcoin is a fairly new financial instrument, we will describe some of its properties first. To a trader, bitcoin is just another foreign currency such as EUR or AUD. Trading bitcoin against another currency is like trading EUR.USD, AUD.USD, or in general, B.Q. B is called the "base" currency, and Q is the "quote" currency. Here is a useful mnemonic: B is ahead of Q alphabetically, hence base currency is always the first symbol. Conveniently, we will always use bitcoins as the base currency, too. For example, BTC.USD is the number of USD needed to buy 1 bitcoin, and BTC.CNY is the number of CNY needed to buy 1 bitcoin. If the value of bitcoin increases against any currency Q, BTC.Q will increase. Other than BTC.USD, BTC.CNY is the most traded currency pair.

(CNY is the onshore version of the currency of China. This currency is not freely exchangeable and its rate is regulated by the government to trade in a narrow band. The offshore version of the Chinese currency CNH *is* freely exchangeable at almost every FX broker. Unfortunately, I know of no bitcoin exchange that allows us to trade BTC.CNH. So unless you live in China, including Hong Kong, trading BTC.CNY is not very practical.)

There are over 40 bitcoin exchanges. As of this writing, the top five exchanges with the most volume (measured in bitcoins) are BTC China, BitStamp, Bitfinex, itBit, and btc-e. The first exchange is for BTC.CNY, and the last four are for BTC.USD. Their latest exchange rates as well as volumes can be viewed on bitcoincharts.com. While currencies typically do not trade from 5 p.m. ET on Fridays to 5 p.m. on Sundays, nor on certain holidays, bitcoin trades 24/7.

Compared to other risky assets, both volatility and kurtosis (which measures tail risks) of bitcoin returns are high. Table 7.1 is a comparison of the riskiness of bitcoin compared to other risky assets. We have chosenMXN.USD as a risky asset for comparison because it is the most

TABLE 7.1 Comparison of Riskiness of Risky Assets

	BTC.USD	MXN.USD	SPY	HYG
Volatility (annualized)	67%	16%	20%	13%
Best daily move	20% (20140303)	18% (20081104)	15% (20081013)	12% (20081013)
Worst daily move	−24% (20150114)	−13% (20081103)	−10% (20081015)	−8% (20080929)
Max Drawdown	−79%	−49%	−55%	−34%
Kurtosis[1] (annualized)	7	8	1	4
Period analyzed	20140120 −20150114	20080102 −20160225	20020627 −20160520	20070411 −20160520

liquid of all emerging market currencies, and it is often used as a proxy for them when traders wish to express their views on this asset class. (ETF data are obtained from csidata.com, FX data are from Interactive Brokers, BTC.USD data are from BitStamp and compiled by Jonathan Shore. You can download historical data directly from api.bitcoincharts.com/v1/csv/.)

Market risk is not the only risk we have to worry about when trading bitcoin: There is also credit risk. According to Johansson and Tjernstrom (2014), 45 percent of bitcoin exchanges fail due to thefts and hacks, taking their investors' deposits with them.

Time-Series Techniques

As was discussed in Chapter 3, if we don't know a lot about an instrument, the first step is to run a time-series analysis on it using ARIMA. Fitting[2] the midprices of BTC.USD one-minute bar data from January 20, 2014, to September 3, 2014, to an AR(p) model (see equation 3.2 and the methodology described in Chapter 3) results in $p = 16$ and $\phi_1 = 0.685$ with a standard error of 0.0001. Hence, this time series seems strongly mean-reverting. We can also run the ADF[3] test for stationarity described in Example 2.1 of Chan (2013) on this time series:


```
results=adf(mid(trainset), 0, 1);
prt(results);
```

which comes back with a ADF test statistic of –3, while the critical value at 95 percent level is –2.9. So the ADF test also confirms that the BTC.USD price series is mean-reverting and stationary. Hence a mean-reversion trading strategy promises to be successful. But before we try that, let's just use AR(16) to predict the next price and buy or sell based on that prediction on the test set from September 3, 2014, to January 15, 2015. (This is the same strategy applied to AUD.USD in the Section on AR(p) in Chapter 3.) The CAGR is 40,000. The equity curve for the test set is shown in Figure 7.1.

Is this return realistic? Of course not. One would need to assume that a limit order at midprice is always filled instantaneously to achieve this result. Nevertheless, it serves to illustrate that a simple AR(p) model has quite a bit of predictive power here.

We should also try ARMA(p, q) on BTC.USD. Following the same steps as we did for AUD.USD in the Section on ARMA(p, q) in Chapter 3, we find that the optimal p and q are $p = 3$ and $q = 7$. We can then estimate

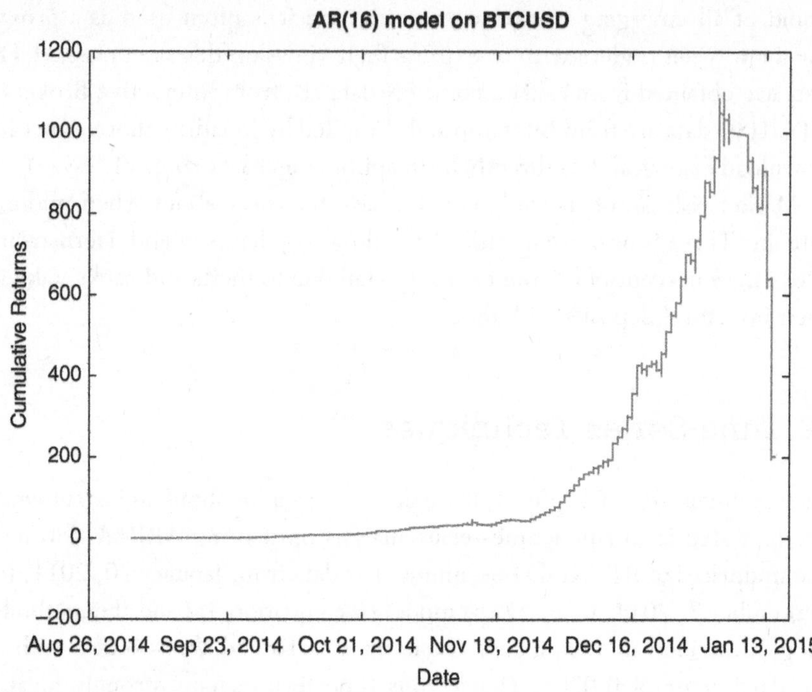

FIGURE 7.1 AR(16) trading strategy applied to BTC.USD

the autoregressive and moving average coefficients on ARMA(3, 7) on BTC.USD, and use the resulting model to make one-step-ahead prediction as in the AR(16) case. Over the same test set, the CAGR is 3.9, which is still fantastic but much lower than the AR(16) model. The equity curve (Figure 7.2) also looks very different.

Mean Reversion Strategy

As we have ascertained via an AR(16) model as well as an ADF test in the previous section, the midprices of BTC.USD is a mean-reverting, stationary, time series. This means a lot of simple mean-reverting strategies described in Chan (2013) can be applied here.

The most well-known mean reverting strategy is the Bollinger band strategy, where we buy a unit of BTC.USD when the midprice is *k* moving standard deviations below the moving average, and sell when it is above. We will exit a position when the price mean reverts to the current moving average. This is illustrated in Figure 7.3. The moving standard deviation

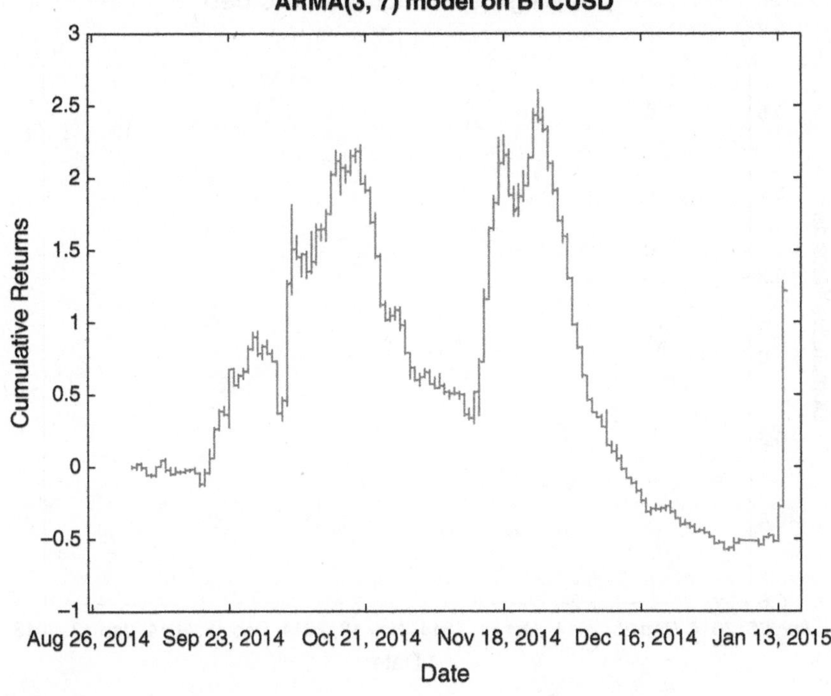

FIGURE 7.2 ARMA(3, 7) trading strategy applied to BTC.USD

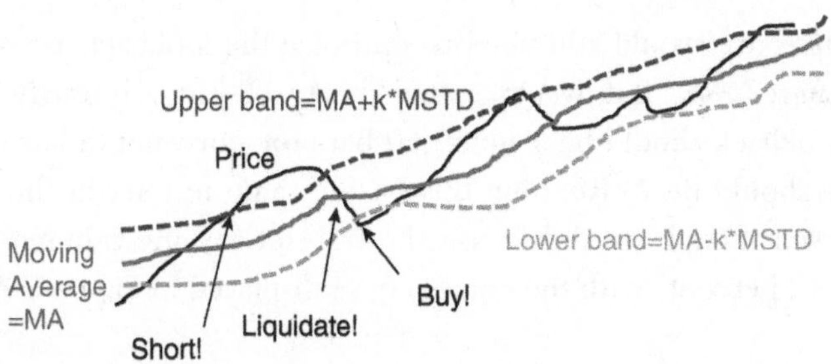

FIGURE 7.3 Bollinger band trading strategy

and average are on prices, not returns. The code fragment[4] that generates the buy and sell signals is

```
buyEntry=cl  <= movingAvg(cl, lookback)-entryZscore*movingStd(cl,
   lookback);
sellEntry=cl >= movingAvg(cl, lookback)+entryZscore*movingStd(cl,
   lookback);
```

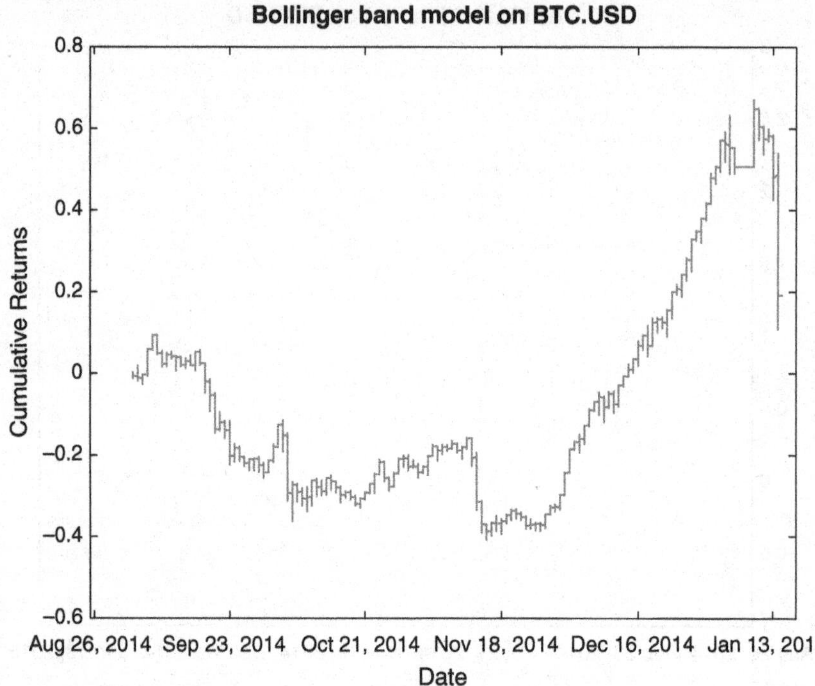

FIGURE 7.4 Bollinger band trading strategy on BTC.USD equity curve

Of course, we would still need to optimize the lookback as well as the multiple *entryZscore*. But we take the liberty of just arbitrarily deciding that the lookback should be 1 hour (60 bars for our minute-bar data) and *entryZscore* should be 2. Running this on the same test set in the previous section (even though we didn't use the trainset for any training) yields a CAGR of 42 percent, with the equity curve displayed in Figure 7.4.

Artificial Intelligence Techniques

Just like time series analysis, machine learning algorithms are another group of techniques that are helpful when we are faced with a market whose behavior is new to us, and we have not yet developed intuition about price patterns and arbitrage opportunities that may exist. So let's apply some of the algorithms we learned in Chapter 4 to the one-minute bar BTC.USD data. To avoid learning spurious effects such as bid-ask bounce, we will again use midprices for our analysis in this section throughout.

The first technique we will try is the regression algorithm with bagging. We merely copy the rTreeBagger.m program[5] to apply to the data here. But instead of using *ret1*, *ret2*, ... , *ret20* as predictors, we use 1-, 5-, 10-, 30-, and 60-minute bars returns. I will not display either the CAGR or the equity curve on the test set (which is the second half of the data set from January 20, 2014, to January 15, 2015), because they are simply too high to be realistic. This strategy clearly calls for a more careful backtest using bid-ask quotes.

The second technique is the support vector machine. We can just copy the code svm.m from Chapter 4,[6] using the new predictors above. Lest you think that everything that worked with SPY will work even better with BTC.USD, here you will find quite negative returns for both train and test sets.

Finally, we will apply the feedforward neural network that we discussed in Chapter 4 as well.[7] We will use a network with just one hidden layer and one neuron on that layer, but we will train 100 such networks with different initial guesses of the network parameters and average the predicted returns over all these networks. The out-of-sample return is as astounding as the one using the regression tree technique above, subject to the same caveats.

Order Flow

We discussed using order flow as an indicator for shortterm prediction in Chapter 6. Recall that order flow is *signed* transaction volume: if a transaction of size *s* is the result of a buy market order, the order flow is $+s$; if it is the result of a sell market order, the order flow is $-s$. Some bitcoin exchanges provide such data feeds with the "aggressor tag" that specifies whether a trade is the result of a buy or sell market order. This is the case with the BTC.CNY feed from BTC China and the BTC.USD feed from BitStamp. We will use a one-month sample of the BTC.USD trade tick data from BitStamp to illustrate a trading strategy that uses order flow as a predictor. These data are time-stamped to microseconds.

The trading strategy is in principle very simple. At the end of every microsecond bar, we look for all trade ticks within the past minute, and compute the order flow in that period. If this order flow is greater than some threshold, we send out a buy market order to buy a unit of BTC.USD, and vice versa for a sell market order. We will exit the resulting position, again using market orders, whenever the one-minute order flow is zero or has the opposite sign from the one triggering the entry. The problem with this algorithm is that there are too many microsecond bars to loop through, and the program may need to run for a very long time. So we will instead backtest a simplified version of this strategy, using an event-driven algorithm where we only compute order flow and decide whether to generate a trading signal when we encounter a trade tick. We also assume that our trade can be filled using this trade price, instead of using the current best bid or offer price. This is the same simplification we made in Example 6.3. The code details are discussed in Example 7.1. Naturally, both the entry threshold and the implicit exit threshold of zero, as well as the lookback period of one minute, should be optimized in-sample and tested out-of-sample.

The backtest shows a profit of US$0.097 per one-sided trade. With 336 such trades in December 2014, this translated to a profit of US$32.54 per coin, or an annualized return of approximately 100 percent. Of course, we should really be backtesting this high frequency strategy using bid-ask quotes, as we have to execute this strategy by buying at the ask and selling at the bid. With a bid-ask spread of about US$0.12, the transaction cost per trade is about US$0.06, which is still lower than the gross profit we computed. So there is hope that the strategy can generate a net profit, depending on the commissions that need to be paid. At the very least, this demonstrates that order flow is a reasonable predictor for bitcoin for this time frame.

Example 7.1: An order flow strategy

This example is similar to Example 6.3. It is very fortunate that we have access to the historical trades data from BitStamp that are time-stamped at microseconds and more importantly, include the aggressor tag. This tag allows for accurate computation of order flow for our strategy. We save the aggressor tag in an array called *side*, where *side* = 1 indicates it is due to a buy market order, and *side* = −1 indicates it is due to a sell market order. We will also save the trade size and price in arrays called *tradeSize* and *tradePrice* respectively, and compute the order flow as

```
ordflow=zeros(size(tradePrice));
ordflow(buy)=tradeSize(buy);
ordflow(sell)=-tradeSize(sell);
```

and the cumulative order flow as

```
cumOrdflow=smartcumsum(ordflow);
```

We will also keep track of the time stamp in an array *dn,* which contains the MATLAB datenum of the trades. All these arrays have the same dimension as the number of trade ticks. But note that trade ticks are not evenly spaced in time: There often are many consecutive microsecond bars that do not have any ticks and will not show up, and theoretically there can be multiple trades that share the same microsecond (though much less likely). If we go through these trades one-by-one, we can easily compute the net order flow within the last one minute:

```
for t=1:length(cumOrdflow)
    idx=find( dn  <= dn(t)-lookback/60/60/24);

    if (~isempty(idx))
        ordflow_lookback=cumOrdflow(t)-cumOrdflow(idx(end));
    end
end
```

The *ordflow_lookback* computed above can certainly be used to trigger a trade, whether for entry or exit. But even if time elapses without trades, the order flow within the last minute still needs to be updated. We are not actually doing that—we loop over only time bars that have trades, otherwise the program will take much longer to finish. What we are backtesting is really a slightly different version of the strategy described in the main text—one which is simpler to backtest. In this version, we only enter or exit when a trade occurs, therefore we only need to compute the order flow in the last minute at that time. For the original version, we will need to backtest with trades and quotes (TAQ) data, in addition to a more intelligent way to "fast forward" when there is no trade tick. (The backtest of this version will be left as an exercise.)

Continuing with our simplified strategy, we can insert the trade signal generator in the if-block right after we compute *ordflow_lookback*:

```
if (ordflow_lookback > entryThreshold)
    if ( pos <= 0)
        if (pos < 0)
            dailyPL=dailyPL+(entryP-tradePrice(t));
            dailyNumTrade=dailyNumTrade+2;
            entryP=tradePrice(t);
        else
```

```
                entryP=tradePrice(t);
                dailyNumTrade=dailyNumTrade+1;
            end
            pos=1;

        end
    elseif (ordflow_lookback < -entryThreshold)
        if (pos >= 0)
            if (pos > 0)
                dailyPL=dailyPL+(tradePrice(t)-entryP);
                dailyNumTrade=dailyNumTrade+2;
                entryP=tradePrice(t);
            else
                entryP=tradePrice(t);
                dailyNumTrade=dailyNumTrade+1;
            end
            pos=-1;

        end
    else
        if (ordflow_lookback <= exitThreshold && pos > 0)
            dailyPL=dailyPL+(tradePrice(t)-entryP);
            dailyNumTrade=dailyNumTrade+1;
            pos=0;
        elseif (ordflow_lookback >= -exitThreshold && pos < 0)
            dailyPL=dailyPL+(entryP-tradePrice(t));
            dailyNumTrade=dailyNumTrade+1;
            pos=0;
        end
    end
```


Before entering into the for-loop, we should first initialize pos=0

```
pos=0;
dailyPL=0;
dailyNumTrade=0;
```

If we set *entryThreshold* to 90 and *exitThreshold* to 0, this simplified strategy generates a gross P&L of $32.54 for one unit of BTC.USD in December 2014, or $0.097 per one-sided trade, assuming that we can get filled at the same trade price that triggered our trade. The complete code can be downloaded as orderFlow2.m.

Cross-Exchange Arbitrage

Cross-exchange arbitrage is only possible when the best bid price of an instrument on one exchange is higher than the best ask price of the same instrument on another exchange, so that we can buy at the market from the second exchange and then turn around and sell at the market on the first exchange, making a riskless profit.

There isn't much opportunity for cross-exchange arbitrage in mature financial markets. Let's take the US stock market as an example. As we discussed in Chapter 6, though there are more than 60 exchanges or dark pools where one can trade AAPL, the "crossed market" situation described above will rarely occur due to Regulation NMS ("National Market System") Rule 610 implemented by the SEC in 2005. Rule 610 requires an exchange to avoid displaying quotations that will cross the BBO quotes of another exchange ("Rule 610," 2005). There goes our arbitrage opportunity!

There is still the possibility of engaging in *cross-border* cross-exchange arbitrage in stocks. For example, since IBM is traded in both NYSE and the LSE (London Stock Exchange), we may be able to spot the occasional crossed market situation after taking into account the exchange rate GBP.USD. But to make this trade really riskless, one has to hedge our currency risk. So, for example, if we bought some shares of IBM on LSE and sold equal number of shares of IBM in NYSE, we are essentially short GBP and long USD. We need to simultaneously buy some GBP.USD in order to hedge this currency exposure. This adds transaction costs and will reduce or eliminate our arbitrage profit.

In bitcoin markets, on the other hand, the opportunity for cross-exchange arbitrage is seemingly abundant. Let's look at one example. At 7 p.m. EST on February 2, 2015, BTC.USD had the following bid-ask quotes on two exchanges:

Bitfinex: 239.19–239.48
btc-e: 233.232–233.546.

Why not sell a coin at $239.19 on Bitfinex, and immediately buy a coin at $233.546 on btc-e, and earn a gross profit of US$5.644? In fact, the market is crossed like this for many days, even months. So why not do this continuously and becomes an overnight millionaire? To analyze whether there is really a free lunch to be had here, we have to look closely at the costs of the trade.

First, there is a commission of about 20 bps per side, which is about $1 for the complete transaction. Second, if we were to execute this continuously, we need to regularly withdraw a coin from btc-e and transfer it to Bitfinex to cover our short position there. This withdrawal will cost about 1 percent, or $2. So we are left with about $2.6 net profit per coin—still excellent! But lastly, we have to be mindful why the quotes are lower at btc-e. That is because the market judges it to have a lower credit rating. Since we have a long position there, we are exposed to credit risk.[8] We have no easy method to compute whether this credit risk is higher or lower than the $2.6 per coin profit.

Summary

I have provided a whirlwind tour of some of the trading opportunities present in the bitcoin market. Bitcoin markets are still relatively immature compared to the stock or currency markets and, hence, there are still many inefficiencies and thus potentially profitable arbitrage opportunities. Some of these profits look outlandishly high—but are they real? That partly depends on your execution software's sophistication, the exchange's API efficiency, and its commissions and other fees, and finally, the credit-worthiness of the exchange.

But beyond bitcoin, we also demonstrated how some of the techniques we developed in the previous chapters, such as time-series analysis and artificial intelligence, can be brought to bear on an unfamiliar market. We also demonstrated the power of a universal short-term indicator—order flow—and pointed out the mechanics of a cross-border, cross-exchange arbitrage that may be applicable to many more mature markets.

Exercises

7.1. Try the AR(p) and ARMA(p, q) models on BTC.USD on lower frequency time series such as 5-minute, 15-minute, and daily bars. Daily data can be downloaded from api.bitcoincharts.com/v1/csv/.

7.2. Backtest the strategy described in Example 7.1 where we may enter a trade even when there were no historical trades in a microsecond time bar. The best bid offer (BBO) data is available to download as 2014-12_bbo.csv. Why must we backtest with BBO data in this case? Are there cases where we would enter into a new position with this strategy while our simplified version described in Example 7.1 would not? Is this version more or less profitable than the simplified version?

Endnotes

1. Kurtosis of a normal distribution is 3. We annualize kurtosis by assuming that it scales linearly with time (Manokhin, 2015, and Carr, 2016).
2. The complete code can be downloaded as buildARp_BTCUSD.m.
3. The *adf* function is part of the free spatial-econometrics.com's jplv7 package. MATLAB's Econometrics Toolbox has the equivalent *adftest* function.
4. The complete code can be downloaded as bollinger.m, together with movingAvg.m and movingStd.m.
5. The modified code can be downloaded as rTreeBagger_BTCUSD.m.
6. The modified code can be downloaded as svm_BTCUSD.m.
7. The modified code can be downloaded as nn_feedfwd_avg_BTCUSD.m.
8. Ironically, Bitfinex is the exchange that was hacked on August 2, 2016, causing bitcoins' value to drop 20% at one point (Tsang, 2016).

CHAPTER 8

Algorithmic Trading Is Good for Body and Soul

Before we start engaging in a complex, time-consuming, and possibly risky venture, it is often a good idea to pause and ask why we should do it. Even if we have already been doing it for years, and have invested countless hours and dollars, it is still worthwhile to ask if we should continue doing it. (Sunk cost is not a rational justification.) Now that we have surveyed the highly technical side of algorithmic trading, perhaps it is time to ask these high-level questions.

Your Mind and Your Health

If you tell an acquaintance that you work as an algorithmic trader, it will likely be assumed that your motivation is primarily financial. However, statistics show that the majority of traders are unprofitable.[1] There are much easier ways to earn a good living that do not involve bankruptcy risks. Of course, the few especially smart and lucky quants will find lucrative jobs at one of the big hedge funds where there is only upside and the downside is limited to getting fired. But then, these elites can also find very lucrative jobs at Silicon Valley, where a newly minted PhD graduate in artificial intelligence was offered more than $1 million annual compensation (Markoff and Lohr, 2016). So there must be more than financial consideration when it comes to deciding to become an algorithmic trader.

From my years of interacting with algorithmic traders, an important motivation for them is intellectual challenge. This is where mathematics, computer science, and economics intersect. Just like science, algorithmic trading offers a lifetime of opportunity for creative research. But unlike most sciences, one can pursue this research with minimal infrastructure, unencumbered by bureaucracy and the need to impress or convince others. One can pursue this research until the last day of one's life (which is my present plan), without needing to ask the government or large corporations for research grants. In short, one does not need *permission* to conduct this research anywhere and at any time. I find this very appealing.

(Of course, this freedom is predicated on the assumption that one's trading strategies are at least moderately successful. But to increase the likelihood of this success is the chief goal of this book.)

You may think that such a lofty goal as the freedom to pursue creative research is not that important to you. You may think that all you want is a stable income and a long and happy life. But how about this: Algorithmic trading is also a good way to improve your *health*. Research has found that having a bad boss is harmful to one's health and longevity (Porath, 2015), and furthermore, time spent with any boss (not just bad bosses) is the top-most reason for unhappiness (Kahneman, 2011). As an independent algorithmic trader, you can escape from boss-related unhappiness. True, one can be an entrepreneur in any field, but few other fields offer the opportunity to extract financial value so directly from one's intellect, and in a very scalable manner, as algorithmic trading. Often, such personal attributes as managerial acumen and marketing skills are equally important to entrepreneurial success. Not so with algorithmic trading.

While we are on the theme of health and the avoidance of (constant) stress, I should note that one of the main benefits of setting up your own algorithmic trading operation *at home* is that you will save time from commuting to the office. Unless you commute to work by walking or biking, that hour or more each day is neither healthy nor stress-free. There are other health benefits to working at home: the ability to get up and walk around regularly. The Mayo Clinic website states, "Too much sitting also seems to increase the risk of death from cardiovascular disease and cancer" (Levine, 2015). It felt strange when I worked at an institutional trading desk to stand up and walk around every half-hour or so, but you can do that at home without embarrassment. Finally, it is common knowledge that owning a pet decreases stress (Doheny, 2012). Our cat, a Ragdoll, not only offers me her support during periods of drawdowns, but also insists that I chase her around the house every half-hour in the morning, compounding the health benefit. You can hardly bring your cat to work on the trading floor of Goldman Sachs. In addition to the presence of a pet, I have also found a continuous streaming of music in my office to be soothing, but wearing a headset at an institutional trading desk is bad optics (and so is wearing pajamas at work).

It may seem counter intuitive, but working at home also enhances my productivity. Many readers or colleagues have asked me how I can manage a hedge fund and separate accounts, write books and blog posts, and teach graduate finance classes, all at the same time. The answer is that working around the clock and on weekends doesn't feel like work in the comforts of home. (Of course, working from home is becoming less possible for me as our team expands to include new members who need to be physically close by to maximize efficiency, learning opportunities, and most importantly, serendipitous idea generation.)

You may like this lifestyle, but you may still hesitate because of the risks of failure. The usual argument of signing up for a steady job is that, well, it is steady. But is it? It didn't work out that way for me,[2] and often not for anyone in a position with P&L responsibility in any institution. Two of the institutions that I worked for have either shut down, or are on the verge of it. The banks that I have worked for have drastically scaled down proprietary trading activities due to the Dodd-Frank Act, and some of my colleagues who worked hard to become managing directors have either been laid off or quit of their own volition. Even if your firm is alive and well, your job typically lasts as long as your cumulative profit is sitting at its high watermark. But if your strategy is profitable, why do you need to work for anyone? Furthermore, by starting up your own algorithmic trading outfit, you can diversify your career risks away from sole dependence on P&L. Nobody can stop you from teaching, consulting, and writing books while building a robust portfolio of strategies. As Nassim Taleb said (Taleb, 2014), running your own business increases normal (read "Gaussian") fluctuations in your income, but reduces tail risks, and is thus *antifragile*. Having a diversified income stream greatly reduces the stress of a drawdown, and in fact, makes you a better algorithmic trader because you can become more emotionally stable. An additional virtue of such diversification is that teaching, consulting, and trading are synergistic. I learn quantitative techniques better by teaching them, and as a result, teaching sometimes inspires new strategies. I also learned much from the investment professionals that I taught and consulted for. That's why some prominent physicists (Richard Feynman comes to mind) prefer to work in universities rather than pure research institutes where they are free from teaching and supervising duties. They have found that teaching and supervising smart students stimulates new ideas and avenues of research. From a business relationships viewpoint, both of my partners in the hedge funds that I founded or co-founded used to be my consulting clients, and some of our largest investors have been readers of my books.

Trading as a Service

Now that we have taken care of the personal benefits of algorithmic trading, are there any societal benefits? Is this all just a selfish but amusing game? If you think the currency conversion counters or ATMs in foreign airports are useless, then you are entitled to think that trading is useless. As a foreign currency trader, I stand as the wholesale counterparty behind these retail counters and machines. Without us, consumers will likely have to pay more for such conversions.

Some people despise trading and finance in general. They think the only honest living is to manufacture physical products. However, our advanced economy today is increasingly dependent on production of ideas and services. If that's the case, why celebrate video-game makers or movie directors but not algorithmic traders? Some argue that trading is a zero-sum game, producing no net benefit to society. But as I have shown above, a zero-sum game is still useful to the society if it provides temporary liquidity to those who invest for the long term.[3]

Another oft-overlooked societal benefit of algorithmic trading is that it is a business, and businesses provide for wages and incomes to their employees and suppliers. In addition to tangible income, we mentor interns who have STEM or business degrees, most of whom find productive jobs in finance or other industries. Sometimes, they even help us create new, profitable strategies.

One reason I offer my investment management service to others is to further enhance the social utility of our trading. I believe I am a competent and ethical investment manager. By offering my service, I hope to displace from the marketplace incompetent or unethical investment managers. Contrary to popular misconceptions, investment management is not just for the wealthy. We are more than happy to manage investments from university endowments or pension funds for teachers, healthcare workers, or other public employees. I feel greatly honored to be entrusted with the task of safeguarding the retirement assets and income of my clients. I will talk more about managing other people's money in the last section in this chapter.

Does This Stuff Really Work?

Readers often ask me: "Are these strategies still profitable?" and my answer is, inevitably, "Some are, some aren't," and that's the truth. Strategies have finite shelf lives, and more importantly, strategies that have been backtested but not traded live (like most of the ones I described in this and my previous books) may not even work at all out-of-sample.

There are two main reasons profitable strategies may stop being so: macroeconomic or market structure changes, and competition from other traders. In response, we can sometimes modify the strategies to adapt to such changes or competition (e.g., entering or exiting a momentum trade earlier). As for strategies that have only been backtested, I have discussed at length in my previous books on how to spot flawed backtests (e.g., avoid survivorship and data-snooping biases), and how to ensure that backtests are more predictive of future returns. A major part of the skillset of a trader is to decide when to start trading a strategy that only has backtest evidence for profitability, and stop trading a strategy that is suffering a drawdown. Often, the decision is partly based on statistical evidence (e.g., we are more likely to start trading strategies with higher Sharpe ratio), and partly based on understanding whether the fundamental economics of the trading strategy still holds for the current market condition (e.g., we may postpone trading a short volatility strategy until the market is calm). This is also the only occasion when discretion meets algorithmic trading. But as with any investment, the key is diversification. The more independent strategies we have in a portfolio, the less chance that they will all stop working or have a drawdown at the same time. I would strive for at least 10 strategies trading live at any moment, with continuous births and deaths. As for the best way to allocate capital among them, I discuss that in Chapter 2.

To illustrate, let's examine two strategies I discussed in my previous books.

One of the first strategies I introduced in Chan (2009) was the pair trading of GLD vs. GDX. In that book, I use the spread between GLD and GDX as the input, and buy the spread whenever it falls below some threshold, and sell it whenever it rises above another threshold. The threshold is determined based on the mean and standard deviation of the spread in a trainset. If we run this strategy again using the first half of the data from May 24, 2006, to May 1, 2013, as a trainset, we will find that the cumulative return is negative on the test set (the second half of the data). This is no surprise if we look at a plot of the spread in Figure 8.1—it has kept increasing from 2011 until 2013 when it stabilized. It would, however, have been a great time to start trading this pair again in 2013!

On the other hand, a similar pair, GLD vs. USO, backtested in Chan (2013) using a Bollinger band strategy (i.e., where we continuously update the mean and standard deviation of the spread in a 20-day lookback period) continues to have positive returns.

If we are running just these two strategies in our portfolio, does it mean that in practice we would have zero or even negative net returns over the out-of-sample period? Hardly: We would have continuously lowered the

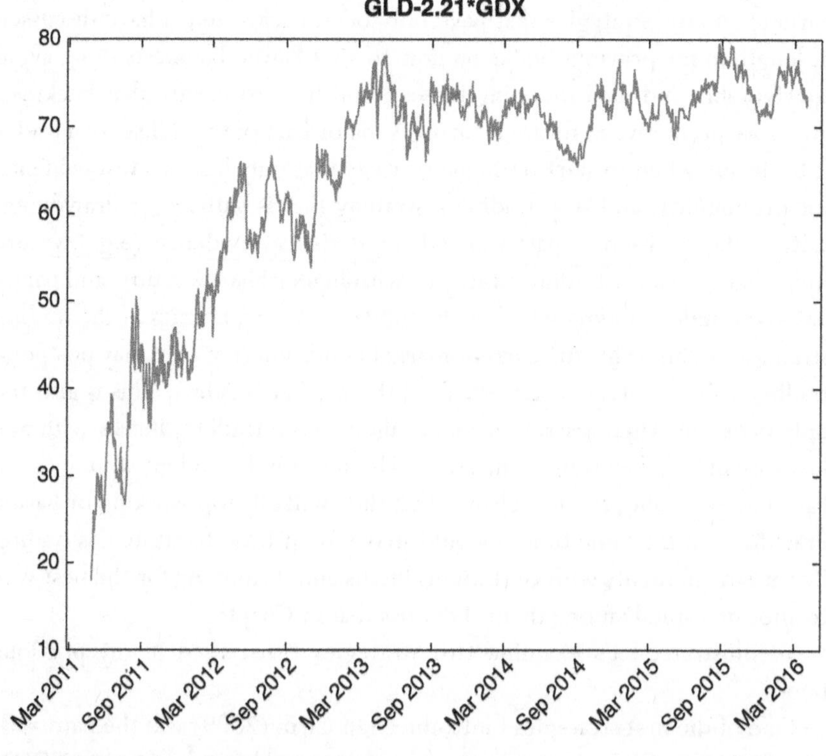

FIGURE 8.1 Spread of GLD and GDX: Out-of-sample

leverage of the GLD-GDX strategy as it lost money, until it was zero. Meanwhile, we would have kept that of GLD-USO fairly constant. (This is the Constant Proportion Portfolio Insurance, or CPPI, scheme mentioned in Chan, 2013.) This, and the fact that new strategies are continuously being created and added to the pool, is how we survive the death of a strategy and maintain net positive return. As Brett Steenbarger wrote in Dahl (2015), " ... traders ... find their ultimate edge in perpetual creativity."

Keeping Up with the Latest Trends

As with any other technology-intensive business, algorithmic trading evolves rapidly. The frequency of trading is increasing, the number of asset classes traded algorithmically is increasing, the variety of available data is increasing, and the variety of algorithms invented is increasing. I discussed in Chapter 6 some of the issues related to the increasing frequency and decreasing latency of trading. In terms of data, the race is on to extract information from unconventional sources. Elementized newsfeeds and sentiment scores are no longer new to traders, and I discussed some vendors who provide that in Chapter 1. But I have heard of more outlandish data that involve satellites and drone images of oil tankers, parking lots of retail stores, infrared heat map of factories and industrial districts, and so forth, all to gain a leg up on official crude oil, retail, and industrial production data releases (Kamel, 2016). A colleague told me about a firm that is even analyzing the voice of company executives during conference calls to detect whether they are lying, hiding something, or just plain gloomy despite the outwardly cheerful projections. Some of these data must be analyzed using machine learning algorithms due to their voluminous nature. Machine learning is used directly in creating trading rules as well, a topic explored in Chapter 4.

Where can we keep track of all these new developments and knowledge? The most efficient way for me is to follow the Twitter feeds of quant news consolidators such as @quantocracy, @quantivity, and @carlcarrie. These consolidators regularly tweet about publications of new papers or blog posts. (I occasionally retweet their posts @chanep.) We can also visit the blogs of jonathankinlay.com, tr8dr.wordpress.com, eranraviv.com, godotfinance.com, quanstart.com, quantnews.com, factorwave.com, or my own epchan.blogspot.com. But the virtue of Twitter is that someone will notify you of new content on any of these and other websites. There are also numerous forums and podcasts, online and off, that have active discussions of trading in general: BetterSystemTrader.com, Futures.io, ChatWithTraders.com, TradersLog.com, London Systematic Traders club, Market Technician Association, Quantlabs.net, and so on.

■ Managing Other People's Money

Suppose you have decided that, like me, you would enjoy using your trading skills to serve others. How would you go about it?

If you work as a trader in an investment bank, hedge fund, or a high-profile proprietary trading firm, the fund-raising process won't be too hard. A typical way to raise money in this case is to pitch your business plan to a prime broker who has a capital introduction service. Many such brokers may not advertise that they have such a service, but they do informally. So there is no harm in asking. Kroijer (2012) detailed the travails of such a route.

But what if you have been an independent trader all along, albeit one with a stellar track record? In recent years, a coterie of services have sprung up to facilitate fundraising just for this type of trader. Most of them take the form of an investment competition over varying periods and will introduce the top performers to various capital providers. Many of them host physical capital introduction events. In alphabetical order, these include BattleFin.com, Battleofthequants.com, Fundseeders.com, Quantiacs.com, Quantmasscapital.com, and Quantopian.com. The last site, of course, offers much more than just capital introduction. It is a full-blown back-testing and live trading portal, as discussed in Chapter 1. In addition, it is backed by $250 million from Steve Cohen (Hall, 2016). There are also sites such as iasg.com, managedfuturesinvesting.com, and rcmalternatives.com that list the track records of futures traders (CTAs and CPOs). Naturally, if you have to go through a capital introduction service to find clients, your take of the fees will be reduced by the amount you have to share with them.

When I started as a fund manager in 2008, most of these services did not exist. So how did I raise funds? It all started with my blog, epchan.blogspot.com. Because of my blog, I got an offer to write my first book. Because of my blog and books, I got offers to consult for other traders or financial firms. Because of such consulting gigs, I got partners who not only introduce capital (their own, and their family and friends') to me to manage, but actively contribute to building up our strategies portfolio and technology infrastructure. Also because of my blog and books, there have been media interviews, invitations to speak at conferences, teach courses, and so on, which naturally generate more publicity for my money management service. Of course, none of this publicity would mean much if I had not treated our investors, consulting clients, and students decently.

Curiously, I have not found that going around town personally meeting with prospective investors yields much benefits. Most of my investors have never met me in person, and some have not even spoken to me on the phone. As I mentioned above, my investors learned about me by first reading my blog and books, taking my courses, or hiring me as a consultant. Many of them did not think that they could tell whether I am a crook or a charlatan from a one-hour meeting. This also relieves me of any pressure of trying to impress people all within an hour. In particular, it is easy to be fooled by charismatic people in physical meetings. I slowly built my reputation on and offline as a decent person to work with over many years. This way of building a business is also recommended by Grant (2014). I am mindful, however, that this way of marketing a money management business may not work well on large institutional investors, and may be too passive as we try to accelerate asset growth. Some people do advise me to "get out there" more.

The relative unimportance of face-to-face meetings in investment decisions does not, however, extend to research and ideas generation. I find it crucial to discuss with people face-to-face in order to brainstorm and have open-ended exchanges of ideas. People seem more spontaneous and uninhibited in sharing ideas in a physical social setting as opposed to an online setting, which perhaps is counter intuitive in this age of social media. We need in-person interactions for serendipitous discoveries. As they say, you don't know what you don't know. Hence, I find my workshops in London highly valuable. I also make sure my partner Roger and I (plus our quant researcher Ray) attend conferences together, as we normally work out of our respective homes at opposite corners of the continent (see a Bloomberg profile of our business in Burger, 2016). If physical meeting of the team is impractical, the new online collaborative platform slack.com is another way to promote such informal communication among colleagues: People are far more chatty with instant messages than with emails.

What is the exact business structure you should set up to serve the investors you have attracted? Despite the common notion that "hedge fund" is the investment vehicle of choice, it is actually far less hassle to first start a service to manage separate accounts. It is far less of a hassle to attract investors, because their money is sitting in their own brokerage accounts under their control at all times. You are only given trading authority over their accounts, but not authority to withdraw money. Many investors also like managed accounts because of their transparency—they can watch every day what is being traded in their accounts, what sort of risks are being taken, and what the daily returns look like. It is also far less hassle to manage separate accounts from a regulatory point of view. In the United States, you do not even have to register as an Investment Advisor with the SEC or a Commodity Trading Advisor with the NFA/CFTC if you advise fewer than a certain number of accounts and meet certain other criteria. Even if you do have to register, there is no required annual audit, no need to hire a third-party administrator to perform treasury functions and to send out monthly financial statements, and so on. You might think that it is complicated to trade in multiple brokerage accounts simultaneously, but many brokers have made it possible for you to just send one large order, and they will allocate the resulting positions and P&L to various accounts under your management according to some formula (usually proportional to the NAV's of the accounts). You may also think that it is complicated to collect fees from multiple brokerage accounts, but again, some brokers (such as Interactive Brokers) have automated this process (as long as you are a Registered Investment Advisor or a Commodity Trading Advisor).

Some clients also prefer managed accounts because of the potentially smaller margin requirement (i.e., they can employ higher leverage). In a fund or pool, the manager decides the optimal leverage. For managed accounts, clients *can* deposit a relatively small portion of their total investment capital into their accounts, and request that the manager trade that at high leverage. However, "can" doesn't mean "should": it is often not optimal to trade an account at a leverage higher than what Kelly formula recommends (see Chapter 1). We constantly adjust the order size for each account based on the account equity and the desired leverage. Readers of this and my previous books will understand that if this leverage is higher than the Kelly optimal, the long-term compound growth rate under this constant rebalancing scheme will suffer.

There are, however, some significant downsides to managing *or* investing in separate accounts instead of a fund or pool. From the investment manager's point of view, it is never ideal to disclose the timing of every trade of every instrument to your investors, as will be the case with managed accounts. These leak your trade secrets. It is also difficult to execute multiple *futures* strategies across multiple small accounts: the broker won't be able to allocate the futures contracts strictly according to the accounts' NAVs.

Some small accounts may be allocated zero contracts randomly, and others may be allocated one contract whose market value may already be bigger than what is warranted.

Diversification is also a problem for managed accounts. In our fund, we have many strategies that are allocated small amounts of capital. This may be because a strategy has a short track record or may be because it delivers good returns but not consistently. The sum total of these strategies may have an attractive and stable returns profile, but they are difficult to replicate in a managed account because many of these strategies will result in zero allocation in a smaller account. Hence, true diversification is very difficult for managed accounts, and this structure is best for investors who have investments in multiple managed accounts with different managers, and who can achieve diversification on their own. But even if an investor can invest with multiple managers, it is a big burden to manage the allocation of money to them actively. In a fund or pool structure, we will manage such allocation on behalf of the investor and will update such allocations regularly based on our continuous analysis. Indeed, capital allocation (as discussed in Chapter 1) is a big part of investment management. This is especially true with the constant creation and destruction of strategies in a fund.

Finally, a major drawback of the managed account structure is the principal-agent problem: The managers do not have skin in the managed account. So it is all upside and no downside for them, and this encourages the managers to take higher risks than may be optimal for the owner of the account. On the other hand, you can choose to invest in a fund or pool[4] in which the managers have substantial personal investment themselves and who will suffer losses in the same percentage as outside investors.

Conclusion

Nobel physicist Hans Bethe, a key figure in the Manhattan Project during World War II and a beloved figure at my alma mater's physics department, was still conducting theoretical astrophysics research and giving public lectures in his late eighties. Though algorithmic trading involves research that is far more mundane, it still offers a lifetime of intellectual challenge and financial reward. This book is just a snapshot of my ideas and thinking at a moment in time during the endless cycles of creation and destruction of trading strategies.

Endnotes

1. An example of such statistics can be found at www.financemagnates.com/forex/brokers/exclusive-us-q1–2015-forex-profitability-report-more-accounts-and-profits/ where it is shown that in a typical quarter, the vast majority of Forex customer accounts across all brokers are unprofitable. A more comprehensive survey that goes beyond Forex trading is available at www.tradeciety.com/24-statistics-why-most-traders-lose-money/, where it is quoted that active traders underperform the market index by 6.5 percent annually.
2. See Chan (2009) for my sorry history working in institutions.
3. I won't join the debate about whether high-frequency traders actually provide short-term liquidity here.
4. In the United States, a hedge fund is typically regulated by the SEC, and a commodity pool regulated by the NFA/CFTC.

BIBLIOGRAPHY

Ahmad, Riaz, and Paul Wilmott. 2005. "Which Free Lunch Would You Like Today, Sir?: Delta Hedging, Volatility Arbitrage and Optimal Portfolios." *Wilmott Magazine* (November 2005): 64–79.

Aikin, Stephen. 2012. *STIR Futures: Trading Euribor and Eurodollar Futures*. 2nd edition. Harriman House.

Aikin, Stephen. 2015. Private communication.

Aisen, Daniel. 2015. "The Genesis of an Order Type." blog.quantopian.com/2015/04/.

Albanese, Chiara. 2015. "Forex's 'Last Look' Practice Gets Curbed." *Wall Street Journal*. May 27. Available at www.wsj.com/articles/forexs-last-look-practice-gets-curbed-1432768404.

Allen, Kate. 2015. "How a Toronto Professor's Research Revolutionized Artificial Intelligence." *The Toronto Star* (April 17). www.thestar.com/news/world/2015/04/17/how-a-toronto-professors-research-revolutionized-artificial-intelligence.html.

Almgren, Robert. 2014. "QB Simulator Performance." quantitativebrokers.com/wp-content/uploads/2014/04/QB-Simulator-Performance.pdf.

An, Byeong-Je, Andrew Ang, Turan G. Bali, and Nusret Cakici. 2013. "The Joint Cross Section of Stocks and Options." Georgetown McDonough School of Business Research Paper No. 2012-10. Available at ssrn.com/abstract=2008902.

Andersen, Torben G., and Oleg Bondarenko. 2014. "VPIN and the Flash Crash. *2013*." *Journal of Financial Markets* 17: 1–46, Available at ssrn.com/abstract=1881731.

Ang, Andrew. 2014. *Asset Management: A Systematic Approach to Factor Investing*. Oxford University Press.

Anonymous, 2015. "Support Vector Machines. Mathworks Documentation." www.mathworks.com/help/stats/support-vector-machines-svm.html.

Aruoba, S. Borağan, and Jesús Fernández-Villaverde. 2014. "A Comparison of Programming Languages in Economics." NBER Working Paper No. 20263. Available at economics.sas.upenn.edu/~jesusfv/comparison_languages.pdf.

Asness, Clifford S., Andrea Frazzini, and Lasse H. Pedersen. 2012. "Leverage Aversion and Risk Parity." *Financial Analysts Journal* 68: 47–59.

Augen, Jeff. 2008. *The Volatility Edge in Options Trading*. FT Press.

Augen, Jeff. 2009. *Day Trading Options*. FT Press.

Baker, Malcolm, Brendan Bradley, and Jeffrey Wurgler. 2011. "Benchmarks as Limits to Arbitrage: Understanding the Low-Volatility Anomaly." *Financial Analysts Journal* 67(1). Available at people.stern.nyu.edu/jwurgler/papers/faj-benchmarks.pdf.

Bali, Turan G., Jianfeng Hu, and Scott Murray. 2015. "Option Implied Volatility, Skewness, and Kurtosis and the Cross-Section of Expected Stock Returns." Georgetown McDonough School of Business Research Paper. Available at ssrn.com/abstract=2322945.

Bargh, John A., and Yaacov Schul. 1980. "On the Cognitive Benefits of Teaching." *Journal of Educational Psychology*, 72(5). Available at dx.doi.org/10.1037/0022-0663.72.5.593.

Bennett, Colin. 2014. *Trading Volatility: Trading Volatility, Correlation, Term Structure and Skew*. CreateSpace Independent Publishing Platform.

Breiman, Leo, J. H. Friedman, R. A. Olshen, and C. J. Stone. 1984. *Classification and Regression Trees*. Wadsworth & Brooks/Cole Advanced Books & Software.

Brown, Stephen J., Paul Lajbcygier, and Bob Li. 2007. "Going Negative: What to Do with Negative Book Equity Stocks." *The Journal of Portfolio Management* 35(1). Available at ssrn.com/abstract=1142649.

Burger, Dani. 2016. "Meet the DIY Quants Who Ditched Wall Street for the Desert." *Bloomberg Businessweek*. www.bloomberg.com/news/articles/2016-03-16/barbarian-coders-at-the-gate-the-inexorable-rise-of-diy-quants.

Carr, Peter. 2016. Private communication.

Cartea, Álbaro, Sebastian Jaimungal, and José Penalva. 2015. *Algorithmic and High-Frequency Trading*. New York: Cambridge University Press.

Chakravarty, Sugato, Pankaj K. Jain, Robert Wood, and James Upson. 2009. "Clean Sweep: Informed Trading Through Intermarket Sweep." Available at ssrn.com/abstract=1460865.

Chan, Ernest. 2009. *Quantitative Trading: How to Build Your Own Algorithmic Trading Business*. Hoboken, NJ: John Wiley & Sons.

Chan, Ernest. 2013. *Algorithmic Trading: Winning Strategies and Their Rationale*. Hoboken, NJ: John Wiley & Sons.

Chan, Ernest. 2015. "Interview with Euan Sinclair." epchan.blogspot.com/2015/09/interview-with-euan-sinclair.html.

Chang, Bo Young, Peter Christoffersen, and Kris Jacobs. 2009. "Market Skewness Risk and the Cross-Section of Stock Returns." Available at ssrn.com/abstract=1480332.

Chattopadhyay, Akash, Matthew R. Lyle, and Charles C. Y. Wang. 2015. "Accounting Data, Market Values, and the Cross Section of Expected Returns Worldwide." Harvard Business School Accounting & Management Unit Working Paper No. 15-092. Available at ssrn.com/abstract=2613366.

Chicago Mercantile Exchange (CME). 2012. Special Executive Report. www.cmegroup.com/rulebook/files/ser-6465_Equity_Index_Futures_Options_on_Equity_Index_Futures_20121114.pdf.

Chicago Mercantile Exchange (CME). 2015. MDP 3.0—Trade Summary Order Level Detail. www.cmegroup.com/confluence/display/EPICSANDBOX/MDP+3.0+-+Trade+Summary+Order+Level+Detail#MDP3.0-TradeSummaryOrderLevelDetail-Example3-OneAggressorTradingatMultiplePricesAgainstCustomerandImpliedOrders.

Chung, Juliet. 2015. "A 'Black Swan' Fund Makes $1 Billion." *Wall Street Journal*. August 30. www.wsj.com/articles/nassim-talebs-black-swan-fund-made-1-billion-this-week-1440793953.

Clark-Joseph, Adam D. 2013. "Exploratory Trading." Available at www.nanex.net/aqck2/4136/exploratorytrading.pdf.

Cont, Rama, Arseniy Kukanov, and Sasha Stoikov. 2014. "The Price Impact of Order Book Events." *Journal of Financial Econometrics* 12 (1): 47–88.

Copeland, Rob, and Timothy W. Martin. 2015. "Hedge Fund Bridgewater Defends Its 'Risk-Parity' Strategy." *Wall Street Journal* (September 15). www.wsj.com/articles/hedge-fund-bridgewater-defends-its-risk-parity-strategy-1442368802.

Cremers, Martijn, and David Weinbaum. 2010. "Deviations from Put-Call Parity and Stock Return Predictability." *Journal of Financial and Quantitative Analysis* 45: 335–367. Available at ssrn.com/abstract=968237.

Dahl, Brady. 2015. "Momo Traders." Miltona Publishing.

Deltix, 2014. "Can You Generate Alpha in US Equities Using Crowd Sourced Earnings Data?" www.deltixlab.com/blog/2014/06/19/can-you-generate-alpha-in-us-equities-using-crowd-sourced-earnings-data/.

Ding, Shengwei, John Hanna, and Terrence Hendershott. 2014. "How Slow Is the NBBO? A Comparison with Direct Exchange Feeds." *Financial Review* 49 (2) (May 2014): 313–332. Available at ssrn.com/abstract=2422136.

DirectEdge, 2015. Order Type Guide. Available at cdn.batstrading.com/resources/membership/EDGE_Order_Type_Guide.pdf.

Doheny, Kathleen. 2012. "Pets for Depression and Health." www.webmd.com/depression/features/pets-depression.

Domingos, P. 2012. "A Few Useful Things to Know about Machine Learning." *Communications of the ACM* 55 (10): 78–87.

Dueker, Michael J., and Christopher J. Neely. 2006. "Can Markov Switching Models Predict Excess Foreign Exchange Returns?" Federal Reserve Bank of St. Louis Working Paper 2001-021F. research.stlouisfed.org/wp/2001/2001-021.pdf.

Easley, David, Marcos Lopez de Prado, and Maureen O'Hara. 2012. "Flow Toxicity and Liquidity in a High Frequency World." *Review of Financial Studies* 25 (5): 1457–1493. Available at ssrn.com/abstract=1695596.

Easley, David, Marcos Lopez de Prado, and Maureen O'Hara. 2015. "Discerning Information from Trade Data." Johnson School Research Paper Series No. 8-2012. Available at ssrn.com/abstract=1989555.

Economist, 2015. "Why the Swiss Unpegged the Franc." www.economist.com/blogs/economist-explains/2015/01/economist-explains-13.

Fama, E. F., and K. R. French. 1993. "Common Risk Factors in the Returns on Stocks and Bonds." *Journal of Financial Economics* 33: 3–56.

Friedman, Jerome H. 1999. "Stochastic Gradient Boosting." statweb.stanford.edu/~jhf/ftp/stobst.pdf.

Galati, Gabriele. 2002. "Settlement Risk in Foreign Exchange Markets and CLS Bank." Available at www.bis.org/publ/qtrpdf/r_qt0212f.pdf.

Golub, Anton, John Keane, and Ser-Huang Poon. 2012. "High Frequency Trading and Mini Flash Crashes." Available at ssrn.com/abstract=2182097.

Grant, Adam. 2014. *Give and Take*. New York: Penguin.

Greenblatt, Joel. 2010. *The Little Book That Still Beats the Market*. Hoboken, NJ: John Wiley & Sons.

Hall, Taylor. 2016. "Point72's Cohen Bets $250 Million on Crowd-Sourced Quantopian." www.bloomberg.com/news/articles/2016-07-27/point72-s-cohen-bets-250-million-on-crowd-sourced-quantopian.

Harris, Larry. 2003. *Trading and Exchanges*. Oxford: Oxford University Press.

Hasbrouck, Joel. 2014. "Securities Trading: Procedures and Principles." (NYU MBA course teaching notes.) Available at pages.stern.nyu.edu/~jhasbrou/TeachingMaterials/STPPms06.pdf.

Hasbrouck, Joel. 2015. "Dark Mechanisms." Available at people.stern.nyu.edu/jhasbrou/Teaching/POST%202016%20Spring/classNotes/STPPDarkLiquidity.pdf.

Hothorn, Torsten. 2014. Machine Learning & Statistical Learning. cran.r-project.org/web/views/MachineLearning.html.

Hull, John C. 2014. *Options, Futures, and Other Derivatives.* 9th edition. New York: Prentice Hall.

Hunsader, Eric Scott. 2015. "eMini on track to set a record low average trade size today (below 2.4 contracts)" at twitter.com/nanexllc/status/643505068550017024.

Hunsader, Eric Scott. 2016. "What % of Nasdaq quotes/trades in NYSE & ARCA symbols arrive at the SIP within 350 micros?" at twitter.com/nanexllc/status/691686389939900417.

Infantino, Leandro Rafael, and Savion Itzhaki. 2010. "Developing High-Frequency Equities Trading Models." MBA thesis. Cambridge: Massachusetts Institute of Technology. dspace.mit.edu/handle/1721.1/59122.

James, Jessica, Jonathan Fullwood, and Peter Billington. 2015. *FX Option Performance: An Analysis of the Value Delivered by FX Options Since the Start of the Market.* Hoboken, NJ: John Wiley & Sons.

Johansson, Nathalie Strale, and Malin Tjernstrom. 2014. "The Price Volatility of Bitcoin." Umea Universitet School of Business and Economics Master thesis. www.diva-portal.org/smash/get/diva2:782588/FULLTEXT01.pdf.

Kamel, Tammer. "The Changing Generations of Financial Data." www.quandl.com/blog/alternative-data.

Kaplan, Ian L. 2014. "Value Factors Do Not Forecast Returns for S&P 500 Stocks." Preprint. Available at www.bearcave.com/finance/thesis_project/factor_analysis.pdf.

Kahneman, Daniel. 2011. *Thinking, Fast and Slow.* New York: Farrar, Straus and Giroux.

Kazemian, Kiavash, Shunan Zhao, and Gerald Penn. 2014. "Evaluating Sentiment Analysis Evaluation: A Case Study in Securities Trading." Proceedings of the 5th Workshop on Computational Approaches to Subjectivity, Sentiment and Social Media Analysis, pp. 119–127. Association for Computational Linguistics. www.aclweb.org/anthology/W14-2620.

Kroijer, Lars. 2012. *Money Mavericks.* New York: Pearson.

Kun, Jeremy. 2015. "The Boosting Margin, or Why Boosting Doesn't Overfit." jeremykun.com/2015/09/21/the-boosting-margin-or-why-boosting-doesnt-overfit/.

Ibbotson, Roger G., and Daniel Y.-J. Kim. 2014. "Liquidity as an Investment Style: 2014 Update." Available at www.zebracapm.com/research.php.

Levine, James. 2015. "What Are the Risks of Sitting Too Much?" www.mayoclinic.org/healthy-lifestyle/adult-health/expert-answers/sitting/faq-20058005.

Lewis, Michael. 2014. *Flash Boys: A Wall Street Revolt*. New York: W. W. Norton.

Lyons, Richard K. 2001. *The Microstructure Approach to Exchange Rates*. Cambridge, MA: MIT Press.

Mackintosh, Phil. 2014. "Demystifying Order Types." Available at www.kcg.com/uploads/documents/KCG_Demystifying-Order-Types_092414.pdf.

Manokhin, Valery. 2015. *Application of Machine Learning Techniques to the Analysis and Forecasting of Commodity Prices*. Master's thesis. London: University College.

Markoff, John, and Steve Lohr. 2016. "The Race Is on to Control Artificial Intelligence, and Tech's Future." *New York Times* (March 26). www.nytimes.com/2016/03/26/technology/the-race-is-on-to-control-artificial-intelligence-and-techs-future.html.

MarketWatch, 2012. "Lawmakers Grill CFTC Chief over Broker Failures." www.marketwatch.com/story/lawmakers-grill-cftc-chief-over-broker-failures-2012-07-17.

McMillan, Lawrence G. 2012. *Options as a Strategic Investment*. 5th edition. Upper Saddle River, NJ: Prentice Hall.

Murphy, Kevin P. 2012. *Machine Learning: A Probabilistic Perspective*. Cambridge, MA: MIT Press.

Murphy, Kevin P. 2015. "Why Matlab." github.com/probml/pmtk3/wiki/WhyMatlab.

Nasdaq, 2014. "Order Types and Modifiers." Available at www.nasdaqtrader.com/content/ProductsServices/Trading/OrderTypesG.pdf

Nimalendran, Mahendrarajah, and Sugata Ray. 2011. "Informational Linkages Between Dark and Lit Trading Venues." Available at ssrn.com/abstract=1880070.

Okendal, Bert. 2014. *Stochastic Differential Equations*. 6th edition. New York: Springer.

Porath, Christine. 2015. "No Time to Be Nice at Work." *New York Times* (June 21). www.nytimes.com/2015/06/21/opinion/sunday/is-your-boss-mean.html?src=xps.

Rechenthin, Michael David. 2014. *Machine-learning Classification Techniques for the Analysis and Prediction of High-frequency Stock Direction*. PhD Thesis. Iowa City: University of Iowa. myweb.uiowa.edu/mrechent/_research_stuff/mrechenthin-thesis-May1-2014.pdf.

"Rule 610." 2005. www.sec.gov/rules/final/34-51808.pdf.

Ruppert, David, and David Matteson. 2015. *Statistics and Data Analysis for Financial Engineering*. 2nd edition. New York: Springer.

Saraiya, N., and H. Mittal. 2009. "Understanding and Avoiding Adverse Selection in Dark Pools." ITG white paper.

Sharpe, W. F. 1964. "Capital Asset Prices: A Theory of Market Equilibrium under Conditions of Risk." *Journal of Finance* 19(3): 425–442.

Sinclair, Euan. 2010. *Option Trading: Pricing and Volatility Strategies and Techniques*. Hoboken, NJ: John Wiley & Sons.

Sinclair, Euan. 2013. *Volatility Trading*. 2nd edition. Hoboken, NJ: John Wiley & Sons.

Sinclair, Euan. 2016. "Why Is Equity Index Implied Volality Skew More Pronounced for Shorter Maturities?" www.quora.com/Why-is-equity-index-implied-volality-skew-more-pronounced-for-shorter-maturities/answer/Euan-Sinclair-2?srid=hDWq.

Taleb, Nassim Nicholas. 2014. *Antifragile: Things That Gain from Disorder*. New York: Random House.

Tsang, Amie. 2016. "Bitcoin Plunges After Hacking of Exchange in Hong Kong." *New York Times* (August 3). http://www.nytimes.com/2016/08/04/business/dealbook/bitcoin-bitfinex-hacked.html?_r=0.

Wang, Sheng, et al. 2014. "The Wisdom of Crowds: Crowdsourcing Earnings Estimates." www.estimize.com/deutsche-bank-research.

Wood, Robert, James Upson, and Thomas H. McInish. 2013. "The Flash Crash: Trading Aggressiveness, Liquidity Supply, and the Impact of Intermarket Sweep Orders." Available at ssrn.com/abstract=1629402.

Zerohedge. 2014. www.zerohedge.com/news/2014-11-21/broken-market-chronicles-third-year-row-most-shorted-names-generate-highest-return.

Zhang, Xiaoyan, Rui Zhao, and Yuhang Xing. 2008. "What Does Individual Option Volatility Smirk Tell Us about Future Equity Returns?" AFA 2009 San Francisco Meetings Paper. Available at ssrn.com/abstract=1107464.

ABOUT THE AUTHOR

Ernest P. Chan has been the managing member of QTS Capital Management, LLC, a commodity pool operator and trading advisor, since 2011. An alumnus of Morgan Stanley and Credit Suisse, he received his PhD in physics from Cornell University and was a researcher in machine learning at IBM's T.J. Watson Research Center before joining the financial industry. He is the author of *Quantitative Trading: How to Build Your Own Algorithmic Trading Business* and *Algorithmic Trading: Winning Strategies and Their Rationale*. Find out more about Ernie at www.epchan.com.

INDEX

Page references followed by f indicate an illustrated figure; followed by t indicate a table; followed by b indicate a box; followed by e indicate an example.

A

B

C

D

E

F

G

H

I

J

K

L

M

P

Q

R

S

T

U

V

W

X

Z